Teaching English
Across the Ability Range

Richard W. Mills

Ward Lock Educational

ISBN 0 7062 3643 2

First published 1977

Set in 10 on 11 point Times
by Amos Typesetters, Hockley, Essex
Printed and bound by Morrison & Gibb Ltd,
London and Edinburgh
for Ward Lock Educational
116 Baker Street, London W1M 2BB
A Member of the Pentos Group

Contents

A note on the contributors

Judith Atkinson is Head of English at Sidney Smith Comprehensive School, Hull, having previously taught in grammar and comprehensive schools.

Shirely Hoole has taught for a number of years in comprehensive schools and is at present Head of English at Maypole Comprehensive School, Birmingham.

David Mears has experience in public and comprehensive schools and is now Head of English at Theale Green County Secondary School, Berkshire.

Richard Mills was formerly Head of English at Shenley Court Comprehensive School, Birmingham, and is at present Senior Lecturer at Westhill College of Education, Birmingham.

Leslie Stringer has a number of years' experience in secondary teaching and is now Head of English at Four Dwellings Comprehensive School, Birmingham.

Gordon Taylor's teaching career has been in comprehensive schools and he is at present Head of English at Blandford Upper School, Dorset.

Introduction

This book has been written for students in training and for secondary school English teachers new to teaching and/or new to, or contemplating, mixed-ability grouping or work with wide ability bands. It has, thus, a two-fold purpose: to indicate some of the strategies which might be used with classes of children whose attainment varies enormously, and also to show some of the ways in which English teaching can be tailored to cater for wide abilities, irrespective of the method of grouping.

All the contributors to this book were colleagues for a number of years in the same 11-18 comprehensive school English department, where initially streamed, and later complete mixed-ability work from first to third years was practised. Since that time, we have each gone our separate ways, adding to our earlier experience, but retaining certain basic common beliefs in the theory and practice of English teaching. The book which has been put together should, then, be internally consistent, despite its nature as an anthology. Certainly, there are differences in emphasis but nowhere, I think, a downright contradiction.

We have endeavoured to act as a team, reading each other's essays in draft form and making suggestions for their improvement, but the responsibility for overall design and structure is mine, as editor. In such a book as this, you might have expected to find separate chapters dealing with such issues as: work cards; marking; remedial activities; homework; record keeping, and it was the original intention to include such sections as discrete entities. However, as the project proceeded, it seemed more natural to incorporate this detail into the body of the text, where appropriate, since none of these matters is, or should be, a wholly separate issue, to be kept in a watertight compartment. You will, therefore, find that more than one contributor touches on these topics but the resulting effect should be one of emphasis, rather than redundancy.

The first chapter looks initially at the theory behind non-streaming, not in a crusading manner, I hope, but merely to provide some kind of justification for the approaches and practices outlined in the later pages. Some breakdown of literacy and oracy skills is offered so that problems facing the teacher may be clearly identified. At the end of this chapter there is a brief consideration of some possible effects of unstreaming, and this paves the way for chapter two which looks at change from the point of view of one particular establishment, formerly a grammar school, now a complete comprehensive school with a measure of wide-ability teaching. Again, strategies are suggested which staff facing similar changes might wish to contemplate.

Part Two of the book moves away from preparation and planning to where the action is – lion's den, chalk face, battlefront – choose your own well-worn metaphor. Some sections are deliberately blow-by-blow accounts of organisation and classroom management since we feel such detail could be helpful to inexperienced teachers and students and since, in general, good teaching presupposes good structure. Judith Atkinson describes a kind of English teaching which stresses the integration of experience through form, genre and medium. Shirley Hoole, who is also in sympathy with such thematic work, concentrates on the appreciation of literature, as something of value in its own right and also as an illumination and extension of awareness. Both draw on past and present daily classroom experience for their detail. So, too, does Les Stringer, whose contribution will offer a perspective which will be new to many teachers. His chapter is not the traditional nod in the drama direction, common in such anthologies. It starts with drama but swiftly moves to the specific area of games and simulations showing, with some detailed classroom examples, how such an approach may be integrated into general English teaching.

Next follows Gordon Taylor's chapter on how to incorporate natural objects, artifacts and visual materials into one's teaching, not merely in order to vary the diet but rather because such stimuli are appropriate and effective in all kinds of situations, but especially with small groups. Chapter seven picks this up and attempts to be both theoretical (in its categorization of small group activities) and practical (in the range of possibilities outlined and in the *modus operandi* proposed). Some evidence is presented to show the kinds of learning that may occur in small groups under certain conditions.

Behind Part Three of the book is the notion of the English teacher as prospector or scavenger, hunting anywhere and everywhere for appropriate and useful material and ideas. The days are gone when your provisions for the term were *Merchant of Venice,* Ridout, Palgrave's *Golden Treasury* and *The Cloister and the Hearth*. Iron rations indeed. You need much more varied fare nowadays in order to cope with the demands, interests and range of your pupils, and the local scrap metal yard may be as appropriate at times as the City Library. It all depends on what you are trying to do. Chapters eight, nine and ten offer a variety of sources and materials for use across the ability range and I hope they will prove to be helpful.

If the methods and materials we describe are appropriate for mixed groups, then they are just as appropriate for streamed forms also, as for and other mode of grouping for learning. Every group is a mixed group; some are more mixed than others.

R.W.M.

Part One: Planning ahead

1 Mixed ability English

Richard Mills

Justification

The Oxford Book of Literary Anecdotes has a story about Matthew
Arnold which has altered forever my conception of the great man. Lina
Waterfield, a narrator, tells how, as a backward child of six, she was
unable to read. It was, apparently, a serious case, sufficient to warrant
the attention of a family friend, known to be a poet and government
inspector. The man was duly sent for and, sitting the little girl on his
knee, he spoke to her of books and poetry. Then he ended with these
words: 'Your mother tells me that you do not know how to read, and
are refusing to learn. It surprises me very much that a little girl of six
should not know how to read and expects to be read to. It is disgraceful,
and you must promise me to learn at once; if you don't I shall have to
put your father and mother in prison.' Within a few weeks Lina could
read Grimm's *Fairy Tales*.

I offer this story not as a code of conduct for inspectors or poets, nor
as the panacea to reading problems, although the threat did apparently
work. Your views of the incident will depend on your preconceptions.
You may see it as a very powerful piece of individualized instruction.
After all, Lina is sitting on Arnold's knee in a one-to-one relationship.
Or you may regard it as yet another Victorian con trick which may have
been successful but which probably set up traumas for life. The point is
that one man's method is another's madness.

Certainly, those methods which my colleagues and I outline in this
book are ones which we believe have been, and can be, efficacious in
producing English work of good quality across the range, albeit
without penal sanctions, and, since every method or piece of practice is
inevitably based on some theory, it is appropriate to put the case for
non-streaming, even though the matter seems to be an ideological
issue, where argument is unlikely to convince unbelievers. Indeed, it
would be strange in a book of this kind if no such statement were to be
made. Nevertheless, I am not arguing the case, but rather making the
assertions briefly, in no particular order of significance, with biblio-
graphical references for those readers who wish to pursue a specific
argument. Eight of these arguments run as follows.

1   Unlike weather forecasting, the system of streaming has a self-validating quality. Children in the A stream behave as such, and those in the D stream (or possibly the fourteenth stream in a very large school) perform according to their label. Teachers' expectations are significant factors in attainment, and such expectations are often conditioned by the streaming process. (Barker-Lunn 1970; Hargreaves 1967; Rosenthal and Jacobsen 1968). You walk down the corridor to teach the top fifth year and may well feel stimulated at the prospect of this intellectual encounter. Forty minutes later you travel the same corridor to a low second-year class, wondering just what you'll be able to teach them. There is a sense in which your expectations should, of course, be different if you are to approach your task realistically, but ideally, no ceilings on achievement should be contemplated. It may be only natural to prefer lively groups to dull groups, but the terms 'lively' and 'dull' are not synonymous with 'bright' and 'unintelligent'. The labelling process is an insidious one.

2   Ignoring all manner of social skills and such characteristics as commitment to hard work, perseverance and honest endeavour, rigid streaming depends on accurate measurement of ability, but no such infallible measures exist. Even the 10+ selection and rejection procedures, known to be very accurate, were subject to an unavoidable error of at least 10% (NFER 1963) which meant that each year thousands of pupils were 'wrongly' allocated. Any selection procedure has a considerable margin of error and any stream, however sophisticated the tests, is far less homogenous than it is thought to be (NFER 1968). Moreover, there is the assumption that intellectual capacity does not alter; it merely has to be assessed and then treated accordingly, rather like the diagnosis of some incurable illness. Such a notion is now out of favour. (Yates 1966).

3   Such selection is, in any event, strongly affected by additional factors such as social class (Douglas 1964; Jackson 1964); by birth dates, i.e. amount of time spent in infant school (Jackson 1964); by language background and parental attitude (Bernstein 1969).

4   A stream of water generally flows in the same direction, over the same ground, at the same speed. A stream of children, it is implied, is expected to pursue activities corporately. The class generally works on the same material at the same speed. In other words, streaming is an organizational device and promotes a teaching style which minimizes individual differences. Under this system children should be dealt with *en masse* and, indeed, if this doesn't happen, then one argument in support of streaming automatically disappears. It's only when we don't know children particularly well that we feel they have a lot in common; the more we get to know them, the more they diverge. Imagine your

own son or daughter to be one of your pupils and you will realise just how little you know of the other twenty-nine in the class, however conscientious you may be. Mixed ability grouping forces us to notice and take into account the specific strengths and weaknesses, interests and idiosyncrasies, of individual children, and treat each according to his need.

5   Streaming promotes a competitive and hierarchical ethos. Top streams have high status; bottom streams virtually no social standing. Children may strive to be promoted but movement is inevitably a two-way process and few, if any, benefit by being demoted. If there is too much movement between streams then, it could be argued, the original division was inaccurate. If there is too little, then, presumably, the system ossifies and those who have aspirations give up hope. Similar problems apply to banding, and setting, which is a more sophisticated form of streaming. Whatever ideological stance one takes here, there is no denying that, logically, mixed ability grouping precludes competition. Non-swimmers and Olympic swimming medalists may do many things together, but they will not compete in the same swimming race.

6   Not only does streaming act as a divisive academic influence within a school but it also has other undesirable social effects. While A streams show high morale (and are often believed by their contemporaries to contain 'snobs'), low groups have a bad self-image (Chetouti 1961), which they may seek to deserve. Such images may be strengthened by teacher expectation. Certainly, there is evidence that mixed ability grouping may have considerable beneficial effects so far as discipline is concerned (Kaye and Rogers 1968; Thompson 1969).

7   Some opponents of mixed ability grouping maintain that, under such a system, the bright pupils will be held back and the less academic will struggle to maintain progress. (What of the majority of 'average' pupils?) Such evidence as is available would indicate that this is an ungrounded fear and that the bright do as well, whereas the weak ones may improve significantly (Banbury 1975; Barker-Lunn 1970; Yates 1966). Perhaps in a *streamed* situation the bright weren't stretched and the weak were under-achievers? There is an obvious need for much more research here and the NFER survey of 1978 should be consulted. Certainly, no professional person would support a system which manifestly led to a lowering of standards and to a general mediocrity of attainment. To oppose streaming is not to oppose high standards. However, behind the misgivings mentioned above, there seems to lie the assumption that in mixed ability work there will continue to be comparison of pupils with each other and the group will be moving along a common path, with the leaders striding out in front and the

stragglers dawdling at the back. Such a notion is a hangover from streamed thinking. In fact, pupils are following a variety of trails, perhaps not all towards the same destination. Each pupil should be engaged on work which is appropriate for him, relevant to his needs and interests, and in such a class atmosphere that each is valued, irrespective of strengths and weaknesses. A very tall order. No attempt should be made, I believe, to disguise differences and to pretend they don't exist; that would be a useless attempt at deception, fooling no one. Rather, a mature awareness of difference, in a non-competitive atmosphere, seems more desirable, and teacher attitude is clearly crucial. Teachers involved in mixed ability work, as in any other system of grouping, must want it to succeed.

8 Points 1-6 are arguments *against* streaming and only by implication *for* mixed ability grouping. We now move away from points of principle, some of them based on notions of equality of treatment and attitude (Bridges 1976), to the question of subject suitability. Whatever the appropriateness for mixed ability work of other subject areas in the curriculum (Bailey 1976; Davies 1975; Kelly 1975), it can be strongly argued that English, by its very nature, is particularly appropriate (Bullock I.6 1975).

Subject suitability
There appear to be five main models of English teaching, none of which is entirely discrete.

(a) **Basic skills** with its stress on a minimum competence in reading and writing so that all school leavers should at least be able to read a daily newspaper and cope with the literacy demands of a bureaucratic and industrialized society.
(b) **Cultural heritage** which argues that all pupils should be acquainted with work by the great writers of their country, and the myths and legends and cultural foundations out of which such writing grows.
(c) **Sociological stance** where the stress is on English as a study of contemporary national and international social issues and the individual in relation to local and more wide-ranging contexts.
(d) **Language/communication** which, for our present purposes, could be defined as seeking to replace the previous notion of grammatical correctness with the more ambiguous, and perhaps at times subjective, concept of appropriateness, and which endeavours to examine and promote genuine language in a variety of real contexts.
(e) **Personal development** where the individual, with his own needs, beliefs and experiences, is at the centre of the stage and where, to

4

use the old terminology, the intention is 'to develop each person according to his full potential.'

These then, very baldly, are five possible approaches to the teaching of English. Any school English syllabus or, more pertinently, the actual teaching which takes place, will show a bias towards one or two of these approaches. However, there can be strengths and weaknesses in each, unless some kind of balance is achieved. Let us assume that we make an amalgam of the strengths of each. Then, in this best of all possible worlds, we shall be endeavouring to develop a range of literacy and oracy skills and an adequate technical competence; to impart some appreciation and knowledge of the prose, poetry and drama of our own and other cultures; to consider and explore matters of immediate and lasting human concern; to look at language 'such as men do use' in a variety of contexts and to attempt to ensure that our pupils can operate well in a range of situations; to assist, above all, in the intellectual, aesthetic, moral and spiritual growth of each boy and girl we encounter. It is this last model, that of personal growth (Dixon 1967) which, in its ideal form, can subsume all the strengths of the other models and it is, for me, synonymous with mixed ability teaching since it places the emphasis firmly on the individual child in all his uniqueness. This approach to English teaching is the premise which underpins the thinking of all contributors to this book.

Although they possess no monopoly on personal growth, many English teachers often lay great stress on the development of individual perceptions and insights and on the maturing understanding of each person. In dealing closely with social and individual concerns of morality, relationship, taste, personal experience and so forth, through literature and the mass media and by virtue of regular contact with pupils throughout the week, English and Humanities staff are often able to develop strong relationships based on mutual trust and understanding. Let me add, many 'non-English' teachers may also achieve such understanding, and perhaps some 'English' teachers do not. I suspect that the role of, say, boys' and girls' craft teachers in this respect has been underestimated. After all, such teachers often work with small groups and individuals, who are performing different tasks at varying speeds. These teachers have an ideal opportunity to foster mutual understanding on a one-to-one basis. In any event, whatever the specialism, the cause of staff unity is hardly served by polishing one's badge of understanding too vigorously.

Transition
In his short story, *Dead Men's Path*, Chinua Achebe tells of the ambitious young Headmaster, Michael Obi, who, in order to fulfil his great plans for Ndume Central School, is scornful of the village's

traditions and sets out to destroy them overnight. Such unilateral action is a recipe for disaster, not because the long-term aims are unacceptable, but on account of indecent speed, a lack of respect for the views of others, and a contempt for older ways.

The moral seems to be: 'Make haste slowly' and it's one which a school changing from streamed to unstreamed teaching might well adopt. Innovation has a threatening quality; it poses a challenge to status, role and previous experience. Like a new friendship, it is often better when allowed time to mature than when embraced too early and too indiscriminately. Moreover, there are so many imposed changes in the educational maelstrom that any additional upheaval needs careful scrutiny in order to measure certain turmoil against possible benefits. The words of Gaius Petronius, 66 AD, have a curiously modern ring:

> We trained hard – but it seemed that every time we were beginning to form up into teams we would be reorganized. I was to learn later in life that we tend to meet any new situation by reorganizing – and a wonderful method it can be for creating the illusion of progress whilst producing confusion, inefficiency and demoralisation.

One way of avoiding this trinity of undesirables is by constant departmental discussion, formal and informal, and I want now to identify some of the areas which might concern an English department contemplating a move to mixed ability teaching. I am assuming that the move has not been forced on them from the top, since there is plenty of evidence that innovation of that kind has little chance of lasting success. The fruit may grow rapidly, but it soon withers. Instead, let us take the case of a department where a majority professes a belief in mixed ability grouping but has little or no experience of it, and where some highly successful and respected colleagues are very sceptical. It's an ideological confrontation where care should be taken to avoid unhelpful stereotypes such as:

Supporters = progressive – child centred – modern
Antagonists = reactionary – subject centred – old fashioned

One way in which a department might proceed, is to contemplate the tremendous variety of literacy and oracy skills which any teacher of a mixed ability class might expect to encounter. What ranges might we find in a first year mixed group of eleven year olds, and what are some of the teaching strategies we might adopt? Let us look at the areas of reading, listening and speaking, writing.

Reading
We could well encounter a span of measured reading age from 7–14 years and a tremendous diversity of interest and taste. Some children cannot read a daily newspaper, nor much else for that matter; some can

6

cope with *The Times* if they wish. Some are hooked on the Famous Five's adventures; others prefer the exploits of Mr Pickwick. Some read no books at all; others devour several a week. Frank Whitehead (1975) makes many interesting comments about the range of children's reading interests and how tastes change with age, and the results of his survey might well cause a department to look critically at its stock, particularly its provision for adolescent specialist interests, which are often of a technical nature. The main point, is that whatever written material we are thinking of – whether it is fiction or factual information; notices on the board; instructions on work cards; newspapers or magazines – there are some boys and girls who will have difficulty with reading matter of any kind. It is probably the inability of some children to read reasonably which is the biggest problem facing the teacher of mixed groups, since so much energy, time and attention, have to be devoted to ways and means of either remedying the deficiency or circumventing it.

In order to do either of these two things satisfactorily we need to have as much information as possible about the weak reader. Ideally, he would have a full medical examination which would involve audiometric, opthalmic and neurological tests. That ideal is rarely attained, except in the case of children with severe learning difficulties or those with parents who are determined to be as fully informed as possible. Here is one example (Gray 1976) of the sort of information which could come from a thorough examination:

> My younger son, Peter (aged 7 years) was assessed by a paediatrician, a neurologist and a psychologist. The three visits were spread over nine months, and we were given no information until the last visit. The centre (a dyslexia clinic) appeared grossly overworked and understaffed.
>
> At our final visit, the neurologist summed up their findings. Peter had a full-scale WISC IQ of 121, verbal 140, but performance below average. He had very poor visual perception, that is, his brain did not interpret correctly what his eyes saw. This explained his constant confusion of 't' and 'f', 'm' and 'w', 'e' and 'g', 'p' 'd' 'b' and 'q'; and his trying to walk through the closed halves of doors when smaller! His hand and eye co-ordination were poor, and he had difficulty with fine finger movements. Regular scanning of straight lines, needed in reading, would be difficult for him for some time to come. They did not consider he had brain damage, but was suffering from a 'maturational lag'.

Comparatively few children get such rigorous examination from medical and psychological experts, but all can be tested for reading age and reading level, and this can be done objectively and subjectively. *Objectively,* you will find a *group* or *individual* reading test which can be administered by a *teacher,* (some can only be used by trained psychologists), which is applicable to the *secondary* range, which will either *diagnose* and/or show *attainment* and, at the same time, is relatively *inexpensive*. The most commonly used tests are those of word recognition (e.g. Schonell and Burt) but they are of limited usefulness. More helpful are those by Neale (1957), and the GAP (1970) and NFER (1966) tests.[1]

It is for you to look at these if you wish and decide on the most appropriate for your purposes. Jackson (1968) and Vincent and Cresswell (1976) give useful advice for those uncertain about testing techniques,[2] and Cotterell's booklet is helpful.[3] The children would then be tested early and late in the academic year. There is nothing incompatible between the use of diagnostic tests and the practice of mixed ability grouping.

I believe we should treat any results, which purport to measure attainment, with respect certainly, but also with a healthy suspension of judgement, being aware of the perils of too dogmatic a stance in this area. Diagnostic information is, in my view, much more valuable. However, what of subjective judgements? What of the teacher's own continuous assessment? Here, I believe, good infant and junior school methods should be used. You can hear the child read aloud, making a mental, and later written, note of the kinds of errors he makes and deducing categories of errors from the clues provided; questioning him on what he reads; or asking about a passage he's just read silently; constantly building up and revising a detailed record which monitors his strengths and weaknesses, his interests and hobbies, books he's read and ones he's failed to read. Open University material offers considerable help in this area of reading and interest inventories (OU 1973). Perhaps it all sounds a little formidable, but what I have in mind is some simple yet useful cumulative record such as David Mears offers in chapter two, and it should not become a burden for the teacher; nor for the children.[4] No child should be required to write about every book he reads. It will only make him read less and there are other, more imaginative ways in which you can check his progress.

When you are aware of attainment levels and interests, look again at your departmental stock to see if it is appropriate and adequate. You will, presumably, have the examination texts you require, but can you offer good factual material as well as satisfying fiction? Are there any useful play texts for first- and second- years? Can you cater for the weak third- year readers? Here you will, no doubt, come up against the old dilemma: should you be happy if the really weak or poorly-motivated ones are reading anything at all, whatever it might be? I'm not just thinking of Enid Blyton. I visited a school recently and happened to see at lunchtime a group of five second-year girls sitting on the lawn, one of whom was reading aloud to the other four. It was an idyllic scene and I don't recall seeing it before or since. Then, as I walked by, I noticed the title of the book – *The Exorcist*.

As you're inspecting your stock, look carefully at the questions in your text books and on your work cards. Are they clear? Have you included a translation of any difficult phrases, so as to accommodate a wide range of children? Let me emphasize that I'm not arguing for a lowering of standards. Quite the contrary. I want standards to be higher than ever, but don't let us correlate incomprehensibility with academic excellence. Colleagues from other departments should look carefully, too, at the language of their questions and their subject and their teaching. The phrase 'a language policy across the curriculum' might then begin to become a reality. Here's one example I came across the other day of a question addressed to eleven year olds based on a prose passage: 'What does Moorehead wish us to understand when he compares the animal's dignity and majesty with that of the prophets?' I'm sure there are better ways of saying that. Perhaps that was a fairly obvious candidate for attention, but we can easily be caught unawares by much simpler constructions. Recently an acquaintance of mine included on a work card the instruction: 'Give the definition of "amphibious" ', and discovered that, while a particular girl knew the meaning of amphibious she was fooled by the injunction, 'Give the definition of'.

Please be clear that I am not arguing for a reduction of all written language to monosyllabic Anglo-Saxon grunts. That way illiteracy lies. Often we must help weak readers through difficult text, but equally we should be sensitive to the problems posed by awkward constructions as well as unfamiliar vocabulary.

Let us assume that we now know the children's levels and interests and we know our stock quite well also. How do we match the stock to the children? I will make some points briefly here since Shirley Hoole deals at length with the subject and, in fact, offers a different emphasis.

Traditionally, we have had class readers and no doubt there are some appropriate for mixed groups but to expect thirty boys and girls regularly to maintain interest in the same book for the same amount of time is probably unrealistic. The short story, if chosen with care, is a much more appropriate form for this kind of treatment and some sets of short stories could be kept together, precisely for the purpose of class teaching lessons, in order to develop skills of comprehension and appreciation and to ensure that all children are introduced to various techniques involved in prose reading, as well as using such stories as springboards for creative activities.

Another method of organization is to have four or five titles in a class (six copies of each book) chosen and distributed on the basis of interest, rather than reading age. Otherwise you are in danger of streaming within your mixed class. Any one small group of six children would work, at times corporately and at times individually, reading their books and completing a variety of tasks, based on work cards.

One advantage of such a system, apart from the element of choice which it may permit, is the more flexible use of stock involved.

Better still, I believe, is a class library where individual informed choice can be made and this means dividing up your departmental stock into, perhaps, sets of thirty separate titles with two copies of each title, i.e. sixty books in all, or more, if you have them. If you ask pupils to donate used books to the class library, as I did on one occasion, I would expect you to pick up some useful material within the lumber. You may also develop a school bookshop[5] and/or develop one of the existing schemes[6] for encouraging children to buy their own books.

Class libraries, alongside school libraries, do mean that more children read more books, but there are still problems to be solved and you do have to devise adequate ways of monitoring what is read, whether it has been understood, and so on. However, we should take care not to kill the habit with pedantic insistence on complete understanding. In an excellent chapter entitled 'Making Children Hate Reading', John Holt (1967) writes:

> Unfortunately, we English teachers are easily hung up on this matter of understanding. Why should children understand everything they read? Why should anyone? *Does* anyone? I don't, and I never did. I was always reading books that teachers would have said were 'too hard' for me, books full of words I didn't know. That's how I got to be a good reader. When about ten, I read all the D'Artagnan stories and loved them, it didn't trouble me in the least that I didn't know why France was at war with England or who was quarrelling with whom in the French court or why the Musketeers should always be at odds with Cardinal Richelieu's men. I didn't even know who the Cardinal was, except that he was a dangerous and powerful man that my friends had to watch out for. This was all I needed to know.

I remember reading those stories about the same age as Holt and being mildly baffled by those same questions, but not sufficiently for it to inhibit my enjoyment. That's probably the key; only enjoyment and high motivation will really develop the reading habit. Recently I came across eight year old Wayne reading these words:

> She sat on her eggs to keep them warm. She sat on them for days and days. The only time she went away was to get some food. She came back soon.

Then he said to me: 'I save eggs, you see. I've got a raven, a woodpigeon, a golden pheasant, tree creeper, a house sparrer, a hedge sparrer, a quail, a coot, a moorehen, a swan, a blackbird, a starling, a thrush, a duck, a hen, a poechard, a twight.' He was, in fact, an expert on the subject, collecting and swopping eggs, like stamps or marbles, as a hobby, and he said that he always chose reading books about birds and eggs. His own knowledge was clearly far in advance of the text of his reading book, *Gertie the Duck,* but the mere subject held his interest.

A last point about class libraries. It's very useful to have suitable reference material in your classroom so that it becomes a natural activity, both in the class and the school library, to look up information, thereby developing a range of reference skills. You might think about the following reference sources as a basis:

a good dictionary
Roget's *Thesaurus*
a Bible (with a Concordance?)
an Atlas
Pears Cyclopaedia
Whitaker's Almanack
Radio Times and TV *Times*
a newspaper
a telephone directory
a dictionary of quotations.

Mentioning the school library leads me to consider in passing its modern development, the Resource Centre, and to refer interested readers to the bibliography for more detailed analysis of this concept. (Beswick 1975; Holder and Mitson 1974; Schools Council 1972; Taylor 1971; Walton and Ruck 1975). Perhaps the very phrase 'resource centre' frightens some teachers, with its transatlantic overtones of high cost, establishment problems, complicated operation, and, perhaps above all, loss of autonomy over one's own materials which, it is feared, will be absorbed into the common pool. Such fears are real enough, but many a good collection started from humble origins and was built up slowly and gradually, as needs were identified and met. (The Schools Council will loan, free of charge, a tape-slide sequence of an unpretentious home-made resource centre at a Ludlow school).

Certainly, such a development is directly in line with mixed ability teaching where you often need to draw on as many kinds of stimulus as are available, and it should be remembered here that some excellent resources are human – pupils, teachers, other adults – and that we should explore this potential as well as any other. All teachers will develop their own personal materials but in the additional central collection one would eventually expect to find a range of books, photographs, charts, worksheets, newspapers, magazines, colour slides, film, film strips, objects, tapes, cassettes, records and folders (produced by pupils). This does not mean that poor readers should be for ever looking at photographs, drawing pictures, or listening to tapes, but such material and methods may be used to develop a range of language skills in the weak and the strong, as Gordon Taylor indicates in a later chapter.

Time and again we return to the weak reader. What do we do about him? The first thing is to recognize that the school exists as much for him as for the 'O' and 'A' Level candidate. In fact, probably more so, but there are no easy answers and I have known weak readers who have improved only marginally, despite great efforts by very hard working staff. Ideally, after the screening and testing which I mentioned earlier, all kinds of strategies will be used, including:

interest based work – (With a boy like Wayne see p.10 this is no problem, but there do appear to be children who obscure their interests remarkably successfully.)

extra tuition – (possibly in some of the time allocated to a subject other than English, if all parties are agreeable. In one school where I worked, the Head of Modern Languages permitted such an arrangement).

devices to build confidence, including encouragement, success at short-term goals, enthusiasm and conviction on the teacher's part and an awareness of the possible value of counselling (Lawrence 1974), and of the virtue of building on strengths rather than stressing weaknesses. In other words, an attempt to deal with the whole person.

use of multi-media materials mentioned above.

use of various kinds of hardware, including the Language Master;[7] the Audio Page;[8] and the tape recorder with junction box.[9]

above all, perhaps, good systematic infant and junior method, without infantile material. (The Open University course PE 261 offers much valuable advice on reading in the curriculum.)

Finally, let me end this section on reading with an unusual testimony to the enduring quality of literature. These are the words of a seven year old boy as he compares comics with books:

I don't like comics. Comics rip too easily, but books are tough. You try to break them, but you can't. I sawed through my book. I tried to sell it, so I sawed through it, in half. My saw was ever so sharp. I couldn't even get through it.

Listening and speaking
Reading and writing are often regarded as the high status skills among the language arts but much recent research has focused on the need

for good foundations in listening and speaking, and it is to these areas that we now turn our attention.

Whatever results may be obtained from listening tests (Wilkinson, Stratta, Dudley 1974 and 1976) we can never be wholly certain of any child's listening thresholds in the day-to-day classroom activity. We can't legislate, mercifully, for what goes on between the ears. However, our experience indicates that some children can apparently concentrate for lengthy periods of time and, subsequently, act upon what they heard, even after long intervals. Others hear our words and those pearls of wisdom sink like stones into cotton wool, provoking no discernible response. Between these two extremes there is every level of listening skill and somehow we must try to provide for such range within our groups. Bullock gives useful advice:

> People listen best when they have to take some action upon the information they have received. Where they have the opportunity to reply or to participate through action their attention is stimulated. (10.19)

So, although I am sceptical of Listening Laboratories of the SRA variety, since these tend to isolate the skill and try to develop it in a vacuum, nevertheless, it does seem sensible to plan for some amelioration in listening skills, within the normal daily work in school. Certainly, many teachers are increasingly anxious about the quality of listening and, despite any hard evidence, attribute a supposed deterioration to the deleterious effect of television.

As with listening, so with speaking, a similar range of skill may be discerned in our wide ability group. One or two may be highly articulate and virtually able to enter into Socratic-type dialogue. Some may speak several languages but not be particularly proficient in English. Some children, not unlike some adults, will utter many words with no thought. One or two may remain absolutely silent, as did one boy I met, for over a year. Many will not understand particular words or constructions which we use. If you, as a teacher, use a sentence such as: 'Presumably you will be familiar with the contextual constraints involved', then you need to translate it in the next breath into something like: 'You'll probably know a bit about how the situation you're in affects what you say.' Then you follow up with some examples. However, in the unlikely instance I've just given, there are obvious difficulties of construction, vocabulary and concept. Our language could be much simpler and still pose many problems for our pupils (Barnes 1969 and 1976) and we need constantly to listen to the words we speak and provide, in a subtle and discreet manner, (unlike my example) a running commentary or translation. Sometimes such a translation may be supplied by a pupil. Shirley Hoole tells me she once participated in the following exchange with some ear pupils:

S.H.	Don't assume that a boy with an upper-class accent is necessarily effeminate. Don't equate class with femininity or masculinity.
Pupil	What does she mean?
Another pupil (Karen)	She means, 'Don't think because he talks posh he's a puff.'

Apparently, they then had a very profitable discussion on why the teacher couldn't (or felt she couldn't) use such language herself, and on the differences between teacher and pupil language.

Listening and talking are two sides of the same coin. Perhaps we have all too readily tried to develop the former skill in our pupils by exercising the latter skill ourselves. 'Who needs the most practice talking in school?' asks John Holt. 'Who gets the most?' (1967). Bullock, less pithily, but with no less concern, states:

> There is research evidence to suggest that on average the teacher talks for ¾ of the time in the usual teacher–class situation. It has been calculated from this that in a 45-minute period the amount of time left for a class of 30 to contribute is an average of some 20 seconds per pupil. (10.4)

As it is, we know that the time in a class lesson is never evenly apportioned in this way, as a wedding cake might be. When we speak of having had 'a good discussion' what we often mean is that we were able to conduct an interesting dialogue between ourselves and three or four articulate pupils, while the other twenty-seven were good enough to be passive, listening or not listening. At least, we may have advanced a little from the time when a pupil of primary school age, questioned as to the worst things he could possibly do, replied: 'Murder, and talking in the corridor'. (Widlake 1971).

Other problems spring to mind. How do we continue to stretch the highly able and articulate pupil while, at the same time, helping him to become sensitive enough to avoid rejection by his less fluent contemporaries? How do we encourage in some children more thought and less talk? How do we develop such a climate that the silent person will feel able to say something with comparative confidence, thereby developing his grasp of ideas which he as yet dimly perceives? How do we grapple with the two or three pupils in the class who need to be taught English as a second language, and for whom there is no peripatetic help? How do we provide such a variety of contexts and situations that pupils have the opportunity to use language in a number of different ways and for a number of different purposes? The questions almost ask themselves, and the list could easily be continued, but let us now consider briefly some of the areas in which the answers may lie, with more detail of strategies in ensuing chapters.

A major requirement is for us all to become more sensitive to language, both our own and that of our pupils and students. One of the ways to do this is, on occasion, to tape record ourselves and the children in the classroom and produce a transcript of part of the lesson. You probably can't do a great deal of this, but an occasional analysis will, like a long week-end, act as a refresher. For example, you will be able to remind yourself of proportions of teacher-talk and pupil-talk; of the pros and cons of open and closed questions; of the virtues of encouragement and praise; of the kinds of language the pupils are called upon to use. Here is a short excerpt for you to analyse. What would you say to (or about) the teacher who figures in this extract? He is working with 42 ten year olds.

Teacher	One, ONE, one good sentence that describes you eating a meal. It, it, it might be, it doesn't have to include the er thing you're actually eating. No. Put up your hand and tell me one. One good sentence that describes what you're eating.
Pupil	Munching, crunching all the chicken away.
Teacher	Munching, crunching all the chicken away. That's good, Paul. Can you think of anything, Clare?
Clare	No, sir.
Teacher	Er, well. Come on, think, Clare. Use your brain. Dominic?
Dominic	Shloshing chips and beans in your mouth, sir.
Teacher	Shloshing chips and beans in your mouth. Can you think of a better word than 'shloshing' 'cause you're, you're tending to get a bit slangy? Dominic?
Dominic	Stuffing.
Teacher	Stuffing. That, er, that's still a bit slangy. Can you think of . . .
Dominic	Piling.
Teacher	Yes, er, that's a little better. Can you think of something, well . . . write down the sentence now that you've now thought of . . . quickly . . . that describes . . . how you're eating a meal . . . describe what . . . go on, say what you're doing. Can you think of some good describing words, to describe the meal? What can you think of one quickly?
Pupils	(unintelligible)
Teacher	Yes. Delicious. Yes, that's a good one. Can you think of er, er a better word than 'delicious?'
Pupil	Luscious.
Teacher	Luscious.
Pupil	Scrumptious.
Teacher	Scrumptious. Can you think of anything else?

I can only speculate on whether you and I would make the same points about that short exchange. It's certainly a salutary experience for a teacher to see his fleeting words frozen in print and assuming a status which he would not have wished for them. But there are compensations, too. We may find some gems. My wife was recently in a class of infants, listening to a music programme on the radio. Towards the end of the programme one of the participants ran his fingers across a harp. The children hadn't been told it was a harp, and a girl in the class, whose command of English was very limited, said: 'It's like water, dingley, dingley'. That seems to me a splendid comment; what you might call 'creative speaking'.

Such tape recording and transcription, then, is one of the ways in which we can 'learn to listen to language' (Halliday 1968), our own and other people's. We must also devise ways in which pupils can exercise their language in differing contexts so that they become practised in adapting to differing language expectations and able to operate effectively in a range of situations. The arrangement of furniture within a traditional lesson – ranks of single desks facing the teacher – promotes a boomerang style of dialogue where virtually every comment from a pupil is mediated through the teacher who redirects it back again, either to the whole class or to an individual, often having passed judgement on it or modified it in some way en route. There is undoubtedly at times a place for this kind of activity, but let us be clear of its language limitations. It is not suitable for promoting interaction between the pupils; it merely sustains action and reaction between pupils and teacher. Hence the need, on occasions, to move to a kind of regrouping which will encourage children to talk.

The most obvious means at our disposal is to work in pairs and in small groups. Good small group discussion can occur spontaneously, and when that happens it's very satisfying for the members of the group and for us as teachers. More often, it has to be worked for and I favour a fairly fixed kind of control early on. The sort of thing I'm thinking of, is where a group of no more than five is given a poem, or a piece of prose, or a short story, or newspaper article, or photograph etc. with several questions they have to answer, within a limited amount of time (say, fifteen minutes, but obviously extended at your discretion). This is followed up later by one from each group acting as secretary and reporting back, or by whole class discussion, or by written work. In other words, the small group discussion has a clear purpose in view. It's an activity intended to train children to focus their thoughts and I like to think it will lead to the situation where they may just be given the poem itself to grapple with, or the short story to relate to their own experience, or the current problem which they try to resolve, or the contemporary issue which they explore and open up. At this stage *process* is more important than *product*. They are, we hope, learning

16

that it's a rational thing to try to bring order out of the chac
mind, and to discuss matters with other people, agreeing p
many occasions to differ. There is no virtue in spurious cons......
the same time, all being well, *process* is refining *product*.

Naturally, there will be times when they 'go off the subject', but that
could sometimes be valuable. If the talk merely becomes the loose kind
of general chat about Leeds or Manchester United or Wimbledon, that
they could have in the playground (and that you and I may have in our
staff rooms) then, generally speaking, that is lesson time wasted.
However, because that *can* happen on occasions I don't think it
invalidates the general view that small group discussion is a very
valuable strategy. After all, in a traditional class lesson, the pupils may
be merely *dreaming* of Leeds, or Manchester United or Wimbledon.
To sum up and develop this point, let me quote James Britton (1970):

> At the secondary school stage, the educational importance of
> good conversation in small intimate groups can hardly be
> over-emphasized. It paves the way for class discussion, which in
> the informative subjects, may be a principal mode of learning,
> but it has its own value as a mode of learning, particularly in
> English lessons, where the main stream of activity will be the
> handling of experiences in the spectator role. This will be no
> unfamiliar occupation for adolescents, whose own conversations
> are likely to be a traffic in what D. W. Harding has called
> 'considered experience' – things that have happened to them-
> selves or to other people, offered in such a way as to involve
> direct or implied evaluation. But they will need a good deal of
> help in moving to general inferences. Left to themselves they
> tend to oscillate between particular instances and vast generali-
> sations taken over at second hand, leaving a gap that needs to be
> filled by intermediate generalisations they must make for
> themselves.

So much then, at this stage, for small group work, and I will return to
the subject at greater length in a later chapter. What else can we do to
encourage awareness of spoken language and to develop oral skills?

Children can listen to and discuss tape-recorded speech from radio
and television and real life[10].

The can go out into the school and the community and interview
people, possibly using tape-recorders as well as note-books.

They can become accustomed to recording material on tape as well
as on paper. At my last school we were in the habit, at one stage of
having fortnightly radio programmes produced by a different
second-year group each fortnight and relayed to the other eleven
second-year groups. Such programmes could be exchanged be-

tween schools. One school which I visit sends our regular radio programmes to the local hospital.

They can engage in all kinds of drama – (Les Stringer tackles this area in chapter five). At times, the really shy ones will participate in a type of drama where they can speak within a group but not be exposed individually. Occasional choral speech, which can easily be linked with mime, offers this kind of safety, as do crowd scenes. Hand puppets, too, may offer an outlet for shy children and I well remember the liberating effect on a timid child of having stage make-up put on her face, along with others, in an ordinary classroom drama lesson.

They can experience all kinds of language games (and there is more detail on this in the Schools Council chapter).

I don't rule out two-minute lecturettes, what someone once described as 'female lectures'. They can have their uses but they often take place in a forced context and I don't think they generally develop natural speech rhythms. Such talks can be of great value where they are spontaneous or semi-spontaneous, arising out of real interest and expertise, and building on personal anecdotes in the most natural way. The kind of thing I'm thinking of is, to use a fictitious example, Billy Caspar's talk in Barry Hines' book *A Kestrel for a Knave* (film titled *Kes*) about how to train a wild kestrel. I have found, as I'm sure you have too, that children often talk very well about their pets, particularly when they bring them into school and demonstrate to the rest of the class. Gerbils, hamsters, rabbits, tortoises are obvious convergent candidates, but I wouldn't rule out the more divergent, such as snakes or skunks, or indeed any animal which is under control. Similarly, photographs and objects from home are often good stimuli for a short talk and more acceptable, to some, than skunks. Each object has its own story. One girl, Ingrid, once brought into school her deceased granny's suede gloves which, I noticed, had three sets of numbers inked on the inside cuff. Two had lines through them and the third remained distinct. This was, in fact, the current doctor's telephone number and Ingrid's granny, so I was told, had never gone anywhere without that information. It was a fascinating insight into another person's life.

What is needed above all, for good talk to flourish, is a non-judgmental kind of atmosphere where pupils can say whatever they genuinely believe to be true, provided we don't get involved in being unprofessional. Most children readily understand a teacher's loyalty to his colleagues when the convention is made clear to them.

Let me stress, too, that encouraging talk in the classroom does not automatically lead to the disorder of a market place or rabble. Good talk necessarily involves good listening and should be as disciplined an activity, according to its own conventions, as any other work in the classroom.

Writing
Having briefly considered the sort of situation a mixed ability English teacher faces in the areas of reading, listening and speaking, let us now move on to perhaps the most traditional activity of the classroom, namely writing.

Differences between children when talking or engaged in drama may not be particularly noticeable, despite the wide ranges of skill, but when they hand in written work, the variations in attainment and proficiency are plain. We meet some who sprinkle punctuation marks like confetti; others so sparing that they never use any. Some who observe accepted spelling conventions; others who invent their own, and change them line by line. Some who cannot transfer the thoughts in their head to intelligible marks on the page and others whose written fluency we ourselves may envy.

Here are four pieces of work which were written by two boys and two girls on the same occasion in the same first year mixed ability class. I include them, not because they represent the work of the most and least able children. They don't. But because they exemplify work which forces the teacher to think of their authors as individual people who need to be guided in different ways. Here is the first piece.

Snow

The snow was ridged thickly on the forked twig,
And hear and there the plump snow falls in
sudden mounds,
The air is silent and eeire with the stillness
of everthing
Where some early footsteps had been made the snow
was drifting over them,
The snow creaked beaneath my feet as I walked
through a field heavly shod with snow,
The robin lay there his song choked in his throat,
This marved glittered in the cold sun such a place
where paradise was.

Stephen

It has a stylistic control but is derivative and strives after a literary effect which takes Stephen away from his own real experience. He needs to be handled with care, so that, when advised that not every noun needs an adjective, he doesn't regard this as a rejection of his undoubted feeling for words. His strength lies in his observation rather than his literary borrowings and this is something to build on. He might even be able to appreciate the notion of pathetic fallacy, and this can perhaps be explained with examples from Walt Disney.

Patricia also writes of snow, and of rain too.

Snow

SNOW
Cold and
soft white
and
light, iciey,
and creystal, wet,
Smoth refreashing
and clear, sour
smell, Gaive

RAIN
Wet and cold, pittering
on the window pain soggey
Shoses, cold hands, wet-hair
Sharp and Jagged, terrible tast

Patricia

She has produced an interesting word list which lacks development. With the help of judicious questioning she could extend some of these single words into whole phrases and sentences which mirror her own experience of snow and rain. Whereas Stephen develops too many of his words into phrases, Pat develops none. Spelling errors also could be pointed out to her and phonic help given, particularly in relation to the 'e' sound.

Denise's work reads as follows:

The Snow

One day my mom said to me can you go down the shops for me please and I said yes I will. But put your boots on because it is snowing and put your coat on and your hat on I got out side the door.

Denise

She writes in a very low level, blow-by-blow, narrative style which, in my experience, takes a long time to remedy. She needs to hear and read a lot of good writing, including that of other children in the class, so as to be clear of the focus for the task. Practice at selecting significant detail, possibly starting with an exercise on the composition of telegrams, should help. All this could only be accomplished over a period of time. Individualized teaching of this kind, when you're dealing with large numbers of children, is very demanding indeed but certainly made more possible in a workshop context where at times you move from person to person.

The fourth piece is by Barry, who produces something extraordinary, but which can hardly be deciphered.

Storm

Now it is almost nigt from the bron Zesofisk jug full ofrer jug full of pure white ligal Fire, bright white tipples over und spillsdown and is gon.

Barry

Perhaps you might start here by asking him to write a fair copy for your own collection. This would give him useful handwriting practice as well as providing you with a remarkable piece of writing for your records. He could develop his skills with practice in more writing of a similar kind, and you might select appropriate snippets from Gerald Manley Hopkins for him to hear or read, since both he and Hopkins have something in common. Obviously your aim is to improve his technical control, while building on his divergent strength.

What considerations should guide the marking of written work? (See Stratta 1969). Certainly, there should be departmental discussion to establish a coherent policy. I think you will find that a numerical mark is inflexible; a grade gives a little more leeway but is still inhibiting; and that detailed comment, oral and written, is most valuable, if you can persuade the children to act on it. This is the ideal. In practice, you are so pressed for time that often all you can do is to indicate very briefly that you have actually read and responded to the piece that the child has written. Over a period of time I do believe it is possible to convince a child that you are very concerned with what he actually writes, not with the mark or grade it might get; that you don't wish to measure him against anyone else, since there's really no point in this; that you are looking for positive virtues rather than merely spotting technical errors; and that your main intention is to encourage him to write as well as he can. It's a long business, but it can be done, with most pupils.

Let me be autobiographical for a moment in order to develop this point. Concurrent with work on this book, I'm learning to play the piano and, after eighteen lessons, have so often been reminded of useful educational points that I'm inclined to feel that any teacher should also constantly be a learner of a specific skill, not only to respond to the Victorian ethic of self-improvement, but also in order to remind himself of what life is like as the underdog. As a piano learner I can testify that encouragement is a great boost; that practice at what I *can* do is satisfying; that the foundations of the civilized world don't crumble when I hit a wrong note. Indeed, I've been told several times that *technique* is more important. Moreover, it's been evident that a sense of structure and sequence and making progress is helpful, and there is great pleasure in successfully playing a small but tricky item, e.g. a run of five or six difficult notes. I have yet to be criticized for not doing enough practice, even though there have been weeks when I've hardly touched the piano. And so on. I could make many more teaching points from this example, but these are sufficient for you to appreciate the classroom equivalent and, even allowing for differences in maturity and motivation between my learning the piano and school pupils learning English, I don't see why my responses in a learning situation should be so very different from theirs. Indeed, I think they are parallel and should be remembered when we act in the role of teacher as critic and mark a piece of written work. Such acts of empathy may affect our teaching behaviour more radically than trying to respond to results of research.

Let us now move on to the setting of written work. I feel we should more often than not offer a choice to the children, sometimes of topic but always of range within a topic. It doesn't mean that they will inevitably opt for the easiest task although this a realistic danger which the teacher must guard against. Hopefully, they will choose tasks which are potentially interesting and challenging to them and to which they would like to respond, given the constraints of the situation.

Here is an example of a number of assignments on part of Philip Larkin's poem *Whitsun Weddings* which might be used by individuals at fourth/fifth-year level. I've included nine questions and would expect the pupils to do several of them, but only after a close reading, and re-reading, of the poem.

1 Is Larkin a snob?
2 What impressions of England does he convey in the first two verses? (Some of you might try to represent parts of the poem in painting, drawing, or collage).
3 Write the wedding speech of one of the broad-belted fathers.
4 Continue the conversation from 'I nearly died . . .'
5 The poem starts in sunlight and ends in rain. Is the poet being pessimistic?
6 Draw up four columns and list the arguments for and against weddings in church and at a registry office.

7 Is the image of the bride in the drawing the same one that Larkin has in mind?

8 Which is the best wedding you have ever been to? Why was it the best?

9 'Marriage is for fools.' Are you one of the wise?

What I have tried to do here is to offer a mixture of creative and critical responses. To offer a range of written possibilities, from a speech, to conversation, notes, continuous prose, and also other responses of a non-verbal kind. To encourage a judgment on the relationship between visual image and written word. To get the pupils to reflect on their own experience and also consider more general implications of the issues. I am not suggesting we do all of this all of the time; the material itself will always impose constraints on the kind of questions asked. Nor am I suggesting that the example I have just given is without flaws, but it is an attempt to encourage what one might call 'disciplined freedom' i.e. to permit choice within a framework, dependent on some detailed study and reflection. If you merely say to your pupils: 'You can write about anything you like' – on most occasions you will get very poor quality responses. However, if some of them want positively to work on something they have thought up, you would be foolish to suppress this.

They can, then, often choose their own assignments, from a number of options, and also, I believe, their own form of written expression – free verse, prose, a play, notes, conversation. They won't always choose free verse on the grounds that it frees them from some conventional writing restrictions. However, in order that their choice be informed, they need to know precisely what is involved in writing a play, or conversation, or free verse. They all need to be shown in the fairly formal manner of traditional class teaching, I believe, how to cope adequately with each form before they can be expected to exercise a proper choice and produce good quality work. This cannot be done at a stroke, and without careful initial and on-going guidance, many will produce rubbish. However, when choice is given, make sure it is a real one. You may remember the Peanuts extract (Reimer 1971):

> I learned something in school today.
> I signed up for folk guitar, computer programming, stained glass art, shoemaking, and a natural foods workshop.
> I got Spelling, History, Arithmetic and two study periods.
> So what did you learn?
> I learned that what you sign up for and what you get are two different things.

Bear in mind that, as with small group discussion, you can have small group production also, as when a group scripts a play, or a pair of children work together to produce a piece of writing. Pupils can be encouraged to read each other's work and suggest improvements.

A more individual activity is involved in the use of work cards and I can hardly discuss writing in mixed ability classes without mentioning them. You can, of course, use professionally produced sets such as SRA[11] despite any reservations you may have. Five which I would want to express are as follows: I am not convinced that they develop skills which will transfer out of the work card situation, although they do focus attention on reading for information. They are invariably unrelated to anything else in school and exist in a vacuum. They have no real audience, other than the teacher as judge or umpire. The focus may fall on completing as many cards as possible rather than learning from them. In one school I overheard a girl say to herself as she looked at her neighbour's card, 'Bloody hell, I'm only on orange'. They have an American origin which shows itself occasionally in some very odd assignments and uses of language, in the predominantly transatlantic context and the American spellings.

Against such points one must set the strengths of SRA and the English equivalents[12]. These are chiefly five. They do cater for children of all abilities; most children and many teachers like them; they offer a sense of progress, to teacher and pupil; they provide the opportunity for independent work, and self checking; they free the teacher to go round and work with individuals. All these are attractions which teachers do not lightly throw away, as sales of the material will testify.

Apart from professionally produced cards, and there are many on the market in addition to those I've mentioned, you can, of course, make your own. It's time consuming and often hard work, but the big advantage is that you can produce particular cards to suit particular children whom you teach, and to reflect local conditions and circumstances. There is a danger that even home-produced materials can themselves take on the status of a text book and become as inflexible. However, they are rarely so attractive as good books, and to replace a colourful, professionally produced, well illustrated book by an anaemic banda copy, apparently written in invisible ink seems a poor exchange. Attractive and well-constructed workcards can be useful but, like all other methods and materials, must be kept in their place.

What of this weak writer? What can we do for him? Again he needs careful remedial attention which first diagnoses the precise problems and, with any one child, there will be several. He also needs a good primary school method which may have to go right back to basics. We have all met secondary school children whose chief writing problem was their inability to form letters correctly. In addition, any confidence boost is welcome and here are two suggestions: a weak writer could, on occasions, produce a photo essay, i.e. a series of photographs or pictures, stuck in his book, with captions underneath (which you perhaps write first, on his instructions, and he then copies), to tell the story. One advantage of this is that it can look very attractive. A polaroid instant camera is very appropriate for this kind of activity and Gordon Taylor mentions other possibilities in chapter six.

Another possibility is that he can say what he wants to say into a tape recorder. You, or another child, can transcribe it and type it out. This is very time consuming and you couldn't do it often, but it can be the means whereby a child who normally produces no writing at all can, overnight, produce an extended piece. Here is an example. It's the work of a nine year old boy, Michael, living in a dilapidated city suburb. His writing ability is so severely limited that he can only manage two or three lines of indecipherable scribble, but here he is describing into the tape recorder the experience he has just had of visiting a demolition site near his school.

And we seen lots of bombed down houses. We seen a dustbin lid full up with dirty, dirty cans. And then we went and took a photo inside of one house. Then we carried on walking and then Miss said, 'Would you like a piece of paper?' and we said, 'Yes'. 'Would you draw a picture of an 'ouse, bombed down house?' and we said, 'Yes'.

There was lots of bricks and lots of slates. We seen a man pulling slates out of roofs and then we seen a man carrying planks of wood. And then, later on, a few days ago, we se we seen bombs. All the houses. And a tractor came in and bombed down all the houses. All the houses was burnt. Then we seen a fire. And then a boy went over and he pulled a stick from the fire and he was playing with it and he was scaring people with the fire. And then he soon got told off by the teacher.

Then we drawed a picture of the inside. It was very good. We seen a man on the roof knocking a brick through the ceiling. Ceilings were fell through. The chimneys fell off and a whole lot of walls were fall down. All all the toilets was broken. No roofs. Broken chains. Broken toilet tops. And then we saw a dirty old bath and we seen lots of mud. We seen lots of bombed down houses and we.

One day we seen a man carrying planks and he fell in a pile of bricks. He hurt himself. And then he got up and carried the plank and then he got up and carried the plank and then he burnt it. And then a man on the roof shouted, 'Are you alright?' 'Yes, yes', he said. 'Come and help me'. 'I I can't. I have to do, knock the ceiling through and throw and throw the bricks all down.'

And then we seen lots of chimneys fell off, falling off. Then we seen a man on a roof knocking slates through. The slates, when they hit the bottom, they went crash.

That's all I've got to say for today.

Despite obvious weaknesses, the strengths of such a spoken utterance are evident: clarity and vividness of recall; power of cumulative detail; interest of personal incident; above all, vitality. Michael has something worth saying, based on real experience, and says it quite well. He can't write about his world so he talks about it. If the student teaching him hadn't appreciated the validity of the spoken word, then we should never have known his responses to what he saw, and he would not have seen his piece on the wall, for the first time ever.

Such ploys obviously cannot constitute the whole answer but they might offer a way in. Certainly, display and presentation of work should not be neglected. If you're using a multi-media approach in your group and if you're working in a thematic kind of way which, as Judith Atkinson points out later, is often very appropriate, since children can be involved in different activities related to the same overall theme, then you'll probably find that exercise books are very limited instruments for this purpose. They're not flexible enough and you need to think in terms of folders or envelopes of material, trying to overcome the problem of having scrappy bits of paper floating about. I like the idea of children producing folders of material which can be displayed when a theme comes to an end and even, on occasion, donated to the school library or resource centre. Secondary school teachers can learn a lot from junior school colleagues about presentation of children's work in folders, on the wall, and in exhibitions. 'Going from a primary classroom to a secondary class-room is like going from home to a British Railway waiting-room. The former is usually colourful and welcoming, the latter often bare and sometimes hostile.' (Walton 1976.)

Alongside this I favour the idea of children having a private exercise book. I'm not thinking of what some people call a 'graffiti book'. That would not have my support, but rather a kind of personal anthology. The book would only be written in when the child wanted to record something of his own or make a copy of someone else's work which he particularly liked. It would remain private unless the child wanted to show it to the teacher. It would not be marked and it would not be forced.

The advantage of such a private record is that it provides a spontaneous but regular opportunity for boys and girls to grapple with their experience for their own satisfaction and for the sake of the activity itself, in a non-judgmental context. They are not writing for the teacher as critic and final arbiter of good taste, but merely for themselves. It is personal writing unprovoked by an artificial stimulus, or an external command.

Any occasion on which a boy or girl can write for an audience other than that of teacher as judge should be welcomed since, as recent research has indicated, the constraints upon a writer are, in certain circumstances, enormous. The pupil may constantly find himself writing what he thinks his teacher wants to read, or merely echoing teacher's language, at the expense of developing his own views and style. There must be constraints acting upon any writer, as I can testify at this very moment, but if we ring the changes in our demands, then the pupils should be better placed to operate in a variety of contexts. I've already mentioned the circumstances in which a pupil may write for himself. He can also on occasions write for other pupils, or for a display or exhibition, or possibly for his parents. Some could also be encouraged to write for specialist magazines, comics and newspapers. I'm not thinking merely of letters to the editor, but factual articles, and fiction, too. Clearly, anyone proposing to operate in this way would need to study the style, format and demands of the publication he was hoping to contribute to, and that in itself would be a useful exercise.[13] Addresses are to be found in *The Writers' and Artists' Year Book,* published annually by A. & C. Black. I am not suggesting for a moment that this idea could ever be realistically adopted on a large scale, but it might be an avenue worth exploring with a few of your pupils, one of a number of strategies scattered thoughout this book for extending the most able boys and girls.

Effects

Such, then, are some of the problems and some of the strategies which may be adopted with a mixed ability class.

I want now to end this chapter with a circular model which may, depending on your point of view, call to mind either Dante's circles of Hell or Heaven, if not Purgatory. What I've tried to show in this model which, for convenience, and in deference to Dante, I'll call 'The Singing Spheres', are some of the wider implications which may be faced by the whole school when one of its major departments moves to mixed ability work.

At the centre is the non-streaming innovation. This has certain departmental ramifications and these are shown by the inner sphere. Each of these may lead to more far-reaching changes and, ultimately, to modifications in the whole ethos of the school. 'The Singing Spheres' model begins from actual changes experienced by the contributors to this book, when the department in which we were working moved from streamed to mixed ability grouping. However, the diagram, as it appears here, has moved on from the actual to the possible and indicates other effects which might reasonably follow.

I am aware of certain internal inconsistencies which are almost inevitable in an educational Aunt Sally of this kind. For instance, no segment should be regarded as discrete; one often merges into another. An outer sphere segment is not inevitably produced only from its adjacent inner sphere segment. Thus, a workshop approach may develop rationally from a diverse presentation of work, but equally, it could also develop from wide provision of multi-media

The Singing Spheres

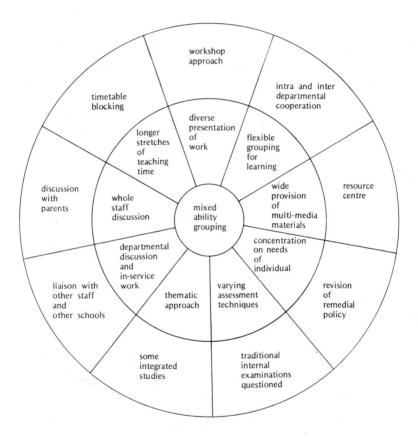

MODIFICATION OF WHOLE SCHOOL ETHOS

materials, or concentration on needs of individual. So it may be helpful to think of the circle almost as consisting of independently moving spheres in a kind of spinning top or roulette wheel. The developing changes aren't so haphazard as that gambling analogy might suggest, but neither are they fixed and inevitable.

Just how far the mixed ability innovation by one department is allowed to affect other areas in the school will depend on many factors. It might be possible to regard it as a departmental aberration, an oddity within an otherwise normal family, to be tolerated, like a mild Early Church heresy, rather than encouraged. In these circumstances, the chain of events mirrored in the diagram would merely remain interesting theoretical possibilities, to be discussed but not pursued, and inevitably there would be dysfunction within the school, with incompatible aims and procedures coexisting uneasily. To give one example, the English department may have replaced traditional end-of-year examinations by a series of periodic attainment tests and constant diagnosis of strengths and weaknesses; the remainder of the school may still be wedded to formal examinations, intended not only to give children exam practice but also to grade them in rank order. Such incompatibility is undesirable but not unknown.

Any innovation within a school – a new style of report book; a system of merit marks; a ten-day timetable; a new course in child care – will have some effect outside its immediately apparent boundaries. Certain of the effects may be considerable, but only if the original innovators find kindred spirits elsewhere among the staff whose own interests may be promoted or, at least, not harmed.

There is no compulsion to develop any of the innovations indicated in the model but, in the situation envisaged, such issues will, almost certainly, become staple ingredients in staff room discussion. Mixed ability teaching constantly forces upon us consideration of weighty educational dilemmas. The model could be regarded as a summary of the practical implications of the transition over a period of time, and, while each of the segments would merit its own chapter, at the very least, I want, finally, to look merely at one part of the school's organization or policy which can hardly remain unaffected. I'm referring to so-called 'remedial provision'.

Under the labelling system which streaming promotes, certain pupils are designated 'remedials' and hived off into a remedial department. Some such departments are even called 'opportunity' or 'challenge' units, in an effort to avoid the pejorative overtones of the word 'remedial'. The apparent function of a remedial department is to restore its pupils to normality as soon as possible and send them back into the mainstream, having recovered lost ground. The notion that they 'catch up' implies, of course, either that they have been moving faster than the more able or that everyone else, meanwhile, has been standing still. It's another of those unhelpful sporting metaphors which bedevil educational debate. Very occasionally a formerly weak pupil goes on to university; but more often than not, 'once a remedial always a remedial' and, reflecting this doom-laden inevitability, a teacher said to me on one occasion, 'Remedials ought to be kept with their own kind'.

This is the language of the isolation hospital, as if those with learning difficulties had a contagious disease and had to be kept apart. In fact, if the very weak pupils are all grouped together, then the problems involved in teaching them are enormous, even if the group is half the normal class size. As Michael Tucker observed some time ago in a *Times Educational Supplement* letter (13.9.68):

Unstreaming should promote *individual* learning, so the precise composition of classes as regards ability is not so important; but to concentrate a lot of less able (and so lower socially, more maladjusted, smaller, sicker etc.) children in one class is to overburden the group and impede their social development, and to increase the difficulties of the teacher in discipline and in attending to children *as individuals*.

It seems preferable to me to try to cope with two or three of the weakest pupils in each mixed group rather than permanently hive off twenty or so and group them together. This is not to deny, or undervalue in any way, the daily efforts of many excellent remedial teachers. However, best of all is a flexible policy where pupils are treated as individuals and regrouped on occasion for a variety of purposes, with the composition of those groups regularly changing. Under such a system, small groups of children with common problems, and common strengths, would be withdrawn at times, *from across the entire ability range,* for special tuition, or attended to in the class itself, perhaps by someone other than the usual class teacher. Such groups could sometimes be self-chosen and sometimes directed. Given the right kind of school ethos, such discriminatory treatment would be acceptable to everyone, particularly since it would be seen to apply to children of all abilities. Under a flexible system, pupils would be regarded, not as competitors to be measured against each other, but as individual people with their own integrity. All staff would share the responsibility for developing a range of talents and ameliorating a range of weaknesses, and those staff with special expertise and experience in the difficulties faced by slow learners would become advisers to their colleagues, rather than members of a separate department.

The logistical, administrative and communication difficulties of a withdrawal system should not be underestimated. In an ideal and well-organized system, members of staff take small groups in time-tabled classrooms, as part of their normal teaching load. Often, however, willing staff seem to lose their free time and have to teach in the foyer, corridor, library or dining room. You need agreement over the time and extent of withdrawal, since to extract pupils from mixed ability English for additional help in reading seems illogical and would suggest failure (of the mixed ability system) to cope with poor readers. You need to know whom to withdraw, and how to do it unobtrusively, and when to change clientele. Above all, you need to know what to do with your pupils and how to link your activities with their normal class work. This presupposes good channels of communication and time in which to discuss individuals, whereas most secondary teachers would claim, with justification, to be very hard pressed indeed.

Some schools, too, positively adopt the policy of withdrawal not to remedy weaknesses only but to extend strengths. To some degree this has operated for years in most schools with academic clubs and societies, and with activities such as athletics, drama, dance, and music. This was not 'withdrawal' in the strict sense of the word, i.e. a taking out from normal time-table, but extra-curricular activity, with the odd period or two stolen just prior to a school production or event. When we speak of identifying pupils at risk, perhaps we should not exclude those who, though academically very competent, are under-achieving. Perhaps additional sessions and/or substitute periods should be arranged for pupils such as these.

One inventive school I visit quite often responds to this challenge on several fronts, withdrawing good mathematicians occasionally from the form or 'pastoral' period, as it is called; providing alternative arrangements for non-PE types and for conscientious objectors during assembly time, and permitting Art and Craft pupils access to the workshops at almost any time. None of this is done with the aim of keeping everyone on an academic treadmill, but rather with the intention of providing what the customers want and need. This same school is about to introduce Punjabi and Statistics o level options, with two sessions in school time and one in the early evening for each subject.

Provided there are equal opportunities for all, any provision of additional hep for those who are already gifted does not seem to me to be at all incompatible with the philosphy of comprehensive education. All pupils need help at different levels. The non-reader must become literate; the highly able scientist must be extended. Some schools are, apparently, able to get round all the formidable organizational barriers and provide a withdrawal service which operates effectively and sensitively, to the benefit of the children and, no doubt the school community.

Notes

1 *Neale Analysis of Reading Ability* Macmillan 1957, 1958, revised 1966. Age 6-12 years. Scored for comprehension, accuracy and speed. It takes up to thirty minutes per pupil.
GAP Reading Comprehension Test, Heinemann, 1970. Age 7½-12½ years. Missing words to be supplied (i.e. cloze procedure) in seven prose passages in fifteen minutes.
NFER Reading Test Ginn 1966. Three tests available for secondary years 1-4. Test 1 – vocabulary. Multiple choice sentence completion. Test 2 – comprehension. Questions based on brief passages. Test 3 – continuous prose, occupying 7 minutes or less.

2 The eventual report of the Department of Education and Science APU (Assessment of Performance Unit, directed by Brian Kay and in existence since 1974), should prove valuable and is certain to be influential.

3 The booklet *Diagnosis in the Classroom* Gill Cotterell 1974, is published by The Centre for the Teaching of Reading, University of Reading School of Education, 29 Eastern Avenue, Reading RG1 5RU, Berkshire. Tel. Reading (0734) 62662. This is a most valuable source for information and advice on reading. Visitors are welcomed to the permanent book exhibition; short courses for teachers are available; and many small but useful and practical publications are on sale. For further details, contact Mrs Betty Root. Gill Cotterell's booklet, which has a useful phonic check list as well as helpful spelling rules, is also available from LDA, Park Works, Norwich Road, Wisbech, Cambs. PE12 2AX. Tel. Wisbech (0945) 2011. This a relatively recent institution, which produces a useful catalogue of Learning Development Aids for language work in the secondary school with children having learning difficulties.

4 See also the Schools Council/NFER report by P. S. Clift on record keeping and the translation from primary to secondary school.

5 For further information, contact School Bookshop Association, National Book League, 7, Albermarle Street, London W1. Or: Books for Students Ltd., Catteshall Lane, Godalming, Surrey GU7 1NG. Or: Schools Unit (School Bookshops), Penguin Books Ltd., Harmondsworth, Middlesex.

6 For example, *Scoop* . Enquiries to Wesfield Road, Southam, Leamington Spa, Warwickshire CV33 0JH.

7 Made by Bell & Howell A/V Ltd., Alperton House, Bridgewater Road, Wembley, Middlesex, this is a kind of tape recorder which uses professionally produced and homemade 'talking cards'. Oblong cardboard pieces carrying magnetic strips, with visual and/or written material on them, are fed through the machine which 'speaks' the appropriate words. It's easily operated by children of any age.

8 Produced by E.J. Arnold and Son Ltd., Butterley Street, Leeds

LS10 1AX, this is basically a tape-recorder which enables the text of a sheet fixed to the machine to be heard aloud by a pupil who is following that text.

9 A junction box (Bell & Howell etc.) is a simple device plugged into an ordinary tape-recorder and enabling up to six children to put on headphones (or make use of stethoscopes) and hear what has been recorded, without outside interference and without causing any noise. It's ideal for small group listening to a story, for example.
More details of these and other useful aids may be found in N.E. Trowbridge *The New Media Challenge* Macmillan 1974.

10 The Schools Council materials *Language in Use,* by Peter Doughty *et al,* published by Edward Arnold 1971, offer many excellent ideas for such work.

11 Details are available from Customer Services Department, Science Research Associates Ltd., Reading Road, Henley-on-Thames, Oxfordshire RG9 1EW.

12 Such as the *Reading Workshops* and *Remedial Reading Workshop* which, in certain respects, are preferable to SRA and details of which may be obtained from Ward Lock Educational, 116, Baker Street, London W1M 2BB.

13 In this connection a Harrap series is to be recommended for able students: *The Writer's Approach to the Short Story; The Play; The Novel; The TV/Film Script, Newspaper Writing* 1976.

Bibliography

BAILEY, C. (1976) Mixed ability teaching and the defence of subjects, *Cambridge Journal of Education*, Vol.6 No.1/2, Lent, ed John Elliott

BANBURY SCHOOL 1975 *The School as a Centre of Inquiry* DES

BARKER-LUNN, J. (1970) *Streaming in the Primary School* NFER

BARNES, D. (1969) *Language, the Learner and the School* Penguin

BARNES, D. (1976) *From Communication to Curriculum* Penguin

BERNSTEIN B. (1969) 'A Socio-linguistic approach to socialisation' in Gumperz and Hymes *Directions in Sociolinguistics,* Holt, Rinehart & Winston 1972

BESWICK N. (1975) *Organizing Resources* Heinemann

BRIDGES, D. 'The social organization of the classroom and the philosophy of mixed ability teaching' *Cambridge Journal of Education*. Vol.6 No.1/2, Lent, 1976, (ed) John Elliott

BRITTON, J. (1970) *Language and Learning* Allen Lane, The Penguin Press

Bullock Report (1975) *A Language for Life* HMSO

CHETOUTI, I. F. 'A study of the morale of A stream and C stream pupils in secondary schools with special reference to any differences in the attitude and behaviour of their teachers' *Education Review* November 1961

DAVIES, R. PETER (1975) *Mixed Ability Grouping* Temple Smith

DIXON, J. (1967) *Growth through English* NATE (OUP)

DOUGLAS, J. W. B. (1964) *The Home and the School* MacGibbon & Kee

GEORGIADY, N. P. and ROMANO L. G. (1963) *Gertie the Duck* Ernest Benn

GRAY, L. 'My Children and Dyslexia' *Where*, ACE No.115, April 1976

HALLIDAY, M. A. K. 'Language and Experience' *Educational Review (The Place of Language)* Vol.20, No.2, February 1968

HARGREAVES, D. H.(1967) *Social Relations in a Secondary School* R. & KP

HOLDER, M. L. and MITSON, R. (1974) *Resource Centres* Methuen

HOLT, J. (1967) *How Children Learn* Pitman

HOLT, J. (1972) *The Underachieving School* Penguin

JACKSON, B. (1964) *Streaming: an education system in miniature* R. & KP

JACKSON, S. (1968) *A Teacher's Guide to Tests and Testing* Longman

KAYE, B. and ROGERS, R. (1968) *Group Work in Secondary Schools* OUP

KELLY, A. V. (1974) *Teaching Mixed Ability Classes* Harper & Row

KELLY, A. V. (1975) *Case Studies in Mixed Ability Teaching* Harper & Row

LAWRENCE, D. (1974) *Improved Reading Through Counselling* Ward Lock Educational

NFER (1963) *Procedures for the Allocation of Pupils in Secondary Education.*

NFER (1968) *Comprehensive Organization in England and Wales. A Survey of Schools and their Organization*

NFER Open University Course PE261, Units 12 & 13 *Individual Progress in Reading* 1973

REIMER, E. (1971) *School is Dead,* Penguin, quoting Charles Schultz

ROSENTHAL, R. and JACOBSEN, L. (1968) *Pygmalion in the Classroom,* Holt, Rinehart & Winston

Schools Council Working Paper 43 *School Resource Centres* Evans / Methuen 1972

STIBBS, A. 'A Scheme of Freely-chosen Individual and Group Work in English with Younger Mixed-ability Groups in a Comprehensive School', *English in Education* Vol.8 No.1 Spring 1974

STRATTA, L. 'Some Considerations when Marking' *English in Education* Vol.3 No.3, Autumn 1969 NATE (OUP)

THOMPSON, D. 'An experiment in unstreaming' *Forum*, Vol.11. No.2, 1969

VINCENT, D. & CRESSWELL, M. (1976) *Reading Tests in the Classroom* NFER

WALTON, J. & RUCK, J. (1975) *Resources and Resource Centres* Ward Lock Educational

WALTON, J. 'Mixed Ability' *Forum*, Vol.18. No.2, Spring 1976

WHITEHEAD, F. (1975) *Children's Reading Interests* Schools Council Working Paper 52. Evans/Methuen

WIDLAKE, P. (1971) 'Deprivation' in *Teachers for Tomorrow* K. Calthrop and G. Owens, Heinemann

WILKINSON, A., STRATTA, L. and DUDLEY, P. (1974) *The Quality of Listening,* Schools Council Research Study Macmillan and *Learning Through Listening,* Macmillan 1976

WRAGG, E. C. (1976) *Teaching Mixed-Ability Groups* David and Charles

YATES, A. (1966) *Grouping in Education* Wiley

2   Aspects of the changeover

David Mears

Colleagues involved in a change from teaching selective to non-selective pupils, or from teaching streamed to non-streamed groups, may feel their experience mirrored in mine.

Six years ago our English department was an important part of a young grammar school anxious to build up a reputation for good learning (and possibly godliness) in the form of sound O and A level results. Ninety senior boys and girls were studying English in the sixth form, two-thirds of them having come up by way of the 'express' streams, who rounded off a four year O Level Language course with a year's preparation for Literature at the same level. Classes were generally streamed, though not rigidly. A legacy of these years in our school's short history – it was founded in 1963 – is to be seen on certain shelves in our stock room, where Graded Comprehension Papers, *Silas Marner* and the *Collected Works* of Pope stare down at us from the heights, accusingly.

Nowadays, a schoolboy generation later, we are nearly a complete comprehensive school. Our pupils come from every conceivable background, ranging from the extremely able to the very dull, and will generally expect to seek jobs after only five years of secondary schooling. The role of the department, especially since the Bullock Report was published, is seen to be far wider than it was assumed by many to be in the past. English teachers have a general oversight of language standards across the school; our function is becoming social as well as academic and we may no longer assume a degree of literacy (let alone a commitment to reading) or an encouragement in the home to speak and write with care and imagination, that in earlier years was taken for granted. Certain shifts of emphasis have taken place in the classroom in the meanwhile, so that cooperation is talked of more than self-reliance, and competition is hedged around by numerous safeguards. The clearest reflection of these changes is seen in the school's commitment (through the Headmaster acting on behalf of the Heads of departments) to mixed ability teaching in the first year across most of the curriculum, and the broadest of banding thereafter. The very weakest, i.e. those who are shown on the Neale Test to have a reading age of under nine years, take most of their lessons from specialist Remedial teachers, until such time as they are equipped to join the mainstream of the school.

I relate this short history of the change in the English department's rôle and the context within which it finds itself, not to point a moral and still less to suggest that the situation is unique. On the contrary, I believe that it illustrates a problem that exists in very many schools today – the job has changed, radically, but the old machine is still around, tampered with, no doubt, revamped, but in essence not very different from the original model. Look at the staff backgrounds, for example. All of us were educated at selective schools. That has not changed, and it will be several years before even a bare majority of teachers will themselves have come through the educational system to which they are professionally committed. The rooms we teach in have not changed, either in size or in number. Through paucity of funds the stock has changed far less than we should wish. But the context within which we work has altered beyond belief. How is the English department to adapt itself to the new world, especially to mixed ability classes?

The English staff
Mixed ability teaching highlights what children have in common. Less appreciated is the fact that it stresses the common interests and experience of the staff too. As a grammar school we tended to appoint graduates to teach the brightest boys and girls, and non-graduates to our single CSE stream. Now as children have found themselves in classes of a similar spread of ability, the staff find that they too are no longer stratified. Though it makes sense to encourage a well-qualified colleague to make full use of his talents with the sixth form, and for that matter to provide another who enjoys dealing with 'problem' adolescents with the opportunity to do so, I make a point of allotting the mixed ability classes to as wide a variety of teaching talents as possible. For such classes give every teacher an insight both into the difficulties experienced by the backward pupil and the particular problems encountered by the very able. They also demonstrate the extent to which basic principles of English teaching apply throughout the ability range. How often have we condemned A level students for their inability to take notes and forgotten that we have assumed lower down the school, knowledge of a skill that did not exist and which is important for schoolchildren of all abilities? Teaching a range of talent in the same class brings such a lesson sharply home to us, by compelling us to consider the fundamentals of all good English teaching.

Timetabling within the department, too, has given us less scope for acrimony than obtained under the old system of setting. Instead of the approach of the bazaar – 'I'll give you refreshing 4A if you're also prepared to taken on dreary 3Z' – we have found almost every member of the department willing to take at least one truly representative class in the year group. The term, 'departmental team' has begun to take on more meaning.

Mixed ability classes have encouraged my colleagues and I to pool our ideas and experience far more readily than in the past. After all, it makes sense to do so when our problems are seen to be similar. On numerous occasions small teams – usually two or three from a department of eleven full and part-timers – have cooperated in planning and executing a series of lessons to a group of sixty or ninety children on a particular topic. Sometimes the initiative has come from me as Head of Department; more often (and with markedly more success) it has sprung from my colleagues as they have come to recognize common aims. I recollect a number of projects connected with the mass media, for example, some of which have resulted in joint publications by the children themselves which have been of a very high standard. One lead lesson, I remember, was given by a parent of one of our fourth-formers, who happened to be a senior journalist on the staff of a popular Sunday newspaper. His Fleet Street tales bordered on the scurrilous, and appealed to the broadest cross-section of his youthful audience!

Now that most of our older pupils sit the CSE examination, we have been able to pool ideas within the department concerning our own Mode III paper. Here again, the fact that staff from a variety of backgrounds have been able to cooperate on a common basis has been good both for the course and for departmental morale.

Occasionally teams of teachers have not 'gelled'; almost invariably this has occurred as a result of extreme timetabling difficulties – teaching rooms have been far apart, or there has been little or no opportunity for those concerned to meet, except at the end of a tiring day. Wherever possible, it is a good idea to provide at least one period a week within this timetable, for those concerned to be freed from teaching in order to consult one another in this way. Crossing the threshold of our colleagues' rooms will no longer be considered an invasion of privacy, but a natural consequence of working together in common situations.

Other colleagues and probationers
Since the publication of the Bullock Report, the staff room has been increasingly aware of the need to cooperate in a language policy across departments. The building of a new lower school complex for our eleven and twelve year olds has enabled us to cut across the established order of subject disciplines by setting up a humanities team of staff from Art, RE, Drama, History and English. The team is responsible for some ninety children, and the English teacher has been able to enlist the support of his colleagues from other disciplines for a joint approach to such general concerns as clear expression – by us as well as the pupil

– and the language of textbooks and duplicated material. These are early days, but the signs are that common planning will result in a far more incisive attack on the problems of English across the curriculum than we have been able to mount by ourselves. For example, we are trying to devise a common spelling policy, with notebooks that are checked regularly by all staff. This may not be the stuff of which English is made but it is clearly relevant. The initiative has come indirectly at least from the changeover to mixed ability teaching, for this has allowed the timetablers to think in terms of the same groups of children for every subject, and as a result, for teachers from different disciplines to cooperate on common language concerns.

Every three or four weeks the English department comes together for a full meeting, which includes staff who specialize in remedial work. Not only is it important for us all to learn of the problems encountered by the weakest children – problems, I suspect, that are different only in degree from those experienced by their abler companions – but equally valuable is their need to feel the importance of their role within the entire English department. Several boys and girls who began as remedial pupils are now in the mainstream of the school. Furthermore, the problems of teaching literacy and oracy skills are equally important at all levels.

Many of our ideas for mixed ability teaching, such as workcards and joint projects, progress sheets, liaison with primary school teachers and the like – details of which are given below – emanated from full department meetings. Among other things this has given all of us a sense of commitment to decisions made. No one can be accused of having taken a line over the heads of those affected.

Finally, a word about probationers and student teachers. I believe that mixed ability organization minimizes the risk of 'sink' classes, with the low morale and preponderance of uncooperative children that go with them. Thus we are free to allocate our classes to new teachers without worrying unduly about that 'class-that-eats-new-teachers-alive'. In the course of teaching mixed ability classes, the student and the probationer will almost certainly have experience of dealing with troublesome boys and girls – an invaluable experience, one might add, for anyone wishing to become a teacher in the broadest sense. But the chances are that the problem will at least be of manageable proportions in a class where the majority of pupils will be cooperative and eager to learn. If the worst should happen, the regular teacher will be able to step in to take the most difficult children on one side without loss of face on the part of the student. At the same time, mixed ability classes also bring the novice teacher face to face with the brightest boys and girls in the age group. In streamed schools, these children have also tended to be reserved for the established teacher. The probationer has not been given a look in, since it has been thought that such children have too much to lose by being taught by the inexperienced.

I have personally found that students and probationer teachers have, without exception, been stimulated by the presence of a variety of abilities within the classroom. They have had much to learn about the particular techniques of such teaching, but have proved keen to experiment.

There will always be some teachers who regret the trend towards mixed ability teaching in English. Our own department probably represents that of many schools; the spectrum ranges from those who embrace it wholeheartedly to those who will have no truck with it so long as they are able to choose. A dogmatic counter-attack is not the answer, but by giving such sceptics at least some experience of what they have only encountered in theory, and by trying to provide adequate facilities and conditions of work – easier said than done – we may well be going some way towards a reluctant conversion. As a department we take full advantage of occasional courses on mixed ability teaching that are offered by the DES, a local University and other similar bodies. Such courses can only be of full use, of course, if what has been learned by the member of staff attending is disseminated among the rest of the department. An opportunity for reporting back must therefore be provided, and we have even been fortunate enough to be able to arrange a departmental residential weekend.

Junior school liaison
It is still hard to realize that much of what is innovatory for secondary school teachers has been common practice among our junior school colleagues for many years, often by virtue of necessity. It seemed to us that as mixed ability teaching was normal in the schools from which our boys and girls came (the small village schools having no choice, through lack of numbers) we should invite representatives from all our feeder schools to join us for a discussion of common problems. The response exceeded our highest expectations. Attendance was very high indeed, and most of the afternoon was spent quizzing one another as to what went on in the other fellow's domain, and what was expected of ourselves.

Several points emerged. For example, a number of conditions apply in primary schools which are favourable to good mixed ability teaching that do not generally obtain in the secondary school. Thus, primary school children are often taught the majority of lessons by a single teacher. This enables them to be seen regularly in a variety of situations so that a composite picture of the children's progress may be drawn. Often indeed the need for fully documented assessments is obviated (and much time normally spent on paperwork, saved), as the teacher sees enough of the pupil concerned to build up an assessment of him that does not need to be committed to paper, except perhaps at the end of the year. Seeing a child for many hours a week means that there is a far greater chance of going through his work individually than is possible in the forty-minute secondary school period. Usually, too, the primary school child is based in a single classroom for the bulk of his working day. This enables the teacher to mount an ever-changing display of work done by the class in several fields, and to engender a class feeling for the room.

As a result of these insights, we have tried to move in the direction of primary school conditions, although we realize that a conflict of interests will often frustrate our intentions. Fewer staff now come into contact with our junior children than used to, so that each one of us will see more of our pupils. With the construction of the new lower school has come a recognition that the child needs a base of his own, if not a single classroom, then at least a relatively small area and the cooperation between humanities teachers mentioned above demonstrates our awareness that subjects need not be sealed off from one another in the way that they have often been in the past.

After our first meeting with the primary school teachers, other decisions were made. We asked for a full record of each child's primary school progress in English to be sent up with him in September, and that this should include an example of his best written work, preferably chosen by himself. One of the problems of a comprehensive intake is that there can be no indication of a child's real ability except through some record such as this. Below, I try to deal with our own progress sheets, by which we monitor a child's progress in English through the school.

We decided, too, that we should twin primary and secondary staff in such a way that every English teacher in my own department would have the chance to spend a day in one of the feeder schools, looking and listening, asking questions and doing some teaching. These visits have been reciprocated by the primary staff, and have proved highly beneficial to all.

Our first-year pupils are grouped, in their pastoral as well as their academic units, according to the area in which they live. This provides continuity between primary and secondary experience, since most children will bring a number of friends with them into their new school. The system also secures a reasonable cross-section of ability in each group, although there is, of course, no guarantee that each group will have exactly the same balance, and there exists the danger that one house will gain a reputation for keenness and another for lack of motivation among its intake. It might be better to test each child upon entry to the school so as to ensure a real balance of ability within each group.

Monitoring progress
English, being a peculiarly public subject, comes under special scrutiny from colleagues and parents. With mixed ability teaching, we must be more than ever aware of the progress made by individual pupils in our

care. The argument goes, that in streamed or setted clases, one generally knows where one is; Class 1A can reasonably be expected to have mastered certain basic spelling rules by the end of the first term, whereas with 1C this will not have been achieved until the summer, and by 1E not at all. But what are we to make of a mixed ability class with no generally recognized 'safety net' below which children must not fall?

Such fears are understandable. Setting enables us to spot the child who is out of step and to take appropriate action. But who is right and who wrong when some in the same group are running, some ambling and a few apparently standing still? The method we use in our department to ensure that each child's progress is under the scrutiny of his teacher is a straightforward, if time-consuming, one. On entry to the school, every boy and girl is allotted a confidential 'progress sheet' (see Appendix One). Spaces are provided for Grades A to E to be entered under various headings, so that aspects of English we consider important, such as breadth of reading, oral ability, technical accuracy and powers of comprehension may be assessed. For the first few weeks of the autumn term it is probably best to try to come to our own conclusions regarding a child's ability and potential; later, however, we find it an extremely useful exercise to compare notes with the primary school record. (See Appendix Two.)

By the end of the first term we feel we know enough about each pupil to be able to fill in the appropriate line in the progress sheet. We have found this procedure to have a number of advantages. Firstly, it compels each English teacher to consider separately the many aspects of English that relate to each of his pupils. Secondly, it provides his successors with information about the child that can be useful in determining what help is needed. Thirdly, it provides other staff, such as those concerned with selecting children for certain academic or vocational courses, with details about the child's linguistic and literary ability which will help them to come to responsible decisions. The progress sheets are kept in departmental files; they follow a child through the school and thus provide a comprehensive record of his progress during the five or more years that he is our responsibility. They also provide a useful addition to the somewhat blunt measuring instruments of formal school examinations.

A glance at the two sheets illustrated in the Appendix will highlight the strengths and weaknesses of the system. Once the format of the sheet has been decided upon, it is best to stick to it, even if we feel certain changes may be advisable in the light of experience. Otherwise we are going to spend an even greater part of our working lives filling in forms than we do at present.

Looking back over the last four years – you will notice that our first generation of students being monitored under this system is not quite through the course – I feel we should have had a slightly different set of headings in the 'writing' section; also the space for 'breadth of reading' is clearly inadequate, and the phrase itself too vague. Nevertheless, sufficient information is recorded for us to gain some idea of each child's abilities.

Looking at Simon's record, one can see a boy who needs to be 'brought out'; although now in his fourth year we do not seem to have succeeded yet, at least we have made ourselves aware of the problem. My early remark about his apparent laziness is seen to be only the beginning of the story; one might deduce from other comments and grades that this boy is very conscious of his weaknesses, and carrots may be more effective than sticks. You will notice that his technical ability – knowing how to spell and to punctuate – is especially weak; a grade E implies the need for immediate remedial action. My colleague who taught him in the third year seems to have had a higher opinion of him. Unless a standardized test is going to be the sole criterion of assessment, we are bound to be to some extent subjective in our views, but I think this is a risk worth taking.

Lorraine is clearly a more able student. One notes from the grades that she is able to comprehend material that is increasingly demanding, and that she writes at length. The Bs and Cs under structure/style suggest that she needs to develop a feel for the right word in the right place, but with her obvious intelligence, high motivation and imagination, she has a good basis for this. I hope she realizes her career ambitions!

One final note: English is not examined formally at the end of the first year, for we have found that the traditional examination is quite inappropriate. Young children find the gap between their classroom experience and the constraints of a formal set of questions too great to make the latter a reliable guide. Besides, the spirit of the examination room is not one we wish to encourage yet. Instead, we set a series of assignments – usually centred on one theme – that can be administered in the classroom by the children's usual English teacher in the course of his lessons. The work is set, and later marked, across the year group by two members of the department. The results of these tests are translated into grades for the progress sheet, so that in the first year at least there is a large measure of objectivity in the assessments. Last year the theme chosen was food (guaranteed to be popular); the material marked by the assessors was often only a small part of the total project – a description of a sweet being sucked, an essay about a birthday feast, a comprehension passage on the same theme – since the extent of the theme was determined by each of the English teachers working on it, and the children treated it as they would any other part of their English syllabus.

Is there ever a case for setting?
I think there is, but it is often outside the classroom. For example, we decided last year that the standard of handwriting reached by our new

entrants was, on average, well below what we had the right to expect. The result was a lunch-hour 'handwriting club' (of which membership for some was obligatory) that attracted a large number of youngsters who recognized their particular weakness in this aspect of their work. The club has been supervised by two members of staff and half a dozen keen sixth formers, and its members copy from writing cards as well as improving upon their own past work. We have found this system far more efficient than one which attempts to grade children in the classroom according to their specific ability in handwriting.

Further up the school, we have sometimes brought a class-sized group of children from within a broad band of ability together for practice in a particular aspect of English, but the virtue of such arrangements has been in their temporary nature. The children know they have been culled from the year group for a specific, limited task. They are not made to feel 'natural inferiors' to their companions, and the spirit in which they enter the task is a positive one.

Resources

It is correctly said that mixed ability teaching makes heavy demands on money and resources, for as soon as we are taken out of a 'lock-step' situation, we find ourselves no longer able to rely on thirty copies of the same piece of material for all boys and girls in the classroom.

The most effective resources are, in my opinion, those devised by the people who intend to use them, and for this reason a large number of books, work-packs, poetry-cards and the like have a strictly limited usefulness. Furthermore, even internally produced sets of workcards may lie dormant in the stock room cupboard. I well remember hours spent in department meetings three years ago devising 'assignment sheets' on such themes as 'coal', 'town and country', 'work and play'. They remain for the most part on the shelves, largely because being everybody's, they ended up by being nobody's. On reflection, I believe their chief value to have been in the questions we were forced to ask ourselves in the course of producing them, namely what aspects of language should be covered? What emphasis should be given to 'free' writing, drama, discussion and research? Should the assignments be graded in order of difficulty? How could they be made visually attractive? Out of these discussions came the realization that each child should be given a variety of experiences, including oral work, writing and reading; that targets should be made clear, with some form of self-assessment built in where possible, and that every assignment should be attractively presented. As often happens, the end result in terms of paperwork appeared less important than the consultation and discussion that preceded it.

In my first school, English teaching was (at any rate in the syllabus) thought to be an extremely straightforward matter: each member of the department was given a list of books – one play, one poetry anthology and one novel – to be 'worked through' during the course of the term. At the end of term we passed those books on to the colleague whose name appeared below ours on the list, and received our next allocation from the name above. Everyone in the department thus knew what his colleagues were teaching (or supposed to be teaching: somehow, one skipped those books for which one had little sympathy). A mixed ability system precludes such organization – even if one wanted it – and it is therefore especially important that every opportunity be given for colleagues to discuss with one another their own classroom practice.

How can this be done? We have tried a number of methods, with varying degrees of success. For example, regular meetings of staff who teach the same year group; possibly a common free period if this can be arranged on the timetable; encouragement of class wall displays and magazines; drama performances and reading of work done, where pupils from one group entertain those from another – and the staff concerned learn a great deal themselves; full department meetings at which topics of common interest are dealt with, e.g. the assessment of oral work; and of course, best of all, the encouragement of an atmosphere in which colleagues feel free to discuss both their successes and their failures.

What facilities should be offered by a department sympathetic towards mixed ability teaching? The short and obvious answer is: anything and everything, a wide variety of material, through books, records, tapes and films. Unfortunately, 'everything' is not normally catered for in present school budgets, so one has to be selective. I would suggest the following as a basis for building up a useful stock of resource material:

1 *Stimulus material* – In this category I would place such books as *Touchstones, Voices* – Penguin English Project Books (now published by Ward Lock). There are many such books on the market as indicated in chapter nine. At least one of these should be offered in a full set, with each boy or girl possessing his own copy. For such books allow class discussion of, for example, the home, in *Family and School*, or animals in *Creatures Moving* – subjects which can bring the class together by drawing on common experience. On the other hand, they permit and encourage individual children to follow up their own interests within the general topic under review.

2 *Any number of duplicated, disposable sheets of language exercises* – The can be rifled (but selectively) from those old-fashioned 'grammar books' that continue to accumulate dust in most school stock rooms, and they should concentrate on particular aspects of language. But for a child who is experiencing a particular language idfficulty at a certain time, an easily accessible exercise, that explains the points at issue clearly and provides a number of carefully devised

examples to be worked through, may be exactly what is needed. It is useful to have a full supply of cheaply produced material of this sort that can be found easily, without the need to refer to a course book (see Appendix Three).

3 *Certain collections of short stories* – e.g. Bill Naughton's *The Goalkeeper's Revenge* (Penguin) for juniors and his *Late Night on Watling Street* (Longman) for older pupils. For other suggestions see chapter 9. A well-written short story can often be enjoyed at several levels. If it has a strong narrative interest, it will probably appeal to the entire class; discussion of points raised, presentation of a particular episode, through drama or readings, and sympathetic questioning – these will draw out a variety of points from children of a wide range of ability.

4 *One-Act plays* – e.g. Longman's Imprint Series. These are well worth stocking, in half sets. Groups of children with a selection of abilities represented in each will take to reading plays with remarkable enthusiasm, and are often keen to present them to others; they also give the weakest children valuable reading practice.

5 *Workcards, poetry-cards and the like* – These too have their uses in that they are easily distributed, cost less than books (though not page for page) and are not so cumbersome.

6 *Audio-visual equipment* – Expensive, but a good investment nevertheless. Small cassette tape recorders can be used with children of all abilities. Short film extracts, taped radio and television programmes can also be used with profit, as indicated in chapter six.

7 *Class Libraries* – These are important in all schools, of course, but no more so perhaps than in classes where it is especially important to cultivate the art, and interest, of extended reading. Library periods can be utilized to the full. The general class absorption in a good book enables the teacher to find time to speak to individual children at some length, as well as to hear slow reading children practise aloud. Boys and girls who are loath to read anything at home may be persuaded to do so at school in the atmosphere of a classroom where reading enjoyment is taken for granted. This is more effective than any number of magisterial exhortations.

8 *Duplicated assignment sheets* – These have been briefly mentioned above. We are fortunate in having a school resources bank that enables us to duplicate material cheaply and easily. I ask all members of the department to issue a copy of all they duplicate to each of their colleagues. This gives us all a bank of material that we can draw upon when needed, and we can run off extra copies if necessary without difficulty.

With the variety of stock implied here – though, incidentally, variety need not involve increased expense, since a single copy of thirty different books costs no more than thirty copies of the same title – a close watch needs to be made on the signing out and return of stock. One needs a system that combines maximum turnover of materials with the maximum flexibility. The method we use is to ask all members of staff to sign out, from a full list of books issued in sets, their name, the title of the book, and the period for which it will probably be required. This way, at a glance, everyone can trace the whereabouts of all stock. If one desperately needs a particular book, one knows with whom to enter into negotiation.

We did at one time consider an elaborate filing system, whereby all material would be indexed and cross-referenced. However, this idea proved unsuccessful in practice since it failed to recognize the amount of time required for such an enterprise. There is in any case no real substitute for each teacher building up his own memory-bank of material that works for him, and we have given examples of such material in our appendices.

Finally, I should mention the department library. New books are expensive, as we know, but individual copies of books well reviewed in *Use of English* (Hart-Davis) and similar journals can be ordered in single copies for departmental use. Details of these may be found in chapter nine. Over the years we have built up a considerable collection of literature both for use in the classroom and for the teacher, recollecting the first part of Chaucer's description of the parson in his *Canterbury Tales* – 'And gladly *wolde he lerne,* and gladly teche'.

APPENDIX ONE: English progress sheets
Notes
This record sheet should be filed in the Faculty Room; it is confidential to staff.

At the end of the summer term, please write in estimated grades (A-E: see below) and add brief comments as indicated: **Attach to this sheet a representative piece of recent writing by the child**. This can be a fair copy of work originally done in the exercise book.
Grades: Grading within the box is by end-of-year assessment across the year group. Other grades are estimates based on the year's work in the classroom *plus* examination results.

Grade A   = very high standard. Clearly 'grammar' ability and likely to take O level in 4 or 5 years.
Grade E   = needs remedial help.
Grade C   = average ability (i.e. *National* average – Grade 4 in CSE).

ENGLISH PROGRESS SHEET

NAME: Simon

YEAR OF ENTRY: 1972

Tutor Group	English Set Master/Mistress	Reading Comp	Quantity	Presentation	Spelling	Punctuation	Structure/Style	Vocabulary	Imagination	Oral, including Drama	Breadth of Reading	Class Readers Studied	Other Remarks (e.g. Behaviour, Contacts with Parents)
1st	1Pb	C	D	D	C	D/E	D	C/D	D/E		Factual – no fiction	Silver Sword	Lazy – not without intelligence.
2nd	2R	D	D	D	E	E	D	D	D	Very quiet. Lacks confidence.	Very fair. Has made use of class library.		Very well-behaved. His written work is very weak but he had made an effort but has had little success.
3rd	3G	B/C	B/C	C	C	C	C	C	B/C	Quiet; rather nervous.	Fair	Huckleberry Finn Animal Farm Kes	Has made good progress this year.
4th	4IV	C	D	D	D/E	C	C	C	D	Quiet still		Henry V Of Mice and Men 20 Short Stories	Spelling really needs attention.
5th													

ENGLISH PROGRESS SHEET

NAME: Lorraine
YEAR OF ENTRY: September '72

	Tutor Group	English Set Master/Mistress	Reading Comp	Quantity	Presentation	Spelling	Punctuation	Structure/Style	Vocabulary	Imagination	Oral, including Drama	Breadth of Reading	Class Readers Studied	Other Remarks (e.g. Behaviour, Contacts with Parents)
1st	17			A	B/C	A/B	B	C	B/C	C				
2nd	2H		B	A	B	B+	B+	B+	B	B+	Becoming more confident and thoughtful.	Sophisticated for class group.	*Lord of the Flies* Read on Bk.II	Potentially a very able pupil.
3rd	3H		A/B	A	B/C	B	B	B	B	A/B	She admits to being very worried by drama and reading aloud, yet is one of the best in the class in discussion. A good cover-up?	Mature and wide. Enjoys fantasy and books on personal relationships.	*Joby* *Animal Farm*	Some highly intelligent and independent ideas. Written work marred by technical weakness. Very interesting girl.
4th	41		A/B	B	B	B	B	B/C	B	A/B	A bit reticent but less worried than earlier in year.	Good – varied	Parts of *Henry V, Mice and Men, Short Stories, Golden Apples* etc	Very keen to teach English at Secondary level. Should be encouraged onto 3 A Levels
5th														

APPENDIX TWO
Confidential
Education Committee primary school record card
1 Name and full Postal Address of Parent or Legal Guardian

This Space to be used for any Subsequent Change of Address

Child's Surname
Child's Christian Name(s)   Nicola _____
Child's Date of Birth   24/6/65
Child's Address (if different from that of parent or legal guardian)

2 *School*
Date Admitted
Date Left
Comments (see instructions)

3 *Head Teacher's Recommendation and Comments* (see instructions)
Nicola works well and is keen to please. Parents are most cooperative and helpful.

4 *School Work* (Subjects to be Assessed A B C D or E see instructions)

	1st Year (8+)	2nd Year (9+)	3rd Year (10+)	4th Year (11+)	*Observations* (see instructions)
English (A) Reading	B−	B	B+	B	
(B) Oral	B−	B	B+	B	
(C) Written	B−	B	B+	B	
Arithmetic	B	B	B+	B	
Art and Craft	B+	B+	B+	C	

5 *Standardized selection test results* (to be entered only on instructions from the Director of Education)

6 *Special Abilities or Disabilities* (other than those mentioned under other headings)

1st Year (8+)	Art, Dance
2nd Year (9+)	
3rd Year (10+)	
4th Year (11+)	PE

7 *Interests* (activities in and out of school such as music, reading, making collections, sport etc.).

1st Year (8+)	Art
2nd Year (9+)	
3rd Year (10+)	
4th Year (11+)	Music Guides

8 *Personality*

	Perseverance	*Self-confidence*	*Initiative*	*Responsiveness*	*Further comments*
1st Year (8+)	Good	Good	Good	Good	Very pleasant, happy, hard working girl. Ideal pupil
2nd Year (9+)	Good	Good	Very Good	Very Good	
3rd Year (10+)	B+	B	B+	B+	
4th Year (11+)	B	B	B	B	

9 *School Attendance* (to be entered as a fraction)

Attendances	*Notes:* (long periods of absence, reason, frequent short absences etc.)
354/372	

1st Year (8+)
2nd Year (9+)
3rd Year (10+)
4th Year (11+)

10 *Health* (see instructions)

11 *Home Circumstances* (see instructions)

Junior progress record

Name: Nicola _____

Date of Birth: 24/6/65

Date of Report: (1st Year)

Date: July 1973 C/A 8yr 1 mth

Reading Age: 9.09 (Holborn)

Mathematics Good. Nicola enjoys Maths and works with care. Tables 2,3,4,5,10. Nicola enjoys problems and will tackle any Maths with a lively open mind.

English Good. Reading good wr4. *Dragon Pirate* D. Written work gay and imaginative. Grammar and spelling good. Nicola takes a pride in producing neat work of a high standard. Works well from SRA Reading Laboratory Brown Cards.

Comments A very pleasant, helpful, sociable girl. Lively and happy in class. An artistic child.

Tests: Name of Test

  Date

  Quotient

Teacher's signature & date 17/7/73

Date of Report: (2nd Year)

Date: July 1974 C/A 9yrs 1mth

Reading Age: 13.00 (Holborn)

Mathematics Steady progress made throughout the year. She is confident to tackle problems and seems to enjoy her work. She is now working on Fletcher Book 3 and maintaining her high standard.

English English work very good and very neat. Her work is a pleasure to mark, her spelling good. Makes good use of a dictionary in her written work.

Comments A very happy helpful girl. A pleasure to teach.

Tests: Name of Test

  Date

  Quotient

Teacher's signature and date July 1974

Junior progress record

Name: Nicola _____ ·

Date of Birth: 24/6/65

Date of Report: (3rd Year)

Date: July 1975 C/A 10yrs 1mth

Reading Age: 13yrs 6mths (Holborn)

Mathematics Nicola copes well with all her maths work.

English   Reading – very good but Nicola needs to build up
             words she doesn't know.
             Writing – she abounds in good ideas for stories which
             are imaginative and well written. Spelling – good.
Comments
Tests: Name of Test
            Date
            Quotient
Teacher's signature

Date of Report: (4th Year)
Date: July 1976 C/A 11yrs 1mth
Reading Age: 13yrs 6mths
Mathematics Good.
English   Slightly immature in her ideas. Sentence construc-
             tion is very basic.
Comments   Neat, enthusiastic, pride in all she does.
Tests: Name of Test
            Date
            Quotient
Teacher's signature

English report sheet
Name: Tony
 1 **Reading**

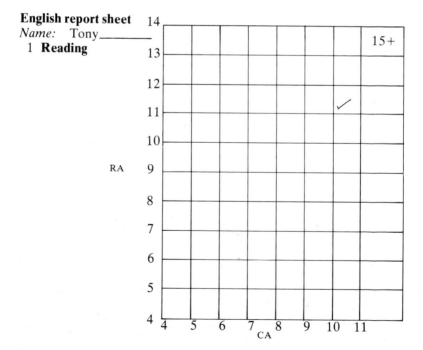

54

2 Comprehension

little or no understanding
grasps only main points
understands most of his reading
full understanding at his own
reading level

5	6	7	8	9	10	11	12
						✓	✓

3 Oral

(a) Class discussion:

takes no part unless asked
directly
occasionally has some-
thing to offer
ready to join in
discussion
partakes fully in class
discussion

5	6	7	8	9	10	11	12
						✓	✓

(b) Language:

barely grammatical
grammatical but poor vocabulary
tries to use more interesting
words
fluent and interesting

5	6	7	8	9	10	11	12
						✓	✓

4 Written

(a) Content

puts very little on paper
tries but lacks originality
– poor vocabulary
good standard reasonable
vocabulary
good fluent work, original
content wide vocabulary

5	6	7	8	9	10	11	12
						✓	✓

(b) Grammar

lacks sentence construction
writes in sentences but little
else
fair use of punctuation and
grammar
very good construction and
grammar

5	6	7	8	9	10	11	12
						✓	✓

(c) Spelling

5 – 6 – 7 – 8 – 9 – 10 – 11 – 12

cannot spell even simple words
sticks to immature words he can spell
basic spelling sound – tries with unusual words
uses a wide vocabulary and spells very well

5	6	7	8	9	10	11	12
						✓	✓

(d) Handwriting

untidy – poor letter formation
neat, but formation poor
formation reasonable but untidy
a delight to read

						✓
					✓	

Tony   (24.2.76)

English   Tony's work is often careless and covered with doodles, and unnecessary marks. He makes very little effort to learn set spellings. He can do some good creative writing but seldom reaches the subject set.

APPENDIX THREE: How to use quotation marks (speech marks).
The following exercises are to help you understand how to use *quotation marks*. Do as many of them as you need to, on the sheet itself, not in your exercise books. When you think you know how to use *quotation marks,* have a word with me when you return the sheet.

Quotation marks enclose the actual words of the speaker.
Albert said, 'Give it to me.'
'No, I won't,' replied Janet.
'Give it to me,' he repeated. 'If you don't, I shall tell the police.'

Now try these. Add quotation marks in each case, but only where they are necessary.

1 Peter said, Let's go out tonight.
2 Where to? Jane replied.

3 How about the Top Rank?
 Too expensive, came the reply.
 Or Mr Smelly's Fish-and-Chip Shop?
 That's more like it. They agreed to go there.
4 She said she had lost her away.
5 She said, I have lost my way.
6 I asked if I could help.
7 I asked, can I help?

You should have *eight* **pairs of quotation marks so far. Have you?**

Notice that you normally begin a new line each time for a new speaker.
8 I asked Mrs Bagshaw for a cigarette.
 Have you got one, I asked? Just for tonight. I'll pay you back in the morning.
 Yes, I've heard that one before, she replied mournfully. Last week I gave you ten, and only five have come back. I'm not made of money, you know.
 Oh, I thought you were, I said rashly. I could have bitten my tongue off. She was so annoyed that she walked away.
 Come back, please I cried. But it was no good.
9 Now write a short conversation between a teacher and a pupil, using *five* sets of quotation marks. (Do this on paper. See me first.)

When to use the apostrophe. Letters missing.
The following exercises are to help you understand how to use the *apostrophe*. Do as many of them as you need to, on the sheet itself, not in your exercise books. When you think you know how to use the *apostrophe*, have a word with me when you return the sheet.

An apostrophe shows where a letter, or letters, have been left out.
'It doesn't (= *does not*) work and I've (= *I have*) only just bought it,' said Lucy. 'It isn't (= *is not*) fair.'
'I'm here and you're over there', shouted Clive. (= *I am*; *you are*).
'You'd like a cake too, wouldn't you? They've got some.' (= *you would*; *would not*; *they have*.)
'Here's the book,' he called, 'but it wasn't on the shelf I'd thought.' (= *here is*; *was not*; *I had*).
'It's cold in here. I'll put the fire on,' said Chris. (= *it is*; *I will*).
'You're first and he's second – but who's third?' (= *you are*; *he is*; *who is*).

Now try these. Add apostrophes where necessary.
1 Im sorry Im late. (*two* examples)
2 Its too late to apologise. Youve held us all up. (*two* examples)
3 Ill sing you a song. I cant wait to see if youll enjoy it. (*three*)
4 He wont play; he doesnt want to; wont you? (*three*)

5 Youre not coming with us, Im afraid. Weve left your supper on the table, and well be in about ten. (*four* – be careful!)

6 Now write a paragraph which includes at least *four* different examples. Do it on writing paper. See me first.

When to use a full stop.

The following exercises are to help you understand when to use a *full stop*. Do as many of them as you need to, on the sheet itself, not in your exercise book. When you think you know how to use the *full stop*, have a word with me when you return the sheet.

A full stop ends a sentence. It tells you where the sense comes to a 'full stop'.

Peter stopped in fear.

He looked warily across the bridge and saw a shape.

It loomed up out of the darkness.

'Don't come any nearer,' he gasped.

'It's only me,' said Mabel. 'It may be foggy, but that is no excuse. You need a visit to the optician, my lad.'

Now try these. Put in the full stop(s) in each case, adding capital letters also where you need them.

1 The girl is crying

2 The girl is crying for help

3 'Why are you crying?' I asked the girl

4 The marathon racer ran, then walked, and finally collapsed at the tape

5 I bought an ice-cream which was ever so cold

6 I bought an ice-cream it was ever so cold

7 Mr Jenkins was running for the bus when he tripped over a stone that someone had kicked on to the pavement picking himself up he grunted I must remember to wear shoes tomorrow it hurts so much when I don't (*three* full stops)

8 He opened the door looked outside and noticed two young boys were running away down the street he shouted at the top of his voice but they took no notice of him he turned back into the house grumbling to himself as for the boys they ran until they were exhausted when the bigger one gasped to the smaller 'do you think he recognised us?' 'I don't think so' replied his companion he was out of breath too 'after all, he can only have caught a brief glimpse of us' (*seven* full stops)

9 I've got the money it's in here in my jacket pocket no it isn't you must have pinched it it was in my wallet half an hour ago (*five* full stops)

10 *Write a paragraph about a thief in four sentences, i.e. with four full stops in it.* (See me for writing paper.)

Part Two:

Inside the classroom

3 Theme and topic work

Judith Atkinson

Thematic work

Thematic work has always been at the centre of my teaching with mixed ability classes in the 11-13 age range. As a way of looking in depth at a chosen subject, it involves the class in a shared exploration; as a way of organizing a series of English activities, it provides a framework for the variety of work I want individuals and groups to explore.

One of the chief claims made for mixed ability teaching is that it allows individuals to progress at their own rate, and clearly one of the teacher's first aims is to provide work which will ensure this. A second, and to me very important claim, is that children will learn from each other in many different, and often unexpected ways. When a class works on a given theme together, both these aims can be achieved. Individual writing, reading, drawing, taping and planning, can go on alongside shared activities because the whole class is focused on the same area and the members of the class are consciously sharing their experiences.

From the point of view of organization, the following of a theme gives the teacher the opportunity to plan a block of work which lasts a reasonable length of time, perhaps for a month or half a term. This has several advantages. I can, in preparing assignments, ensure that the varied activities which come under the title of 'English' will be covered, and that the balance of these activities will be right. Through giving plenty of choice I can provide work for different levels of ability. I can also give myself, and the children, the feeling of continuity and purpose which a series of 'one-off' lessons will not do.

This way of working is sometimes criticized by those who suspect that the theme chosen by the teacher is merely a convenient organizational aid. They argue that the link between given assignments is often tenuous and contrived, and that the children will rarely see these links and will come to the end of the theme without having gained any greater insight into the subject. It is true that if a subject is wrongly chosen for the age level or character of a group, it will not engage their interest, despite the organization which went into it. Equally, children will gain little from a month spent on a theme which was not sufficiently thought out, with materials haphazardly chosen and presented, and the structure of which was not carefully planned.

With successful theme work, though, a sceptical observer would only need to watch a mixed ability class at work to see and feel their involvement. The kind of classroom scene I'm thinking of has an atmosphere of purposeful activity. In one corner, individuals are writing, sometimes breaking off to read each other's work, or to try out an idea on someone before they use it, or to ask for help with spelling or the choice of a word. A group of four in another corner is preparing 'speeches' for a class discussion the following day. Two children are collecting a cassette tape recorder to take into a stockroom where they will record the play they've been writing together. Two more children are pinning up the mounted work they have finished. Another group are talking to me about an idea they've had for their next assignment; it isn't on the work sheet but they think it's a good and workable idea. It's at a stage like this, when the children begin to interpret and explore the theme for themselves that the teacher, and the observer, must realise that the theme has 'taken off'.

Another misgiving expressed is that the informality I've described is often, in reality, sloppiness. With so many different activities going on, with so much emphasis put on children directing themselves, won't the result be unfinished or unfocused work, children who achieve nothing, noisy confusion and limp, exhausted teachers? Again, all this could be true, and only thoughtful preparation and organization will ensure that it isn't. I hope I can show how this can be done by describing in some detail the preparation and working of two different themes I've used with mixed ability classes. They could equally well have been used with loosely banded or streamed groups.

Other worlds was a theme which a group of 13 year olds used in the second term of the third year. The work lasted for a month. I spent two lead lessons providing stimuli which I hoped would give the class an imaginative grasp of worlds other than their own. In the first lesson I read to them an extract from *First Men in the Moon* by H.G. Wells, the passage which describes Cavor and his fellow astronaut making their first steps on the moon. As a whole class we then discussed the sights and sensations the two men met. In pairs the children then compared Wells' imagined moon with the real moon as seen in a series of space photographs in *Things Working* (Ward Lock English Project, Stage One) and the lesson closed with me listing on the blackboard, following the pupils' suggestions, the experiences and sensations which the American astronauts must have had.

In the second lesson I asked the class to think of other, different worlds and, as I played them a tape, to write down what kind of world the sounds suggested to them. The tape contained three extracts: the first from the second movement of Shostakovitch's 'Cello Concerto', an eerie cello solo; the second from Debussy's 'La Mer'; and the third, a sound effects passage of dripping water and voices echoing and resounding in an underground cavern. After listening and writing, we compiled a list of suggested other worlds. I then asked the children to choose from the list a world to study for themselves.

At the beginning of the next session I seated the children in groups according to the world they had chosen. There were some difficulties, as the dreamworld group had to be split into two, whereas the underwater group had only three members, which was just workable. Eventually we had six groups studying five topics: dreamworlds, underwater worlds, underground worlds, space and other planet worlds, and explorers' worlds. I handed out worksheets to each group, two for each child.

Creating and wording worksheets like these obviously requires particular thought when they are to be used with wide ability groups. There are, I think, two alternative approaches. The first one is to provide several different sheets graded in difficulty and either colour-coded so that children can pick one in 'their' colour, or handed out to appropriate children by the teacher. The second, is the method I more often adopt, which is to create open-ended assignments which can be treated by children at different levels, and worded clearly and simply so that weaker children can grasp the basic meaning and can begin work without needing the teacher to start them off. Although I provide several choices for work, I limit the number I give, as I think that a long list of suggestions overwhelms even the most able. This is one of the weaknesses I've found with commercially produced workcards; the list of possible activities is often bewilderingly long.

Here are two of the writing worksheets I used for the **Other worlds** theme. I structured the work so that all the children could start with a visual stimulus. Abler children would then move on more quickly to other assignments while those with more limited vocabulary or initiative could spend longer with the pictures to provide them with initial ideas.

Underwater world

1 Before you start work, look at pictures of the underwater world. Read the story called *Through the Tunnel* or the extracts on pages 19, 23 and 26 in *Thoughtshapes*.

2 With the help of the pictures, imagine yourself underwater. Make a list in rough of words and phrases for the following:
  (a) colours and lights under water
  (b) the difference between sound above and below water

(c) movements of humans and of sea creatures

(d) things and shapes seen under water.

Then, choose one long, or two or three shorter pieces of writing.

I   Write a poem or short story called 'Underwater World'. Use the words and phrases you've collected to help you.

II Write the daily journal of someone who is a member of a team in an underwater lab; or investigating the reports of a monster, perhaps the Loch Ness monster; or exploring the wreck of a ship, perhaps a treasure ship, or a Viking ship.

Remember to include descriptions of what you do; the new and strange things which happen to you; what you see; what it feels like to be diving and swimming; the dangers; how you feel about everything that happens.

III Write a fantasy story about a human discovering a kingdom underneath the sea. (Ask me for a poem called *The Forsaken Merman* to give you ideas.)

The world of space and other planets

Study the photographs in *Things Working* of the moon's surface, and the astronauts in space and on the moon. In rough write down words and phrases to describe what you see and what you imagine the astronauts feel like as they move. Think also about their feelings, their fears, their excitements. Remember television films of their life in the space capsule.

Then, choose one long, or two or three shorter pieces of writing.

I   Imagine that you are an astronaut on a moon mission. Write your daily journal, starting from 'blast-off' day.

Remember to include descriptions of what you do; the new and strange things that happen to you; what you see; how it feels to be weightless in the space ship and on the moon; how you feel about everything that happens.

II Write a poem or short description called 'Moonworld'. Use the words and phrases you've collected to help you.

III An astronaut has returned from the moon or from a previously unexplored planet and he is interviewed on the radio. Write the interview and, if you wish, borrow a tape recorder and, with another person, tape the interview.

IV Ask me for the copy of *Other Worlds* and read the story about Mars. Think about it. Think also about the H.G. Wells story we read. Then write a story about humans on an unexplored planet. Remember to give your reader a vivid impression of what the planet looks like.

The materials I provided in the classroom were a book box containing 6 copies each of:

Other Worlds English Project Stage One Ward Lock Educational
Things Working English Project Stage One Ward Lock Educational
The Nightmare Wang Yen-Shou in *Voices II* G. Summerfield Penguin
You be the Judge Brian Peachment Arnold
Through the Tunnel Doris Lessing in *Spectrum I* Longman
The Forsaken Merman Matthew Arnold in many anthologies
Thoughtshapes Barry Maybury Oxford
Ernie and his Incredible Illucinations Alan Ayckbourn in *Playbill* Heinemann

In addition to these texts there were library books on sea creatures, space and exploration; colour supplements and *National Geographical* articles and pictures on remote tribes, space, Jacques Cousteau etc.; cassette tapes of three BBC *Listening and Writing* broadcasts including *Ernie's Incredible Illucinations* (Autumn 1975) and *Space Poems* (Autumn 1975); and a radiovision filmstrip and tape, *The Colour of Light* (Spring 1975).

Instructions to the class were that as individuals, they were to choose a minimum of two written assignments and a minimum of one group activity. Once each group and individual had started work, my next concern was to keep a hold over the activities of the class as a whole. I let the work continue for a week or so, and then had a class lesson in which the Underwater group introduced facts and opinions about the Loch Ness monster and then directed a class discussion. At a session a week later one of the Dreamworld group performed part of *Ernie's Incredible Illucinations* to the rest. Although these sessions meant that some individual writing had to be interrupted, they achieved the aim of involving the whole class, giving groups an audience, and providing variety. The completed written work was eventually presented as an illustrated wall display. The following extracts should give some idea of the range of work produced.

Astronaut's diary (extracts from)

Jan 1   Everything went well so far. The lift off felt strange straped up to the seats the pull of the gravity agains you. We had a sleap and dinner it was mixed veg and spuds gravy, and for dissert it was rice pudding suposed to be any way.

Jan 2   Then in the morning music wok us up We did our exercises they was quite simple we then had breakfast which was grapefrute and coffee. Just after eating we ran into a meteorite storm it sounded like a bome going of but time after time, we was in it for about 5 minutes then silence again, nothing but space when we looked out of the portholes. I then sat and read for a while my mate played a mouthorgan.

Jan 3   Slept badly as if I was being suffocated

Jan 7   Orbiting the moon now looked as if as soon as we land on it, it will swallow us up. We landed. I opened the hatch and started two walk down, then I jumped and I went about 5 feet across the surface.

Neil

Underwater

It was a very hot day, the sun was shining very brightly, so me and my companions rented a boat to go out and explore under the sea. On the way out me and one of my companions put on our diving outfits so that we would be ready when we arrived at the spot that we wanted to be. When we arrived at our spot we both dived in, and started to explore the undersea world. The things that we so was brilliant, everything was very quiet and still. The colour of the water was dark blue. Then we went deeper down to the bottom of the sea, all of a sudden a scole of fish came swimming by us, they looked like spadefish but I wasn't show. Then all of a sudden my companion pointed behind me to warn me that there was a shark going to attack us. When I saw it coming it looked like a great monster coming to get something to eat, its razor sharp teeth was sparkling like diamons. So we had to swim for our lives, just then we so a holed out coral so we hid inside it until the shark got fed up of chasing us. Then we got out of the coral and made our way back to the boat because our oxygen was running out.

Nicky

Colours and light under the sea

Seaweed a field of green,
specks of colour of tiny fish,
glowing fins and tails,
reds, oranges and yellows,
bands of greens, blues and blacks.
Shiny vicious teeth,

beading, staring eyes,
the murky rocky kingdom.
Shining stones and shells,
transparent creatures,
greeny, black eels,
delicate feelers of anemones.
The screen of light resting on the top,
speckles, stripes and spots flash past,
dull camouflages,
a trailing stream of bubbles,
slight swaying of the plants,
dazzling couloured coral.

Sylvia

I felt pleased that all three writers had made imaginative efforts to
enter the 'other world' they'd chosen. Neil and Nicky clearly needed
help with technical mistakes in their writing. It was interesting to me
that Neil spelt 'meteorite' and 'suffocate' correctly, obviously because
these were important but also difficult words which he recognized the
need to check. In this case I therefore pointed out to him the careless
errors like 'sleap', 'grapefrute' and 'two' and he corrected them before
copying the work out for display. Nicky's problem was different. I
pointed out and corrected the spelling of 'diamons' as this was
obviously a word he'd chosen with care. He made mistakes which are
common in the area of the school, such as the phonetic spelling of 'saw'
as 'so' and 'sure' as 'show', so, as David Mears suggests in chapter two,
I directed him to the appropriate workcard on common errors. Here it
is:

---

so/saw/sew/sore

These words are often confused because they sound similar, but it's
important to spell them correctly because their meanings are so
different.
Fill in the gaps in the following sentences with the right words, then
correct your own work.

1 It's impossible to   without a needle,   I asked
   her to   this hem for me.
2 They   many ladybirds during the summer.
3 The bathers   the shark's fin gliding   smoothly
   through the waves.
4   when the doctor   that the boy's toe was
              , he agreed to help him quickly.

5 When Robert had finished his work on the chair, his hand was
from putting pressure on the

Friends, enemies, fans and gangs was a theme I used with a second
year mixed ability group for four weeks in the summer term. The title
was rather unwieldy, but I wanted the children to think about their
relationships with other people, both in personal friendships and in
larger groups. At a time when the class seemed equally divided
between Bay City Roller mania and Leeds United fervour, I hoped
that they might be able to look more objectively at their own feelings
and behaviour.

I introduced the theme with three whole-class lessons. In the first I
played a tape of one of the BBC *Listening and Writing* programmes
(Autumn 1974) and the class followed this in the accompanying
pamphlets. It was the first part of a trilogy by Peter Fieldson called
Another Saturday, in which the central character, an unemployed boy
straight from school, has his only excitement of the week, his trip to
watch his football team play an away game. The form of the play suited
my purposes particularly well, because most of it was first person
narrative with individual short scenes, for example, at home, on the
train, at the ground, threaded into the story. This meant that the hero's
comments and explanations on his own and his friends' behaviour in
the crowd provided good starting points for later discussion. As the
tape lasted twenty minutes I followed it with a class discussion, first of
the play itself and then of the children's own experience of crowd
behaviour at football ˑmatches. This discussion continued in the
following lesson, widening out to include the behaviour of fans at pop
concerts, and I drew it together to prepare for a piece of writing to be
done by the whole class, a description of their own experience of being
part of an excited crowd. This was begun in the lesson so that I could go
round and talk to most of the children about their ideas and help the
weaker writers to plan their work and find the words they needed. The
writing was completed at home so that I could move on to the next
stage with the whole class.

Next lesson I handed out three worksheets to each individual. Here
they are, reflecting the range of choice of assignment and mode of
expression advocated in chapter 1. These were:

1 Writing for yourself
2 Reading and writing
3 Talking and reading.

1 Friends, enemies, fans and gangs *Writing for yourself*

Stories and descriptions
1 Choose a picture. Study it carefully and discuss it with me or a neighbour. Write the story or poem the picture suggests to you.
2 How you made a friend, or lost a friend.
3 A portrait of a good friend of yours – first discuss what you'll include in your portrait.
4 Our gang – the story of a gang you were in when you were younger, or now. How did you join? Where do you meet? How do you spend your time together? Are there any rules? Who is the leader? Are there any disadvantages about being in the gang? What are the advantages? Any memorable incidents? etc.
5 Write a story in 2 or 3 chapters about the forming of a gang, or fan club – include some of the ideas from question 4. You might write the story as though you are a member of the group, perhaps the leader or a new recruit.
6 Write an account of a memorable day spent with a few of your friends, perhaps a day last holiday. Remember to include conversations in your story.
7 Write about a time when, either in order to be accepted by a gang, or because you were a member of a gang you did something which you know to be wrong.
8 The good and bad things about friends.
(Several of these ideas could be expressed in poems)

Explaining things
1 First discuss in pairs, then write down your ideas as lists and explanations. How would you find or build an ideal gang headquarters? Equip it? Keep it secret? Use it?
2 Find out about the different 'uniforms' gangs and groups have worn since the 1950s. Draw and describe them, then try to explain why you think people have worn clothes in this way.
3 Discuss in pairs the problem of football hooliganism – talk about why it happens, what you've seen happen and the remedies you would suggest to the Minister for Sport. Then write a report of your discussion.

---

2 Friends, enemies, fans and gangs *Reading and writing*

There is a list of stories, extracts and poems about the topic in the box of books. Try to read several. Choose one that interests you particularly and ask for suggestions for further work.

BOOKLIST

BOOKLIST	**STORIES AND EXTRACTS**

Thoughtshapes   B. Maybury
Wordscapes   B. Maybury

Goalkeeper's Revenge
B. Naughton
Imagine   R. Protherough,
J. Smith

Late Night on Watling Street
B. Naughton
First Choice   M. Marland

Explore and Express 3
R. Adams, J. Foster, R. Wilson
Listening & Reading
Summer 1972

Listening and Writing
Spring 1972

Listening & Writing
Spring 1968

Scene   M. Marland

STORIES AND EXTRACTS

The Dress
The Fight
Lovejoy and Tip

In the forest of the Night
Red Lights
City Boy
Childhood stories

Through the Tunnel
One of the Virtues
Section *Gangs and Victims*

The Dog with a Million Fleas
Tupenny Rush
Joby and Gus
The Otherday
The Gang

PLAYS

Julian
The Chicken Run
The Car
Last Bus

NOVELS

Magnolia Buildings   E. Stucley
Gumble's Yard   J. R. Townsend
The Balaclava Gang   George Layton
The Twelfth of July   J. Lingard
One Hundred Million Francs   P. Berna
The Outsiders   S. E. Hinton
Tom's Midnight Garden   P. Pearce
The Children's Crusade   I. Serraillier
Louie's SOS   E. W. Hildick
Birdy and the Group   E. W. Hildick
Sell Out   R. Maddock
The Cave   R. Church
Joby   S. Barstow

3 Friends, enemies, fans and gangs   *Talking and reading*

1 In a group of 4 or 5 read the play *Julian* together. Then, choose one part of the play for taping. Rehearse it, tape it and follow it with a taped discussion about the play, particularly about Finch and Julian. Who do you sympathize with? Why? Would you have followed Julian out? What do you think of Sandra? And her action at the end of the play?

2 In a group of 4 or 5 tape your discussion about *one* of the following topics:
(a) Being a fan   (b) Being a supporter   (c) Making friends.

3 In a small group write, rehearse and tape a play about a gang and an outsider. (You could get some ideas from *Julian*.)

4 Make up a programme of reading about the topic – your own and poems and stories you have read. (*The Fight* on p.33 of *Wordscapes* is a good one to choose – you could read it as a pair.) Then rehearse the readings and tape them.

5 Imagine that you and 2 or 3 other people are experts on different aspects of soccer hooliganism or of pop group fans. With one person as an interviewer, tape a programme in which the experts argue about one of these subjects.

I read through the assignments with the children, adding further information and answering questions, then explained that each individual should complete a minimum of one assignment from each sheet, so ensuring that three kinds of work would be covered by each child and that all would take part in at least one group activity and at least one individual assignment. The material I'd prepared for the class included a book box referred to on the worksheets, containing individual copies of novels and sets of six copies each of short story collections, plays and source books. There was a folder of picture work cards, made from newspaper and colour supplement photographs. In another folder were newspaper cuttings about hooliganism, gang warfare etc, and, from the school library, a *Socio Pack* called *Violence in the Sixties*, which included useful material about gangs and fans during the fifties and sixties.

I find that I can rarely predict how children will take up a theme and interpret the ideas I give them. This theme was no exception. As the class enjoyed reading plays in groups, the play *Julian* was soon being read by nearly every child in the room. After the first reading (which takes about twenty minutes) several children wanted to write about the play rather than tape and discuss it, so I had to make my first additions to the worksheet. One able boy became so interested in the characters and the ambiguous situation left at the end of the play that he decided to write another play of his own as a sequel. I underestimated, too, the amount of interest shown, particularly by the boys, in the history of gangs and of their characteristic 'uniforms' and this showed up the lack of factual material I'd provided for this assignment.

After about a fortnight it was clear that, although work on fans and gangs was progressing enthusiastically, only a few thoughtful girls had given any attention to reading, thinking and writing about individual friends. As this seemed an important element to me I drew the class together for an input of new material. We read together the extract from *Joby* by Stan Barstow, in which Joby and his new 'hard' friend Gus get caught shoplifting and Joby realises Gus's unreliability as a friend. This had the right effect of reawakening interest in this aspect of the theme, and sparked off new written work and, for some, an enthusiastic reading of *Joby*.

When I finally drew everything together at the end of the fourth week most children had completed four or five varied assignments. Written work was either on display or collected together as booklets, and several tapes made by the children had been played or were still to be heard. Not surprisingly with a theme about communicating with other people, a lot of good work was on tape. Some groups were familiar enough with tape recorders to have been able to discuss friendship and crowd behaviour with great sense and thoughtfulness. The following pieces of children's work should give some impression of the different kinds of writing attempted during the theme. The titles are as follows:

1 My Views on Football Hooliganism   Philip
2 Head Quarters   Paul
3 The good and Bad things about friends   Susan
4 The New Reckrute   Kevin
5 A Portrait of Jane   Alison

My views on football hooligisim
Some examples of football hooligmism. I myself have not seen much football hooliginism but I suppose thats because I havn't been to many football matches. But I have heard a lot of stories about it. For instance the main reson hooliganim starts is becaus of a goal or from losing.

The crowd just go mad such as when a goal is scored for one side, the opposid teams fans turn around and just start scraping. Thene there is retaliation from the winning side.

At Derby matches which is teams from the same area such a a London Derby which involves clubs such as West ham, Arsenal, Fullam, Spurs Chelsea, and Q.P.R. In these sort of matches it doesn't matter which team is at home or away because the support is about eaqull because they dont have far to come. In these matches win, lose, or draw there is always a riot.

Usualy when a team loses they go on the rampadge. There was an incident at York an old man had a lot off to the hooligans who were on the rampage and they threw his car into the river Oose.

Resons for hooliganism
People who go to soccer matches in a gang just go to fite hard with their friends.

But if they were on their own they would most probrably behave.

If a side looses they go looking for trouble and usualy find it. On a TV programe a few months ago there were boys talking to an interviewer and they seemed very pleased with themselves because they had to got a fine of £80 for damages.

This is my way of showing that fines wont help.

I think that every supporter should have a special pass with their name, a photo of themselves and the main details about themselves. These passes can only be bought from a special office where there is a file on every supporter. If this supporter does misbehave he can have his pass taken off him for the rest of the season.

Philip

You explain your ideas very clearly and sensibly – Good.

Head Quarters
It was a monday morning, me and my gang where going to find anew Head Quarters. So we split up and went to look for a new one. As I was scrambling along a back of ariver I suddenly noticed a cave in the side. I quickly ran back and group the gang up. We set off with shovels and bags so we can make bigger. I toke all morning to make the hole big enough for us all. In the afternoon we took boxes and old stools to sit on. We manged to take a table in and a chest of drawers. We dug a small a hole and layed our secret information in and then buried it. Then we found a

big round stone in the ditch. We was just about to move it when I came up with an idea. We could use this as a door way. The next thing was to bring the rest of the stuff from the old Head Quarters. We did not have to bring much because the day before someone burnt most of the stuff. We then decided we better camoflage it because by now it was getting dark. We finished the Head Quarters at about 9.00. All that was need to be done now was to make traps for the enermys. The main gang was the Bashers we were always fighting them. So we had to make traps so we were show that their was nobody their. We had servaral devises to show were the bashers where. One was to have cans tied to gether so when erybody walk that way they could hit a can. The second one was to have sheets of metal along all the paths and put soil over them. The way was to have trip wires laided in the grass. The most important was was to have spys in the trees to spy out the Bashers. The most sucsesful by miles was a trap we called the death Trap,which was hole bedded in the ground and straw put over. So when some one walk over the hole they would fall in. The only danger was a attack from the stream end. The only way was to protect it was by fighting we had a old drain pipe which we used as a perascope to scan the area.

Paul

Excellent piece of work, Paul. You've explained everything very clearly.

The good and bad things about friends
Friends are people who you can trust. You need friends to talk to, and turn to. They should understand problems, or if you are in difficulty be able to talk and understand the problem. Its no good having a friend if you don't understand their problems as well as them understanding yours. Friends are for helping you if your boyfriend has packed you in and you darnt ask your mother or father about it because you get unbrassed.

You may find that your friend will like you to go places with them. Such as town, Fair, School. I sometimes ask my friends about homework and school problems. These are good things about friends, but you may find that there are many bad things about them as well.

The good and bad things about friends
Some friends like to climb apple trees and play at ringing door bells and running away I agree this is fun but it is also cruel and silly.

Some people use a friend for school. There are many people who do this. They play and mess around with them and then when the home time bell goes they usually say. 'Get lost or Clear off'. This is cruel. You must tell your friend, well I'm your school mate but I have another friend for playing with at night and out of school. I like to have friends, some for the class and some for night, I like to be friendly with every one instead of leaving someone out.

Susan

The new reckrute

now you say you want to be a member of the gang o yes thats right who told you about this gang my Brother did i see and who is you Brother? Alan has alan told you anything else about the gang? No good. Now if you join the gang you will have to be excepted By the cormity and you wont have to say a word to anyone about the gang understand. yes i under stand allright Blindfold him you understand why we are doing this dont you? Yes it is for i dont know where the den is untill i have been swarn in. all-right in the car to the den driver. very well Sir allright, get out now take him inside lads now befor we start you have to fill this form in i have sent for you to come here today, to say that your qualifications are right, i here By sware you in as, a member of the gypsyvill gang.

Kevin

A portrait of Jane

This is a portrait of my friend. She is called Jane. Jane has blue eyes, brown hair and her skin is fair. She has a face covered with freckles. Jane's height is 4ft 4 inches. She is quite chubby. Jane's family is not very big. She has two sisters the youngest is 7 years old her name is Debra thee other girl is called Dawn she is 11 years old. Her father is very good at jodo and her mum is very good at wakling backwards on her hands. Her mum and dad are quite big her mum is chubby and very funny. I go down to Janes on saturdays and sometimes sleep the night. She has a dog called patch. She is called patch because she had some different colodired patches. Jane's disslikes are people who swear theif and lie. So are mine. The things she likes are ridding houses and swimming. The food she eats is mostly meats and vegetables. She likes sweets as well also fruit.

Alison

There are several general points about the handling of theme work in the classroom which will not have emerged from the particular examples I've described. The success of a theme depends as much on the organization of the work in progress as on the preparation for it. To describe an English classroom as a workshop has become something of a cliché, but I can think of no more appropriate word. What the teacher has to aim for, is a classroom environment where children can start or continue work without needing the teacher to switch them on. English work in secondary schools is always fragmented by the subject-based timetable and the continuity of theme work will be completely lost if children cannot pick up easily and in an independent, businesslike way, from where they finished in the previous lesson.

This workshop environment can't be created immediately. The first consideration is the room itself and the furniture the school puts into it. Very few secondary school English classrooms are naturally right; most are too small, have heavy, unwieldy desks, no blackout, no shelves, and little display or storage space. Many teachers of mixed ability classes have the even greater misfortune of having no rooms of their own and of roaming the school followed by bearers with boxes. In an ideal situation a room which lends itself to this kind of work should be large enough to allow children and teacher to move about and talk quietly without disturbing others. The desks or tables should be light enough to move into different blocks according to the activity. There should be shelves or a cupboard where books and materials are clearly displayed and easily obtainable and there should be a well placed table where materials particularly relevant to the theme can be looked through. Even more ideally, the room should black out easily, and there should be an adjoining stockroom, broom cupboard or corridor alcove where small groups can make tapes without disturbing others or being disturbed. Very few English teachers will have rooms like this and probably have little hope of achieving them, but reorganization of existing facilities and some persistence in asking for more can help.

Even with ideal facilities, though, confusion can still reign if the children's attitude to the work is wrong. Children unfamiliar with mixed ability classes and theme work will not automatically work responsibly at their own pace, choose appropriate assignments, plan out their own work to keep the right balance when they make their choice. They have to learn to work in this way, and it will probably take at least half a term to teach them.

As the teacher obviously cannot supervise each individual's work programme all the time, it is important, particularly during the first term with a group, that the work should be structured in such a way that children are steered into making the right choices, both according to their ability and to their individual needs. For instance, I usually build in conditions about the choice of assignments. I stipulate that a certain number of individual and group topics should be covered, or that a minimum number of different kinds of writing should be done. Alternatively, as children finish work at such different times, I ask that they should consult me each time they intend to move on to something new. I soon know the group well enough to be able to anticipate where difficulties will arise, so I keep a particular check on children like Kevin, a boy of limited ability and enormous ambition, who would always choose work far too difficult, or Vanessa, an intelligent, lazy, dreamy girl, who would always choose the first assignment on the list, whatever its suitability, because that would take less energy.

Even when children have the habit of moving on responsibly to the next activity, there will still be situations, for example, near the end of a lesson, or when an individual is waiting for others in his group, in which time could be wasted or in which the quiet lazy ones could escape notice as they sit 'waiting to get on'. For times like these the classroom needs to be equipped with a class library of novels chosen with different abilities in mind, with stories on tape, and with boxes of graded cards, preferably made by the teacher, on dictionary work or common errors, an example of which I included earlier.

To help both the teacher and themselves, children should be aware of their own programme. I ask children to make a checklist, in their folders, of work to be covered, which they tick off as they complete assignments. For example, this would have been Alison's checklist during the **Friends and enemies** theme:

1 *Talking and reading* 4– taping a programme of poems and extracts with Jayne
2 *Writing for yourself* 3 – a portrait of Jayne
3 *Explaining things* 2 – about fans' uniforms
4 *Reading – Joby* and writing about Joby's first shoplifting adventure.

A regular reporting-back session could replace or add to this. I've often been pleasantly surprised by the responsible way children explain to the rest of the class what they're doing.

Children's work does not fit conveniently into the compartments imposed by a timetable, and theme work could become disorganized if one piece of work was left unfinished because the lesson came to an end or because the other three children in a group were ready to start a shared assignment next lesson before a child had finished his individual work. It's at moments like these that I use homework during a theme. I rarely set homework in the traditional way for a mixed ability group, but I very often ask children to finish work at home. Many do this willingly, and make the suggestion before I do. When the work is done with enthusiasm there's no need to check it in the following lesson. I make a mental or written note of lazy children who have been given work to do at home and ask to see the results the next session.

The collecting in, marking and handing back of written work could be a problem when a theme is under way. I keep a folder on the front desk in which children put work they wish to be marked. I hand back and discuss work with individuals and, when it's necessary, direct them to the appropriate work card if I think the correction of a technical mistake needs reinforcement at that moment.

I put no numerical mark or grade on written work, but always try to write a full comment, including enough constructive criticism to be helpful to the child if I can't discuss the work with him for any reason when I hand it back. I mark recurring technical mistakes and give the correct spelling of words which children have either struggled with, or which are newly acquired. I discuss basic punctuation mistakes with individuals and ask them to rewrite part or all of their work for display. For example, Kevin, the author of *The New reckrute,* rewrote his story, correcting spelling and setting out the conversation correctly. The dialogue in the story seemed to me to have considerable style and was worth improving. Kevin saw the need to improve it when a friend found the story impossible to understand.

In my mark book I give a grade indicating effort so that I have a record of each individual's attempts to achieve his best. Alongside this, on another page, I keep a record of each child's attainments and problems in writing, reading and oral work. For example, this was the entry during the Autumn Term for Paul, the author of *Head Quarters.*

Written work Competent. Careless spelling mistakes through haste: was/were/where sure/show/their/there. Paragraphs.

Reading Fluent and lively.

Oral Work Logical and alert. Better in small groups than in class.

This picture of the child is, of course, built up gradually during the first few weeks with a group and I keep it up to date by, for instance, recording if a child has mastered a particular technical problem like the proper use of capital letters or of paragraphs.

Some activities can't be 'marked', so I make sure that there are regular sessions in which we play and discuss the tapes children have made, read work out, perform prepared plays and draw attention to work which has been displayed.

When habits and routines have been established and a theme is in progress, classes organize themselves at the beginning of each lesson. I lay out the work in progress, the paper, book box and other material before, or as the class come in. Without waiting for me, they collect work and pick up where they left off. If some are working in groups they assemble themselves, perhaps with the need to rearrange furniture. Although I usually say nothing at the beginning of the lesson, I always speak to the whole class after a few minutes, once everyone is established in their places and remind them about the level of noise, the amount of time the theme still has to run and the importance of setting themselves an aim to achieve in that particular lesson. I find that the right level of noise, when group work is going on alongside individual concentration, is again an element of this kind of working which requires practice and training. Groups are rarely larger than four or five and, once discussion is an accepted way of working and not a safety valve from strict silence, as it could be in some lessons, then children soon realize that they can work more satisfactorily with quiet talk than with raised voices. I don't find that individuals concentrating on reading or writing are disturbed by a working buzz of noise going on in the same room. Many children find this a natural environment. If a group has chosen an activity which is noisier than usual, for example, rehearsing a short play, I move them into an empty classroom, a stockroom or the corridor. With some schools and some pupils this would not be possible, in which case I would ask the group to postpone this activity until a session when most of the class are doing work in groups and the noise level would be naturally higher than normal.

Another element of classroom organization which needs to work smoothly is the forming and maintaining of small groups. As group work is a characteristic of all the work I do in English, classes soon become used to it. Sometimes I organize the groups. For example, if I hand back a piece of writing to the whole class at the same time I might form groups of children with similar technical problems, who will work on them together, or I will form groups according to aptitude or interest to look at a particular short story together. When children choose a group work option from a work sheet, I generally leave them to arrange their own groups. These are usually friendship groups and are nearly always small mixed ability groups in themselves. Once a group like this has been established in the first term, it often works together efficiently for much of the year.

Perhaps it sounds as though my chief objective has been to organize myself out of a job. When most children in a class have become independent and responsible, aren't I redundant? In one sense, I am. When I started teaching, in nearly every lesson I was the focus of all eyes. I read, performed, steered class discussion, questioned, gave information, played to the gallery. Now I find my role is very different, less taxing in one way, much more so in another. It will only be in the lessons which introduce and spark off a theme, and in the later input sessions, that I will be at the front of the class and in the spotlight. In many ways this is a relief, but I exchange this for the equally demanding role of peripatetic adviser, corrector, exhorter, and resource centre. It is the role which for years many primary school teachers have taken for granted. For me it has become one of the chief pleasures of mixed ability teaching.

The social and educational benefits of mixed ability learning seem to me to be very closely intertwined. When a group is thoroughly involved in work of the kind I've been describing, the atmosphere produced in the room by the blending of such a variety of abilities and personalities is very different from that produced by a streamed group. The sense of sharing learning together is strong, and the teacher in the midst of the room becomes part of it in a direct and close way.

At the end of the summer term a group of five children from a third year mixed ability class I'd taught for a year taped a discussion about English and English lessons. They were a mixed ability group in miniature, and they talked by themselves with some questions to prompt their thoughts. What surprised me about the talk was their consciousness of the learning process they'd been taking part in during the year. I think some of their comments will illustrate the teaching and learning approach I've been describing.

Andrew is an alert, intelligent boy who is 'good at English' in the conventional sense. These were his comments on the variety of work within English and on working together. 'You learn more things. You go in different directions instead of just going on writing and reading . . . You know more, because you've been talking to them all.'

Julie, a lively, noisy, bright careless writer enjoyed English lessons because 'they're more friendly'. She also recognized that the friendliness had a positive learning value: . . . 'You all muck in together and sort things out together.'

The most perceptive comments came from Mark, a very articulate boy whose writing never succeeded in being an adequate vehicle for his considerable insight. His comments included these: . . . 'It's like all the subjects in one really, isn't it? . . . You can discuss it without the teachers going on at you . . . You work as if you want to get on with it, you work so that you can enjoy it . . . In History it's by yourself. It seems to be a more sociable lesson, English.'

Topic work

English teachers and writers of books about English teaching all seem to use the phrase 'topic work' in different senses, so it seems sensible to begin this section with a definition or explanation of practice. For me, topic work is an inquiry into a given subject by a class of children. It is very close to theme work, but there are differences in choice of subject and approach. I choose subjects for theme work which are general, wide-ranging, and capable of being interpreted in several different ways. Subjects for topic work cover a more closely defined area and are more factual in nature, for example, the production of newspapers; the development of the local neighbourhood; dialects; school buildings; television. Inquiring into topics like these requires a particular range of language skills. In theme work, children use language in a wide variety of ways. A single worksheet, as part of a theme on 'water', may ask a child to write a poem about the sea and to design and explain a canoe. In topic work, language is used mainly to interpret and present facts and opinions. The written source material children use will be mostly factual: reference books, pamphlets, maps, newspapers. They are likely to spend time collecting evidence for themselves; studying their school buildings; interviewing local inhabitants; making up and filling in questionnaires. During a theme, individual children complete several different pieces of work; during a topic they will probably complete for themselves, or contribute to, a single 'product' like a magazine, a survey, a debate or a tape.

Topic work, as I have described it, plays an important part in many streamed class activities but, like theme work, I find it well suited to mixed ability groups, particularly because many of the activities I prepare require cooperation and shared research. Discussion about the material and methods of work, is an important part of most of these activities. Children are also called upon to use other skills: to become editors, secretaries, group organizers or spokesmen. It will, therefore, be the kind of work in which oral ability, practical and organizing skills, and personality play as important a part as the abilities more traditionally associated with English.

Let me now describe the working of some of the topics I've used with mixed ability classes, namely, **town planning**; **television viewing**; **newspaper writing**; **the development of language**.

Town planning was a third-year topic, but other teachers in the department have used the same idea and similar approaches with fourth years. I hoped to make the class aware of the problems of town planners, to see the effects of new development on people and to apply their understanding to the particular problems of their town, Hull. They would be required to use language for argument, both in discussion and in writing, and for presenting research and observation.

In the first lesson I drew on the blackboard a map of a mythical village in the East Riding and indicated the site of a new commercial airport, proposed as part of the plan to make Humberside 'The gateway to Europe'. Also on the map I marked the properties belonging to people in the village who would be particularly affected by the airport, its approach roads and low-flying aircraft. The class provided a name for the village and its people, and were soon able to suggest additions to the villagers I'd already created. These were some of the affected inhabitants:

The Vicar – in charge of an ancient church with a very high steeple and delicate medieval stained glass windows.
A local market gardener – owner of a very large expanse of greenhouses.
A prosperous farmer – the airport would take some of his fields and the approach road would separate the farm buildings from most of his land. He is also Master of the local hunt.
A retired businessman – living in a manor house which had been bought for its quietness and beauty. He is also a keen fisherman and ornithologist.
The postmistress – has lived in the village for sixty years.
A publican and his wife – 'foreigners' from Leeds who have modernized one of the local pubs and turned one of the High Street

shops into a boutique.

Another publican and his wife, – 'natives' in charge of the genuine local.

The headmistress – of the village primary school which would be divided by the proposed approach road from the small estate where most of the children live.

Mothers and teenagers – from the estate.

Each child in the class was now given the role of one of the listed inhabitants and two I knew to be fluent and confident speakers were made representatives from the Department of the Environment and the Ministry of Aviation. (You will notice certain similarities here with Les Stringer's description in chapter five of how *Tenement* operates). I explained that a public hearing was to be held next day for everyone to express their opinions about the airport. I gave out paper and asked each child to list either their reasons for supporting the plans, or for attacking them, with detailed reference to their own situation. I had tried, in introducing the characters and their situations, to give only information and not to suggest too clearly the stand each might take at the hearing. I had also made sure in handing out the roles that I made the less confident children part of a group, of mothers or teenagers, so that they could support each other, both in preparing their evidence and in speaking to the rest. I asked the two government officials to prepare short talks explaining their concern over the plans and the villagers chose two of their number as leading spokesmen to prepare speeches against the plans. I circulated, helping with lists where necessary and also checking that enough inhabitants would defend the airport to make the hearing a success.

I chaired the hearing in the following double lesson so that I could encourage any timid speakers and also introduce new issues if this proved necessary. Fortunately, the landlord of the Green Man Inn spoke so ardently in support of the airport that a heated argument soon developed which involved most of the inhabitants. At the end the village voted a resounding 'No' to the plans.

In the next lesson I gave the class a piece of written work as the outcome of the hearing. They chose from three assignments:

1 a local newspaper's report of the hearing
2 a statement by the character assumed during the hearing
3 a letter to a friend or relation about the plans for the airport and the hearing, by the character assumed during the hearing.

As the report and the letter were the more difficult assignments, I checked quickly that the weakest writers hadn't chosen something outside their abilities.

These three or four lessons served as an introduction to the problems and princples involved in developing areas where people live and work. Another equally successful way into the topic was used by another member of the department who read *Carrigan Street* by John Pick in the Macmillan Dramascript series. After reading this play about the demolition of slums and the rehousing of inhabitants, the class carried the parts they had read and acted through into a public hearing.

The next stage was to list on the blackboard the areas in Hull where development was planned or was taking place. Three main issues seemed most important:

1 the plans for Hull's Old Town, a fascinating, decaying area, much neglected by the council
2 the rehousing of people from inner city slums
3 the building of new estates like the vast Bransholme, to the north-east of the city.

I directed the children into six mixed groups of four to five and gave each group their assignment. Two groups each worked on options one and two. These were the four options:

---

1 Study the maps of the old town. Read about the work that needs doing there and the plans for the future. Discuss the way you would develop the area, taking each section in turn. Once the group has decided on an overall plan, take a section each and explain and draw your ideas clearly.

2 Hull is changing a lot and many people hold strong views about the new development. Make a list of adults you could interview about their views, particularly on the areas we've talked about. You'll need to spend some time wording your questions and making arrangements to talk to people. Then you'll need to write up your findings.

3 Using the old photographs, the reference books and maps, prepare a talk for the rest of the class about the way that landmarks or popular places in Hull have changed. Hull-born grandparents may be able to help you with this.

4 Find out as much as you can about the buildings, layout, facilities, atmosphere etc. on Bransholme estate and in an area where old houses are being demolished, e.g. near Hessle Road. When you are sure of your facts, make two of the group into people who are to be rehoused from Hessle Road to Bransholme, and two into officials from the housing department. Tape a discussion in which the officials try to persuade the people to move.

The groups spent nearly a fortnight on this work. They used books and relevant newspaper cuttings from the school's library, a set of old maps and photographs of old and new Hull, and information from organizations like the Central Library, the Information Bureau, and the Civic Society. Group two's interviews with staff and friends took place in lesson time, but most of their interviewing was done outside school, and lessons were used for writing up their findings. Similarly, group one did most of their fieldwork in the old town in their own time, although it would have been possible to spend lesson time taking the whole class round the area. At the end of the topic, written work was displayed, group three gave their talk, and group four played their tape to the rest of the class.

A study of television viewing was a topic I used both with a second-year group in their final term and with a third-year group. Television is obviously a big element in most children's lives and I hoped through this work to enable the class to look more objectively at their own viewing and to see this in relation to the rest of the class.

In the first lesson I handed out duplicated copies of a questionnaire and asked each individual to fill it in. As all the children had television at home, (several had more than one set) there was no problem about non-participants. This was the questionnaire.

---

1 What is the average time you spend watching TV during a week night?
2 What is the average time you spend watching TV during the weekend?
3 How are decisions made in your home about the choice of channels and programmes?
4 Which channel is watched most?
5 Do all your family watch the same amount of TV?
6 List your 5 favourite programmes in order of preference.
7 List your 5 worst programmes, worst first.
8 What kind of programme do you like best? Why?
9 What kind of programme do you like least? Why?
10 Are there enough of the kinds of programmes you like?
11 What is there too much of?
12 Are there enough programmes which cater for people of your age? Should there be more?
13 Do you consider you watch:
   (a) too much (b) the right amount (c) too little?
14 Do you think you could survive if TV were abolished? Give your reasons.

84

The class took a lesson to fill this in.

The next stage was for each child to tear up the sheet into sections of related questions, i.e. 1 and 2; 3, 4 and 5; 6 and 7; 8 and 9; 10, 11 and 12; 13 and 14. The torn off slips were collected together in their sections and I organized the class into six working groups of four or five children and handed out a section of answers to each one. I gave these instructions to the class:

1 Find out all the information you can from the answers and note it down in some form in rough.
2 Discuss your findings. Try to explain the reasons for them and decide what's most interesting about your discoveries. Think of possible ways of presenting your findings and your comments on them.
3 After four or five lessons you should be ready to present your material in two ways:
   (a) to go up on the wall;
   (b) as an explanation to the rest of the class of what you've discovered.

Most groups coped efficiently with the first stage of extracting information and had little trouble with the 'mathematical' presentation of these facts. Sections 1, 2, 4 and 6 seemed to be best presented in block graphs. Section 3 needed a complicated votes system to discover the class's top and bottom five. Difficulties arose with the second stage when the statistics had to be interpreted, so my chief job was joining in discussions with each group and drawing their attention, where necessary, to the significance of what they'd discovered. They also needed help with finding the right language for writing and talking to the class. Some groups were dissatisfied with the amount of information they could find from the questionnaire and followed it up with interviews. So, for example, children in section one and six wanted to talk to the student who was also working with the third-year class and who, in her questionnaire, had declared a lack of interest in any television programmes but BBC 2 classic serials.

At the end of the second week of the topic a wall display was put up and the groups reported back on their research. I found many of the results predictable, but to the children they were often new and surprising. The general level of class discussion after the talks was high, both because it was informed discussion and because the experiences were common to all.

Another media topic was **newspaper writing** – second-year work. The end-product of the topic was to be several group newspapers, but I wanted these to be based on an examination of the contents, style and layout of real newspapers. I wouldn't expect children of this age to do more than discover something about the arrangement of material; the purpose of headlines and photographs; and the different styles of reporting used by different kinds of journalists. Some of the able children would be able to recognize the differences in composition and style between the 'popular' and 'serious' newspapers.

In the first lesson I organized the class into groups of four to five children and gave each group one or two newspapers and a worksheet. I had already told the class what we would be doing and several children had brought papers with them, usually local evening papers. I tried to ensure that each group had at least one local and two national papers, one 'serious' and one 'popular'. The leader, or secretary, of the group was to fill in the worksheet with information given by the rest. These were the questions:

---

1 Make a list of the different 'ingredients' in your papers, e.g. sports news; crossword; editorial etc.
2 How are the ingredients arranged on the different pages? e.g. what kind of news is on the front page? in the middle?
3 Look at the front pages. How did the editor decide which stories should be at the top of the page? at the bottom? at the side?
4 With a ruler measure the space taken up on the front page by headlines and then by the actual reports themselves.
5 Now look at the wording of the headlines. What's the purpose of them? Could the papers do without them?
6 Read two or three news and sports reports from your papers. Make a list together of the things reporters do to make their stories interesting to the reader, e.g. how do they start their stories? What kinds of words do football reporters use to describe goals?
7 What do the photographs in your papers add? Could papers do without them?

This work took most of a double lesson, and in the last quarter of an hour I asked each group to report back to the class on one question, and encouraged the rest to make additions to lists read out, or to disagree with conclusions made.

In the following lesson I talked to the whole class for ten minutes about the production of newspapers. I'd drawn a plan of the different stages and people involved on the blackboard, to make it as clear as I could. I explained that each group was going to produce its own newspaper during the next fortnight.

To avoid confusion and a waste of time in the initial stages I gave them a set of instructions. Each group was to appoint an editor to be in charge of production and chairman of the group. The list of ingredients on the worksheet would form the contents of the newspaper and the group were to divide the reporting jobs between them. They had to make a decision about the kind of newspaper they were going to produce. Was it to be:

(a) a national newspaper with imagined news stories?
(b) a local newspaper with a combination of imagined and real stories?
(c) a school newspaper with real stories?

The page arrangement they had noted down on the worksheet would form the plan of their newspaper. Preliminary discussions and organization took up the rest of the period.

In the third lesson production began. I had provided several different sizes of paper, sugar paper and card, scissors and glue. My first job was to get a progress report from each group. This enabled me to check that children had opted for the reporting and writing jobs they were capable of and to make sure that no one was doing less than his fair share. In the following lessons I spent a period of time with each group, reading work, making suggestions, providing books and ideas if they were necessary, and chivvying any lazy members of the group. Only one group chose to compile a school paper, and they made arrangements to interview staff and other children, and sometimes did this during lesson time. At the beginning of each lesson I reminded the class of the deadline date and asked each editor to report briefly on the progress of his group. The completed papers were collected in at the end of the fortnight.

Looking at **The development of language** as a topic was again different in aim and practice. It's a topic I've worked on with both third- and fourth-year groups and I hoped to give children some idea of the nature and growth of language, culminating in a study of their own.

The first stage was to lead the children into situations in which they would question the nature of language, discover its importance and begin to wonder how it first began. I took the class into the hall for the first lesson and split them into pairs with the task of taking it in turns to communicate to each other some information or ask a question without using language. After five to ten minutes of animated gesticulation and expressive grunts I brought the class together again to discuss what they'd discovered. Pairs then joined into groups of four and were asked to improvise a situation in which one of the four was a foreigner in England, trying to communicate information or a question to the other three English natives without speaking any English. The foreigner wasn't allowed to give up, or hand on to one of the others until the communication had been successful. Again, findings from this situation were discussed. Finally, the same groups of four went away to discuss, and act out if they could, the 'birth' of language in a group of prehistoric men. After discussion of this I asked each child to do one of two pieces of research, as preparation for the following day's lesson.

87

They either had to find out and copy down the words for different relations within the family (e.g. uncle, daughter, cousin) in four or five different languages, or, to copy down words from languages such as Greek, Chinese or Russian which use different alphabets from ours.

Using the children's findings as a starting point, the next session was a whole-class lesson in which we looked at the words they'd collected, on the blackboard, and discussed similarities and differences between languages. I wanted to do little more than arouse interest in language itself and to give some idea of the 'families' of languages. The fourth-year group contained a Chinese boy who held the class spellbound with his talk about Chinese characters. This aroused so much interest that we continued talking in the following lesson, helped by further examples brought in by a boy with a Polish grandfather, one with a sea-faring father and a girl who'd made a special visit to the Indian family who lived down her road.

The next stage was to focus on English, and in another whole-class lesson I built up, with the children's help, a picture of the different invasions which have helped to form modern English. I duplicated a sheet of extracts to illustrate what we were finding out. These included sections in Anglo-Saxon from *Beowulf* and *The Seafarer,* and we also read them in modern English translations (i.e. in the Serraillier version of *Beowulf* in *The Windmill Book of Ballads* Heinemann, and in *Voices I* Penguin). There were also short extracts from Chaucer's *Canterbury Tales,* both in Middle English and a modern translation (i.e. parts of the descriptions of the Prioress and the Miller in the *Prologue*). All the children seemed to enjoy the detective work of sorting out meaning and tracing signs of modern English and French.

In the next session I gave each pair of children an etymological dictionary. Their work was to find and write down five words derived from each of the following languages: Anglo-Saxon, Latin, Greek, French and German. This took about twenty minutes and I then collected some of their words on the blackboard in order to show two things. Firstly, the kinds of words which different languages had contributed, e.g. Anglo-Saxon words for tools and basic household implements; Greek for aspects of medicine and learning. Secondly, how different languages have contributed to idiosyncratic English spelling, e.g. psychology, beautiful, science, etc.

Extended group assignments began in the following lesson. I had booked the library for four lessons and asked the librarian to prepare the appropriate books. I gave each group one of the following subjects: Christian names and surnames; place names; food; sports; musical instruments; hobbies and arts; medicine; buildings. Their task was to explore the derivation and history of about twenty words connected with their subject and to prepare to give a talk about their findings to the rest of the class.

The work lasted for between two and three weeks, and with the third-year group I finished the topic at this point. As the fourth-year group still seemed interested I introduced a new piece of group work involving, this time, written work. I gave a dictionary to each child and asked them to look up a newly-coined word, e.g. 'moon buggy' or 'monkey boots', which I knew they would be unable to find. We discussed the problem of keeping dictionaries up to date and then compiled a list on the blackboard of as many new words as the class could think of. Suggestions were made for the derivation of some of them and I chose one word from the list and asked pairs to work together on writing a definition. These definitions were compared and put alongside a dictionary definition so that I could introduce the different components of a definition and the idea of economic and precise description and explanation. I then gave each working group of four or five a subject from the following list: clothes; transport and roads; food and drink; pop music; space exploration; shops and amenities; weapons and war. Their assignment was to produce a modern dictionary of words associated with their subject. The editor or leader of the group was to be in charge of handing out and organizing the presentation of the work. This part of the topic lasted for about a week.

I'd like now to draw from these examples some general points about the preparation and organization of topic work. Several of the points have been made more fully in the first section on theme work.

In one sense, the preparation for a topic takes me less time and thought than that required for a theme, because the topics I've used last for a fortnight of lessons or, at the most, three weeks, whereas a theme which is working really successfully could be used for half a term. Most of my thought, though, goes into the structuring of the topic. I prepare the three or four opening lessons carefully, with the aim of giving the class information and of leading them to think closely about the issues which they'll later explore for themselves. This is unlike the opening lessons of a theme, in which I would aim to provide the kind of open-ended stimulus which would encourage the imagination and spark off related feelings and ideas. As most of the work is done in groups I don't prepare graded worksheets and questionnaires as I know that groups will sort out any difficulties together. However, I do take care to try to word them as clearly as possible. The questionnaire I prepared for the television study was badly worded as there were several questions which proved confusing to all the children. I tend to hand out assignments to particular groups, rather than give a choice, as I would in theme work, and again I take care to word the instructions clearly and explicitly so that groups can start work without needing to consult me immediately.

The amount of material needed for a topic will vary according to its nature, **The town planning** topic needed more preparation in this sense than the **television study**, which tapped the children's own experience.

Other kinds of arrangement often need to be made before a topic can begin. For example, one may be organizing visits out of school, arranging interviews with adults, or providing several working tape recorders and/or cameras. The school library will probably play an important part in topic work. I'm fortunate enough to teach in a school with a permanent librarian who considers it part of her job to help provide relevant books and resource material and also to help children find books and use them. We can make arrangements to use the library in two different ways; either to take it over for the whole class for several lessons, or to send small numbers of children out of the classroom to do their own research by themselves or with the librarian's help.

The problems of organizing topic and theme work in the classroom for a mixed ability group are similar, so many of the points I'm about to make now are by way of reiteration, since they will have been considered in the earlier section on theme work.

The room itself needs to be suitably arranged and equipped. For the kind of topic work I arrange, the children need to have learnt how to work independently and in a self-disciplined way. Once the group work has begun I lay out all the necessary material at the beginning of each lesson and I expect children to find what they need, arrange the group's seating, and start work straightaway. I usually have a quick word with the class as a whole after they've settled and at the end of the lesson to remind them of the time left, of any particular problems connected with the topic and to answer any questions.

The initial arrangement of children into groups is an important part of the organization. The kinds of activities I set, work best when the small groups are mixed in ability, unlike some other activities in English where the ability composition of the group is of less significance. The work usually requires a combination of skills such as writing, thinking, reading, discussing, illustrating, operating machines, organizing, leading, and story-telling. Such skills are best provided by a group which combines varied intelligences, interests, practical abilities, experiences and personalities. To ensure this, I arrange the groups myself, but I've often found that friendship groups are usually naturally unstreamed, as concerns outside the classroom bring them together, so there is often very little organizing to do. It's also true that, if mixed working groups are arranged at the beginning of the year, they will often work amicably and efficiently together for a lengthy period of time, although it's useful to ring the changes on group composition every now and again, in order to provide a range of experience.

Once the second stage of the topic, i.e. group work, has begun, I spend each lesson moving from one group to another with several jobs to carry out. I check first that, if the assignment has required the allocation of different tasks to members of the group, this has been done sensibly. This would be particularly important, for instance, with the newspaper writing. During the course of the topic I discuss each individual's work with him and, where this is written work, I read it and make suggestions and corrections. I shall know already which children have difficulty with writing so, for instance, during the newspaper topic, I helped one boy who was writing a report about the loss of a trawler at sea, by writing the stages of the story for him as he explained it to me, so that he could build up his report from my notes. Similarly, I would watch for the poor readers during work which required research and help them either by providing, if possible, a simpler book (e.g. one of the *Ladybird Leaders* series) or by asking them to retell a short section of what they'd read. Many children who write imaginative work of high quality without any help from the teacher, find logical reasoning difficult so, for instance, during the preparation for the airport hearing, I spent time with several individuals to help them to deduce information from the facts given and to think out their point of view and their reasons.

My job with the good writers and able thinkers is not usually to correct them, more often, to question them, in order to extend their capabilities and to make sure that they are seeing all the possibilities in the work. For example, in the newspaper topic I discussed with them the possible ways of interpreting news and of suggesting bias in reporting style and attitude. One able girl had done so much interviewing of friends and relations during her work on the town planning topic, that she needed help with handling the voluminous material, with sorting out the important from the irrelevant, and with finding a way of summarizing her conclusions.

Most children need help with using reference books for their research. Too often, factual information is copied out from a relevant book and little understanding will have been gained from the exercise. The skills of note-taking and summarizing do not come naturally to most children and have to be learnt. I spend lessons on these skills with the whole class, timed, where possible, to come before work which will need them. For one exercise in summarizing, for instance, the children work in pairs. They both read the same short passage of information, perhaps from another subject's text book or extracts I've duplicated from newspapers and reference books. Then one hands over her copy and repeats the main points of the passage from memory, while her neighbour checks the original. They then discuss the points which were left out and decide how important they were to the meaning of the passage. They follow this by reading a second short passage and, without consulting each other, make a list, in their own form of notes, of the points they consider important. Then they exchange lists and comment on each other's choice of points and note-taking style.

One important aspect of this kind of work for a mixed ability group is that children, through collaboration on a topic, learn from each other. When a child is working by himself he is working to his own time scheme and achieving, or failing to achieve, his own goals. When he is sharing in the production of a piece of group work he is working to the group's time scheme and towards the group's goals. I've found that this stimulates most children to their best work. When they have a double audience, consisting of the rest of the group and the teacher, or other interested readers, they need no urging to write clearly and correctly, to copy out work a second time, and to present their writing attractively.

The sense of shared effort also promotes the kind of atmosphere in which weak writers ask for, and receive, help from the competent writers. There is mutual help in other directions, too. The good leader or organizer is often not the most intelligent child in the group, nor is the tape recorder expert, or the child who is gifted at displaying material. In discussion, for instance, of the newspaper worksheet or at the airport hearing, children who normally struggle painfully to express their thoughts on paper often talked articulately and fluently. They often expressed quick, intuitive insights which a more rational child could then take up and develop.

In one way, keeping a check on the class's progress during a topic is easier than during a theme, as they are working on a more closely defined area and often in quite similar ways. Watching individuals is sometimes more difficult, when each one's contribution is not necessarily a readable and markable piece of writing. Sometimes the written or spoken result of a fortnight's work will seem small. For example, the editor of a group newspaper or collection of material might seem to me to have produced very little, unless I've watched him at work regularly and seen the way he has read others' contributions, organized the next stage, and suggested new ideas. Much topic work is difficult to mark in the traditional way when there is individual written work, e.g. that set after the airport hearing. I read it, write comments on it, and record an effort grade in my mark book. Group written work is usually displayed and read by me and the rest of the class. Talks are listened to, and tapes played back, and, at the end of the topic, I encourage the class to discuss critically their own work and that of others. Where relevant, I add to a child's record card any particular comment about his strengths and weaknesses and his contribution to group work during the topic.

Topic work is only one of the several English activities I use with mixed ability groups. During one year with a group I would probably cover one topic of the kind I've described each term.

APPENDIX Possible themes and topics
The topics suggested for fourth- and fifth-years are generally not suitable earlier on in the school but, apart from this, many of the other subjects could, with a little thought and ingenuity, be adapted for almost any age. Thus, the indications given here are merely guides

which will depend, above anything else, on the understanding, awareness and approach of the class and on the attitude, outlook and preferences of the teacher.

First year (11-12 years)
1 My neighbourhood
2 Taste/touch/smell/hearing/sight/sixth sense
3 People
4 Bonfire night/fireworks/fire
5 Travel and transport
6 Fair/circus/pantomime
7 The sea
8 The desert
9 Discoveries
10 Public servants
11 Words and word games
12 Animals/birds
13 Cowboys and indians
14 My family
15 Spring/summer/autumn/winter
16 Comics
17 Adventure
18 Games
19 Lost and found
20 Myths and legends

Second year (12-13 years)
1 Friends, enemies, fans and gangs
2 Newspaper writing
3 Christmas
4 School/teachers
5 My Village/town/city
6 Heroes and heroines
7 Visits
8 Predators
9 Night
10 Wanderers
11 Food
12 Strange creatures
13 Machines
14 Underground
15 Unusual hobbies
16 Contests
17 Shops and shopping
18 Tall stories
19 Folklore
20 The elements

Third year (13-14 years)
1 Other worlds
2 Superstitions
3 Town planning
4 Television viewing
5 A Day in the life of my street/village/town/city
6 Exploration
7 Dreams/fantasy
8 Growing up
9 Rooms/buildings
10 Parties/celebrations
11 Earthquake/volcano
12 Disasters/accidents
13 Festivals
14 Fish/fishing
15 My autobiography
16 Power and authority
17 Advertising
18 Magazines
19 Men and animals
20 What's funny?

Fourth year (14-15 years)
1 The development of language
2 Social class
3 Family and personal relationships
4 War and peace
5 Rebel/outsider
6 Births/weddings/funerals
7 Part-time jobs
8 Stories: ghost; detective; horror; humorous
9 Town and country
10 Farm and factory
11 Marriage
12 Fashions
13 Sports/athletes
14 Pop culture
15 Education/planning the perfect school
16 Old age and youth
17 Leisure
18 Communications
19 The mass media
20 The social services

Fifth year (15-16 years)
1 Other cultures/third world

2 Crime and punishment
3 New and old
4 Man and science
5 Rituals
6 Moments of truth
7 People's beliefs
8 The future
9 Handicapped people
10 Meetings and farewells
11 Black/white/yellow/brown
12 Life and death
13 Poverty and wealth
14 World of work
15 Censorship
16 An author or genre
17 Moral dilemmas
18 Films: the western; horror; comedy; war; musical etc
19 England and the English
20 The people, music, stories, sights of ? (e.g. India; United States etc.)

4 Literature as literature

Shirley Hoole

In the kind of English teaching discussed in this book children from their first year in secondary school will be dipping into literature in the way Judith Atkinson describes in her essay. Since the 1960s there has been a continuing supply of excellent and beautifully produced source books, usually arranged thematically and using literature from the Sagas to Sylvia Plath.

Much of the work I do with mixed ability groups is on a thematic basis, and part of the enjoyment is 'to invade literature like a monarch' and take whatever one wants. Decide to explore with a fifth-year group the theme of parents and children and it's sheer self-indulgence to think of ideas: *Lear, Romeo and Juliet, Dombey and Son, Père Goriot, The Rainbow, The American Dream, A Taste of Honey, A Night Out.* A dozen other possibilities will spring to mind, and this is before even considering short stories, poetry, and film. There is likely to be time to read only one novel or play in full, and generally extracts will be used. Against the understandable accusation of 'instant packaged list', I would argue that all the children will at least have heard or read *something* of Shakespeare, Dickens, Balzac, Albee, Delaney, Pinter. For abler or interested readers I would have copies of the books and others on the same theme, or by the same authors, available in form and school libraries, or have my own copies available. With such a system, less able readers will come into contact with literature they could not tackle on their own and which, because of the assumptions we make about such children, they would be unlikely to meet outside a mixed ability group.

The great drawback to using literature in thematic work is, of course, that it is a Procrustean process, as Bullock pointed out: literature cut or stretched to fit the theme. It seems perfectly valid to consider the tragic course of Lear and his children in exploring the love, conflicts, and roles within the family. Yet I am aware of the absurdity of cutting down Lear to this size. It is the *reductio ad absurdum* of thematic work to debate whether to slot *King Lear* into outsiders, old age, or parents and children. It could be argued, too, that in using extracts we are butchering literature, that whether it's a Shakespearean play or a children's novel, a work of literature is a work of art, and is meant to be seen as a whole.

The radical reappraisal of the aims, content and methods of English teaching in the last twenty years has brought about a long overdue reaction against a literature-dominated curriculum. New ideas about the scope and range of activities in English has meant that in many classrooms the emphasis has been on direct experience, imaginative writing, thematic work, individual and group assignments. The acknowledgement of the need for oracy as well as literacy has developed from the work of Wilkinson and others in the sixties, and particularly since the publication of D. Barnes *et al* (1969) *Language, the Learner and the School* (Penguin). Many teachers have arranged their work to include opportunities for different kinds of talking and listening, especially exploratory talk in group discussion. This sort of teaching obviously involves changes in classroom organization, and, especially in mixed ability classrooms, frequently a 'workshop' situation with a range and choice of activities going on simultaneously, with an emphasis on individual and small-group work.

In all this multiplicity of activities, it is easy to lose sight of literature for its own sake. My concern is that it should still play a vital part, involving individual, group and class reading. What is needed, for literature as for other activities, is a flexible approach to work and organization. Sometimes a child will be with the whole class listening to a story or reporting back from discussion groups; another time she will be tape recording a play with a small group; another time reading on her own. In the hectic school day, I think children need the occasional quiet time when everyone is reading or working quietly alone. There has been much stress recently on the need for children to talk in school but in acknowledging and implementing this we need to remember the need for peace, time to read and time to *think*. For some children the concentration-span will be short, but it's possible to make sure that everyone reads for, say, a quarter of an hour, then those who want to continue do so, while others get on with some quiet work. It's vital with mixed ability groups always to have work in progress; an assignment on a theme or a book, or a topic, set over several weeks so that everyone doesn't have to do everything at the same time or, more important, at the same pace. There is always work to get on with, so that abler children don't have to waste time and less able children can work at their own speed, changing activities when they need to.

It's essential, too, to have a variety and choice of books available in class libraries to cater for a wide range of interests and reading abilities. At the same time, the shared experience of reading a book together as a class can have an enjoyment and a value of its own. I'm not advocating a return to the old class readers, often read a paragraph at a time round the class, slogged through word for word at a uniform pace. But what was wrong was not the idea of sharing a novel together

– it was the approach, the method, and often the choice of book. A traditional method, as David Mears points out, has been to issue each class with one novel or play, one poetry anthology, and one course book to be used concurrently for a term or even a year. (A colleague remembers, for instance, having *The Merchant of Venice* for a whole year.) It is not a system I would ever use, and it's unthinkable for mixed ability teaching. In my own department we have, firstly, a very large and varied stock of source books, anthologies, thematic materials, and audio- visual aids of different kinds, freely available from stock-rooms and meant to be constantly in circulation. Secondly, as wide a choice as we can afford of full sets of novels, short stories and plays allocated to each year. Each of us chooses what we will read and when, reserving sets of books in advance with the colleague who organizes stock. People are asked to keep them, with rare exceptions, for not more than half a term, to allow maximum choice to everyone. Except for Heinemann Windmill, all the books I have bought have been paperbacks: Penguin (including Puffin), OUP, Fontana, Longman, Macmillan Topliners and so on. They last quite well when covered with mercury film, and although prices have soared one can still buy three sets of paperbacks to one of hardbacks. Thirdly, each English group has every term a new form library with between thirty and fifty different titles (from one to six copies of each).

Having the books is, of course, only the first step and it's of little use unless children really want to read them. Before going on to suggest what books might be read, and ways of tackling them, a look at some of the things which could get children 'hooked on books', might be helpful.

Ways of stimulating interest

I have found that children of all ages have enjoyed visits to book bonanzas, to central and local libraries and to bookshops. One of our main booksellers is very pleased to have small groups of children from schools browsing around his shelves. In school, bookclub schemes, talks and readings in the school library, visits by children's writers and by librarians, all help. There is a new generation of children's librarians in public libraries, who are enthusiastic, informed and very ready to meet and talk to children and to give staff advice on books for children of different abilities. A school bookshop is ideal. Children can order their own copies of books which are in the news, besides having the opportunity to browse at leisure in familiar school surroundings, whereas they might find a visit to a city bookshop somewhat daunting on their own.

The school library can, of course, play a vital part in encouraging reading in school, and block loans of books from public libraries are always available to augment stocks. Often, I think, these are arranged for topic work and are mainly non-fiction; we should also take advantage of their supplies of fiction, and use their expertise when buying books for less able children. The Schools Council Working Paper 52 (1975, p. 46) on children's reading interests comments on one school, where the amount and quality of books read by children was quite outstanding. The library was well-stocked with 'quality' children's books, including loans from the public library. Equally important, the library was run in a flexible way and was easily accessible to the children. This is an ideal situation of course. Many schools find libraries timetabled as teaching rooms, and open only out of school hours.

We need school librarians who are knowledgeable about children's as well as adult literature, and who are available to give guidance or advice. As English teachers, we need to know the library, and to know what there is for children of differing reading capabilities. I prefer this to the system of coding books (by coloured labels for example) according to reading difficulty. It is very important to make sure in any comprehensive school that there are reference books, and a large number of non-fiction books in general, which are easily readable. Often subject teachers set children topic work involving the use of reference books and it is not unusual to see children who have severe reading problems trying to cope with the *Junior Oxford* or even the *Encyclopaedia Britannica.*

When a children's book is serialised on television I buy a copy to read to the class, or a few copies for the form library (using a lost-books fund for petty cash). Then, as soon as money is available, I buy more copies or a full set. I have done this in the last two or three years with Penguin copies of *The Diddakoi, On the Run, Carrie's War, Marianne Dreams, A Pair of Jesus Boots, Pollyanna,* and others. There have been some brilliant television adaptations of children's novels and I find that children, including many weak readers, become very much involved and keen to read the book. The same applies to older pupils and adult novels. My first experience of this was a few years ago when a boy in a CSE group borrowed my copy of *Germinal* to read, after seeing it serialised on television.

Schools broadcasts offer a great deal. Television's *English* (for ages 14–17) has in recent years shown *Zigger Zagger, A Taste of Honey, Hail Caesar,* and *The Government Inspector. The Plough and the Stars* and *The Long and the Short and the Tall* are included in the 1977–9 programmes. *Scene* (14–16), though not a literary series, has included programmes on W. H. Davies and Morrison's *Child of the Jago* (effectively introduced by David Essex). *A Collier's Friday Night* and London's *The Law of Life* were offered in 1976–7. I have found these series very successful with mixed ability groups, and further details are given in chapter ten.

Television's *Scan* and radio's *Adventure* (13-16) and *Inside Pages* (10-12) include contemporary children's literature. Radio's *Books,*

Plays, Poems, (14-16) includes in its current programme *A Man for All Seasons, A Place to Live* (how Scots and Welsh poets see their rural and urban landscape) and *Coast to Coast* across the USA in poetry (a radiovision programme). Other radio series, for instance *Living Language* (9-11), and *Listening and Writing* (11-14), include some radiovision broadcasts.

Listening and Reading, (11-13) for slow and reluctant readers, records readings at a deliberate pace which children can follow in the text. These can be taped and used by individuals or groups of children during a workshop period. The headmaster of one of our local primary schools taped himself reading stories which his children enjoyed hearing and following – a much more interesting and personal approach than the commercial listening labs they also used. The same man held spellbound an audience of mixed ages and abilities when, in the secondary school, he read Dylan Thomas's *Memories of Christmas*.

Given time, we can read and record stories, poems, and plays ourselves. The many advantages of doing this include recording one's own choice of literature, saving on commercially-produced materials, providing a variety of source materials, and being in several places at once – if only as a recorded voice. One of the criticisms of mixed ability teaching is that the teacher has not time to get around to see all the children who need help. By recording like this, we can be with different groups at the same time. Just as important one can avoid 'death by workcard' or children reading literature 'cold'. The teacher's voice will read a poem or tell a story, provoke discussion, and so on, for an individual or group. Cassettes are cheap, cassette recorders very reasonably priced and capable of being operated by people even as mechanically hopeless as I am. Children often have their own recorders and I have found that they are quite ready to bring them into school.

The BBC sells or loans recordings of radio and television programmes, and local authorities' libraries of other commercially-produced recordings are a useful source of supply. The ideal, of course, is for the school to have a videotape recorder. Some of the slide/film strip with tape/cassette background material I find very helpful with older groups. Of course it's possible to produce this oneself, particularly for fairly local writers, given time, some money, a camera and a recorder. It is a good opportunity to work with the children and to cooperate with history, art, and music departments. All this is obviously good practice with any sort of teaching group; we often assume a background knowledge which children don't have.

There are, of course, some excellent (and some appalling) films of novels and plays. The Education Department of the British Film Institute has a checklist of British and American literature on film. Though chiefly using film as stimulus, *Lookout* R.W. Mills & G.T. Taylor (Harrap) includes the brilliant film of Ambrose Bierce's

100

Incident at Owl Creek Bridge, which has the added virtue of being a sensible length for showing in school time. The main difficulty (given the facilities) is that most films of novels and plays last at least an hour and a half. A school film society can show them after school and I have found that a local youth centre will often cooperate, as will a local cinema. In Birmingham, we have an Arts Centre and an Arts Lab; both very ready to hire films on request and show them to children at a reasonable cost.

Unlike film, television and radio, the theatre is not part of children's everyday experience. Yet it is the most dramatic way (if the pun may be excused) of bringing literature to life, and theatre visits have been a regular activity in the English departments I have worked in. My experience is that in a streamed school it is generally A stream children who join in, whereas with mixed-ability groups a cross-section of the children become involved. Unfortunately there are few plays produced which are suitable for younger children, so that theatre-going, unlike other activities, cannot be built regularly into the programme, and there is often an initial reluctance to join in such a foreign activity. I have found several things help to break this down: being involved in drama themselves; seeing 'theatre' in familiar surroundings when youth groups, theatre-in-education groups, or the RSC Theatre-go-round have come to the school to perform; visits to the local drama centre and to studio productions which are less formal than those in the main theatre; and playdays when actors, in a relaxed atmosphere, talk to the children about the play before giving a performance. We are lucky in the West Midlands in having the Belgrade Theatre at Coventry and the Birmingham Rep both regularly organizing play-days.

The simulation games which Les Stringer discusses in his essay can usefully be applied to literature. For instance, if we 'set up' a parallel situation to one which arises in the book they are about to read, or are reading, children can discover for themselves the analogy and better understand the concepts underlying the book – and perhaps their wider relevance.

Children are involved from their first year in school in reading, acting, improvising their own plays, writing their own poetry, short stories, novels, and their own drama scripts. Adapting part of a novel, or short story for stage or television is another activity which makes them aware of the different techniques and forms of literature. Longman's collections of television scripts, for example *Z Cars* and *Conflicting Generations* (both edited by M. Marland) include examples of camera scripts. All these activities make children aware that literature is something which is going on here and now – that it's alive and kicking. Particularly important, I think, is to make them aware of themselves as writers, not shutting away their stories, plays, poems in old exercise books but displaying them, publishing them in broadsheets and magazines and making annual collections and binding them to put on the library shelves with other writers' work.

All these approaches are, I believe, good practice in teaching any English group. The vast majority of the children we teach, live in a non-literary, even anti-literary, world and need to be convinced that books are for pleasure. It seems to me particularly foolish not to accept and use whenever possible the powerful oral and visual media which are a central part of all our lives, when in so doing we have the opportunity to break down barriers between different cultures, school and home, 'us and them'.

Suitable material

What can one read with a mixed ability group? In my belief, almost anything one would judge worth studying with a streamed group. The powers which are needed in responding to literature – such as, sensitivity, perceptiveness, imaginative insight, the ability to realise implicit as well as explicit meanings – these do not necessarily correlate with technical proficiency in reading. It would be interesting to consider how many of the 'semi-literate' children we describe as 'good orally but . . .' do in fact have these gifts. Their oral contributions to lessons, frequently show considerable insight. One of the most interesting lessons I have observed was a reading and discussion of Lawrence's *Snake* with a third-year mixed ability group in a large comprehensive school. I recorded and analysed the lesson, and so it is not just from fleeting impression that I remember that some of the most perceptive comments were made by two boys who had most of their other lessons in their stream in the remedial department. Their measured reading ages were about ten. Of course, other very literate childred showed insight, but my point is, that children who, it is usually assumed, cannot read literature, do in fact show understanding and can enlighten others who are apparently more able.

There may well be remedial teachers who have read *Snake* with their groups, but my experience is that children in such classes are usually given poor quality material produced by some of the publishers and writers who cater for this section of the market.

When I've had the opportunity to meet a remedial group of younger children in a school, I have often used the time to tell them stories of Beowolf, Sir Gawain, Troy, and I have never met a group who had been told any myths or legends before. Recently I came across a series aimed at such groups. The cover and illustrations are of strip-cartoon characters – Achilles as Mr McGoo – and of course there is no trace of the heroic spirit. A thematic booklet on Love and Marriage for older pupils spent some time, quite seriously, with the birds and the bees; the fifteen year old found it too boring even to be amusing. It did include an extract from Barstow's *The Desperadoes*, but none of the great love poetry and prose. To be fair, it was probably meant to be read by the children alone. But any literature these children meet in such schemes is likely to be of the Salford/Bradford school of the sixties – probably because of its limited vocabulary and working-class setting. Because the teachers of remedial groups are rarely English specialists, and because of the assumption we make about 'lower streams', such children are likely to be starved of good literature and of good films, television and radio.

The Newsom Report (1963), quoted again in Bullock, claimed that all children, including those of very limited attainments, need the civilizing influence of contact with great literature, and can respond to its universality'. We might quibble today with the leavisite 'civilizing' but otherwise I would only make it even stronger and say that all children have the *right* to come into contact with such Literature. Not the least of the many arguments in favour of mixed ability teaching in English is that it can make certain that they will do so.

In mixed ability groups there will of course be children who find difficulty in reading at all. But this should no more prevent their hearing and discussing literature than the fact that a child is crippled and unable to climb a mountain should prevent his being helped up so that he too can see the view. The most important consideration in reading a book together is not that every child should be able to read it in the technical sense, though of course it is desirable. That problem can be overcome when a book is serialised, read aloud in the classroom, heard on tape and so on. The less able readers, like the abler ones, will be engaged in close reading of their own form library books at the same time, so reading will not be neglected, and the next book shared by the whole class may be easier. The really important factors, in my view, are that the children should enjoy the book, that our enthusiasm should arouse their interest, and that its content is emotionally and intellectually appropriate.

It is unlikely that in any group of thirty or so, streamed or unstreamed, everyone will be equally enthusiastic about a book. Individuals in the groups will have very different tastes, and will be capable of reading at different intellectual and emotional levels. I have met children of eleven still hooked on Paddington Bear and others who enjoy Dickens and the Brontes. The form library is there to provide a wide range of books for individual reading and I would read neither *Paddington Bear* nor *Jane Eyre* with eleven year olds as a group. I find it difficult to believe that the eleven and twelve year old mixed ability classes who read *David Copperfield* and *Macbeth* with their teacher (*Use of English,* Vol. 25, No. 1, Autumn 1973) enjoyed them as they might have done a few years later. A very bright eleven year old told me that she had loved English at primary school but found it dull and boring in her first year at a direct grant school where her class were reading *Romeo and Juliet.* She could, of course, 'read' it perfectly well.

Many of the schools have been using contemporary children's literature with young classes for some time, and 'literature' is a word not lightly used here. Reference books such as Margery Fisher's *Intent upon Reading* (Brockhampton) and John Rowe Townsend's more recent *Written for Children* (Penguin) are very helpful, as are the journals *Children's Literature in Education* (APS Publications) and *Growing Point* (published by Margery Fisher and available from her at Ashton Manor, Northampton NN7 2JL).

Lists of suggested books for different years appear in chapter nine I should like to mention here some which have a success when studied with mixed ability groups in first and second year. In historical fiction, for instance: Henry Treece's *Viking Trilogy* and *Horned Helmet;* Barbara Leonie Picard's *Knight's Fee.* In fantasy: Lloyd Alexander's *Book of Three;* Alan Garner's *Elidor;* J. R. R. Tolkein's *The Hobbit;* Catherine Storr's *Marianne Dreams.* In a realistic setting: John Steinbeck's *The Red Pony;* Wolf Mankowitz's *A Kid for Two Farthings;* Nina Bawden's *Carrie's War;* Ruth Underhill's *The Antelope Singer* and *Beaverbird.* A. Rutgers van der Loeff's *Children on the Oregon Trail* and Ian Serraillier's *The Silver Sword* are particularly good examples of the popular theme of children coping alone and triumphing. All these are available in paperback (and several in Heinemann Windmill), and all can be read to be enjoyed just as tremendously good stories. All, however, have depths which are worth exploring and, naturally, one explains them in different ways at different times. I find it valuable sometimes to give a carefully-structured assignment based on the book and I have produced at least one example for each year which members of the department can then employ, adapt, dip into and, I hope, use as a loose model for their own schemes on other books. The example for a first year assignment given on *Horned Helmet* starts with notes for the teacher and goes on to provide work suggestions for the children. Here it is.

First Year   An assignment on Horned Helmet
The assignment includes opportunities for talking, listening, writing and reading in a variety of ways. For instance, there is *talk* in pairs, in small groups, and to the whole class; imaginative reconstruction of the story, improvised drama, logical argument and factual reporting of research. *Writing* includes poetry, imaginative and factual prose, a play script, and a written report on research. Again, some work is done alone, some in pairs, some in small groups. *Reading* involves the novel itself, poetry, reference books; reading for imaginative understanding, for the implicit as well as the explicit, and for factual information. The children are encouraged to think and to use language on a variety of levels. They are, for instance, selecting and ordering relevant information, making analogies, exploring their own as well as literary

104

experience, making evaluative judgements, all, I hope, on appropriate levels.

There are opportunities for collaborating with the history, geography and art departments. The children may have learnt/be learning about the Vikings in history, and the department is most helpful.

Drama possibilities include starting with individuals wielding, in slow motion, 'Brainbiter', the great two-handed axe, building to pair work and to group fights; the villagers creeping stealthily up to surround the Vikings at the Howe (in a darkened drama hall with pool of light on the Howe) and the voice coming out of the darkness as the Vikings are about to leave – it's a dramatic scene! Among other things, the children are learning about movement, control, contrasts, timing. There are opportunities, of course, to invent their own situations or to use their own experience (a raid on an apple orchard, fights, bullying, etc.)

All good children's literature will involve people, problems, situations which have a wider relevance, and which we should bring into the children's own lives and experience. Of course, children need fantasy, adventure, escape and the stories we read with them are enjoyable simply as stories. After working on an assignment such as the one suggested here for *Horned Helmet,* we might like to use the next book we read together just as a cliff-hanging serial.

The last but one suggestion in the list of assignment possibilities is finding out about gods and heroes. This could be developed as a whole new area of work. There is much to be done on Norse and Teutonic mythology. Great opportunities for drama, illustration, model-making, writing alliterative poetry or prose.

I would always include an element of choice, making clear which questions were compulsory and which were to be left until we had read/discussed them together.

1 When we've read about Beorn being chased by Glam, write about a time when you were being chased, or were afraid, or were being bullied. Remember who was there, what happened, how you felt; how did it end?
2 When you've read up to chapter 4, write a *factual* description of Reindeer.
3 Draw her. If you'd like to – make a model.
4 Later (page 81) Beorn lies on deck stroking the planks as if stroking a horse, saying 'Oh Reindeer my sweeting'. Read the poem on page 58 again. Notice the alliteration as we saw it used in Beowulf; notice the names the Vikings give things (e.g. Swan's Path, Whale's Way for the sea). Now try to use this sort of language to make up a poem about Reindeer as Beorn might have done.
5 When you've read what Gauk says about Starkad as a baresark, write a poem or a vivid description – Baresark.
6 Draw one, or decorate your work.

7 As you read the book, collect in your preparation book all you discover about the Viking way of life: beliefs, how they behave and talk, etc. When you've finished the book, write all you know about them, giving examples from the book. Then say what you admire and what you don't like about them, and why. See also in class libraries *Viking's Dawn, The Road to Miklagard, Viking's Sunset,* by Treece.

(This could be used for group discussion, or for two sides collecting and arguing the good and bad points.)

8 What bring Starkad and Beorn close, and leads Starkad to give Beorn the stag?

9 Have you ever been given, or do you own, something very special? It may not be worth much money, but it may mean a lot to you. Write about it, saying how you got it and why it means so much to you. (Some people might like to bring in their 'treasure' and talk to the group about it. For others, of course, it may be very personal and private.)

10 When we've read chapter 8, 'Dead Man's Howe' – divide into pairs. One be a villager and tell the other all about what happened. Include how these strangers behaved in the face of death; and your opinion of them.

11 Drama: in pairs, in groups, or the whole class.
e.g. – Beorn's escape from Glam (improvise another chase/escape adventure)
– the raid on the Howe and the rescue
– the raid on Starkad and Katla's home
– Beorn's return.

12 When you've read to the end of chapter 13, 'Blind Beacon', think: have you ever felt fierce jealousy as Beorn does? Perhaps hurt someone's feelings as he does? Write about it (as a poem if you like).

13 Collect examples of the Viking way of speaking, for example, when they're in a tight corner or when things are going really well. What do you notice about them? How do they compare with us in the sort of things we say when things are going really badly, or very well?

14 You are Beorn. Write about your return to Starkad and Katla (story or poem). Look back on your adventures, your decision; include your feelings when you arrive home.

15 When we've read together part of *The Seafarer* and Kipling's *Harp Song of the Danish Women,* and heard about the first Viking raid on Lindisfarne, in groups devise scenes for a television film about a Viking raid.

16 Research on the Vikings. Ask history teachers, use libraries. On your own, or with a partner, choose an aspect of Viking life: clothes and jewellery; weapons and fighting; homes and way of life; journeys and explorations; ships; Vikings in Britain and what

they've left us. Write up and illustrate your findings, and prepare to report back to the class.

17 *The Gods and Heroes.* Find out all you can about: Odin; Thor; Loki; the Valkyrie; Freyja; Tiw; Asgaard (treasure of); Beowulf; Siegfried. What connections are there between our days of the week, some place names, and the Gods?
Use the library – ask the librarian for help.
Use: *Brewer's Dictionary of Phrase and Fable*, Encyclopedias: history section.

18 Design a new dust cover for *Horned Helmet* and/or illustrate any scene from the book.

It is difficult to find books of myths and legends for this age-group which keep something of the heroic spirit yet don't confuse less able readers. Old faithfuls such as Warner's *Men and Gods* (Heinemann) and *Greeks and Trojans* (Heinemann) are tough going for them, as are Greene's retellings of Greek, Norse and Arthurian legends. Simpler versions usually reduce the stories to comic-strip level, or to the cosiness of *Tanglewood Tales*. The obvious way around this is to learn from the best primary school practice and to develop skills as story-tellers ourselves – something I believe we should do throughout the school.

The Beowulf story is beautifully told by Rosemary Sutcliff in *Dragon Slayer* (Penguin) and Serraillier's version in the *Windmill Book of Ballads* (Heinemann) keeps the spirit and form of the original, including the long alliterative line. I have sometimes told the story including extracts from both; at others I have used the full versions with mixed ability classes, and they have enjoyed it and the ensuing drama, art work, writing of their own versions, and experimenting with alliteration.

I find that well-liked children's books such as *The Secret Garden* F. H. Burnett (Penguin) or *Treasure Island* R. L. Stevenson (Penguin) are still enjoyed by younger children. Of course, the language, particularly Stevenson's, is difficult for less able readers. With such an author I prepare the material as if I was reading to them, rather than with them; cutting, serialising, inserting link-passages on page-markers so that the book bristles with slips of paper. By using this method it's possible to give less able children some experience of the book, while abler readers can read it all. I've used *Treasure Island* in this way and found that second-years enjoyed it, including work which arose from it:

Second year   An assignment on Treasure Island

1 (a) When we've read about Billy Bones and the visit of Black Dog,

imagine you are either Jim or Billy Bones. Work with a partner. Tell him/her about what happened.

(b) Act the scene of their meeting and the fight.

(c) Write as a play script. You might like to discuss television scripts with your teacher. Watch some scenes on television *carefully* and see how cameras use different shots etc. A third year book, *Conflicting Generations*, explains the words television people use, and shows you a camera script. You might look at them, then try your own for the scene from *Treasure Island*.

2 When you've read about the death of Blind Pew talk and write about it in different ways:

(a) Work in groups. One be a newspaper reporter, interview Jim and Mrs Hawkins and perhaps one of the Excise men. Tape what they say then play it back. Work together to prepare a radio news report, or work out a television news item with interviews included. We'll discuss this first.

(b) You are Jim. Think about Blind Pew and how you feel about him. Write (as a poem?): Blind Pew. Make people's blood curdle.

3 The Black Spot!

Make one, with a warning message on it. See who you can plant it on. (One boy slipped one into the deputy head's hand during school dinners. It said: 'You will not live beyond midnight'. Did he think there'd be poison in the rice pud?)

4 Make your own treasure map. It may be the actual *Treasure Island* one, or one you invent. Notice the symbols, and the decorations on old maps. Ask history department staff. A piece of strong paper or thin card can be soaked in milk then scorched over heat. Take care – have parents handy. One girl set her map on fire – dropped it into the freezer, which was badly scorched. Try using a quill pen (goose quills are available). Learn how to prepare and sharpen them. You may use red ink for blood – we don't expect the real thing!

5 Long John Silver. Collect notes about him as you read the book, and when you finish it write a pen portrait of him. Despite everything, Jim has a soft spot for him. What do you think about him?

6 Do you know a real 'character' like this – someone who's a rogue but you can't help liking in some ways? Write about him/her.

7 The apple barrel. Have you ever overheard something, maybe about yourself? Or hidden away, and seen or heard something frightening? Use your own experience, or make up a situation where this happens and write the adventures which follow. Before you start, look carefully at the way speech is set out and punctuated in *Treasure Island*. Try to make sure you do the same.

8 When you've read about Ben Gunn – imagine you're marooned on a desert island. Look in an atlas and choose a possible island. Write a note to put in a bottle (bring in a bottle!) as an sos, trying briefly

to give some information about where you are.

9 Alone on a desert island. Discuss in your group how you would cope: consider shelter, food, drink, clothes, keeping yourself from going mad. For ideas read extracts from Robinson Crusoe in *Project Survival* or the book itself, extracts from *Lord of the Flies* (ask for a copy). Write an account of how you'd cope.

10 What and who would you miss most? Think about people, places, things you enjoy doing, food and drink. Would you ask for cheese, like Ben Gunn . . . if you were ever found?

11 In groups or pairs, choose your favourite episode and either improvise a play to act for the others, or make a script and tape it – or both. Remember sound effects. Ideas include Blind Pew's visit and his death, the apple barrel, the battle of the stockade, Jim and Israel Hands in the 'Hispaniola', the march to find the treasure . . .

12 When you've finished the book, imagine you are Jim. You're back in Bristol and you send your mother a letter telling her you'll be home, saying something about your marvellous adventures and the surprise you have for her. Again you might try a quill pen. No envelopes in those days – letters were folded over and the address written on the outside. They were then sealed with sealing wax and seals. (We have both available.)

Everyone wanted to make the Black Spot and the treasure map, of course, and enjoyed writing Jim's letter, and sealing it. I asked everyone to do the pen-portrait of Silver, and to choose at least one from 1, 2 and 11; so that everyone was involved in some discussion and drama work. It is important to allow for choice, but equally one must make sure that no one can spend all his time drawing treasure maps or doing improvised drama. I agree with Judith Atkinson that a lengthy assignment can be daunting, and it's necessary to allow plenty of time as well as choice; my own method is to set outside time limits, within which children can work on different things at different speeds. Sometimes everyone is doing the same thing – for instance the children write about Blind Pew immediately after reading or acting the episode. Some people will have difficulty in reading the assignment and understanding it, and of course it's necessary to sit down with individuals or a small group to help them. In the cooperative situation one tries to build, children also help each other. There is absolutely nothing wrong in giving the same work to everyone in a mixed group, as long as we do not expect the same quantity and quality.

I think it's all too easy in English, without realizing it, to have an unbalanced programme of work. At least in the old days the system made sure that everyone did poetry on Tuesday and grammar on Monday and Friday. Devising assignments, like the knowledge that one is to be hanged the next morning, concentrates the mind wonderfully. A variety of groupings and a cross-section of activities in English are consciously included. We can again use the best primary school practice in keeping records of the different types of work each child has covered in a term, noting strengths, weaknesses and progress in each aspect of English. This seems to me much more useful than recording strings of grades. For reading I keep notes under headings: measured reading age; (only useful if it's regularly measured over the years to show progress) amount read; comprehensions; written work arising from books; reading aloud. In other words, a rather different record system from that described by David Mears in chapter two.

There is so much one wants to do in English that I would work on novels in the depth suggested for *Horned Helmet* and *Treasure Island* no more than twice or three times a year. There are plenty of other novels which can be read just to enjoy as a story, perhaps as a serial, and there are of course some collections of short stories for this age group, including David Jackson's *Springboard* and Naughton's *The Goalkeeper's Revenge*.

The shorter concentration-span needed may be useful for less able readers but I find that children often have difficulty in seeing the point of a short story. It is of course a mistake to suppose that short means easy; difficulty is often in inverse ratio to length, in prose as in poetry. Short stories can be good starting points for discussion and writing (as *Springboard*'s title indicates) and since we often ask children to *write* short stories we ought to give them the opportunity to read some.

As for drama, some English teachers feel strongly that with younger children improvisation should replace scripted plays, and doubtless they would claim this especially for mixed ability classes. I find that children very much enjoy reading plays – as a completely different type of experience from drama lessons. Bolt's *The Thwarting of Baron Bolligrew* Ayckbourn's *Ernie's Incredible Illucinations* and the old favourite A.A. Milne's *Toad of Toad Hall* are all plays I've used in first and second years, either with the class as a whole, or in small groups. *Ernie* especially lends itself to tape recording as a radio play – or at least to the lavish use of sound effects. There are plays by Aidan Chambers aimed at less able children in this age-group which some teachers (and certainly some children) like, such as: *Johnny Salter, The Car, The Chicken Run* (HEB paperbacks).

The scripted plays included in Adland's *Group Approach to Drama* series have evolved from improvisations, and groups can do this themselves, particularly since the shy or inhibited who do not shine in active drama can write down scripts or help with sound effects and recording.

Reading and acting plays with the younger ones is I think entirely for enjoyment – it's certainly preferable not to explore the anti-populist elitism of *Toad of Toad Hall*! But children enjoy drawing or modelling stage sets or characters, writing pen-portraits or their own scenes for

110

the play, and going on to write their own plays. In discussing Toad, Ratty, Bolligrew or Oblong they are beginning character evaluation.

In reading a play or novel aloud with a group there are obviously problems. I always keep one part myself to hold the thing together and to set the pace. There are always the extroverts who volunteer to read, the shy ones who can read well when gently pressed, the poor readers who *will* volunteer, and those who find difficulty in reading at all. It is vital to build an atmosphere of tolerance and cooperation; this is not easy especially when the school itself is streamed though the English department isn't. In any sort of group I have found that children become impatient with poor readers. It's possible to avoid discouraging them and tactfully to allot small parts to such children. The reluctant reader presents a different problem. He may, however, be more ready to read in a small group and we need to provide opportunities for such group work, using stockrooms, corridors, colleagues' rooms. (See chapter 7 for more discussion of small group work.)

I feel very strongly that the dramatic presentation of literature should not be merged with practice in reading, as in the old 'reading round the class' system which, unfortunately, is still with us. With a little initial help most children can understand the idea of a dramatised reading of a novel with a narrator, and actors reading the different characters' dialogue.

With poetry, as with novels and plays in these early years, there is nothing I'd use with a streamed group which I wouldn't use with a mixed ability group. Most children of this age enjoy choral verse, ballads, haiku, concrete poetry, limericks, free verse, nonsense poems, and riddles. It's chiefly poetry for sheer pleasure at this stage, but I find that children of all abilities can appreciate, and begin to use in their own poetry, imagery, sound and shape, rhythm, alliteration.

It's a good idea to include poetry books in form libraries and to have an assortment freely available in the form room, including funny ones like Spike Milligan's *Silly Verse for Kids* and *Milliganimals* (both Penguin), books of riddles, puns and limericks. We tend to use full sets of poetry anthologies, but it's useful to have these small sets of a variety of books for the children to read for pleasure, to find a poem on a theme, or to copy out and illustrate a poem. Children's own poems can be 'bound' in hard covers and used in the classrooms in this way.

Lists of suggested anthologies are given in a later chapter but I should like to mention especially for the younger children Maybury's *Thoughtshapes* and *Wordscapes* (Oxford), Williams' *Tapestry* and *Dragonsteeth* (Arnold), the Bentons' *Touchstones* (EUP) series, Summerfield's *Voices* and *Junior Voices* (Penguin). All are beautifully presented and illustrated. *The Windmill Book of Ballads* (Heinemann) has delightful woodcuts and an excellent version of *Beowulf*.

The third year is an in-between stage whatever the organization of teaching groups. For the first two years, there is the whole of children's literature; for older pupils there is much adult literature to choose from. But it isn't easy to find novels and plays for study with third years. Hines' *Kes*, (Penguin) and Waterhouse's *There is a Happy Land* (Longman) I have found successful. Both are good for encouraging children to explore their own experience, and write autobiographies. *Kes* especially has a wide appeal, as does Steinbeck's *The Pearl* (Heinemann), in a very different way. Zindel's *The Pigman* (Macmillan) and Lingard's *The Twelfth Day of July* (Penguin) both explore relationships, loyalties and betrayals. The first between young teenagers and an old man, the second between Catholic and Protestant youngsters in Northern Ireland.

Among plays I have found useful with groups of this age are the Longman's television series, for instance Marland's *Scene Scripts* and *Conflicting Generations* and one-acters in collections such as Mansfield's *Play-makers* (Schofield and Sims). I have also used shortened versions of plays which would be too difficult as a whole – for instance Shaw's *Androcles and the Lion* (Penguin). A cooperative venture is for the group to write and produce their own play – a melodrama often works well. There are activities for people with very different abilities and interests, and at the same time they are learning about a special form of drama.

In this year I think one can begin to look more closely at literature, including poetry. I would stress that as with all teaching it is important to be well-organized but flexible, to have a firm but friendly and encouraging classroom atmosphere in which one has developed attitudes of mutual tolerance and respect, and cooperation. The lesson on Lawrence's *Snake* which I recorded is an example of what can be done in this sort of classroom. The lesson began with a friendly interchange of people's feeling about snakes, including some factual information by one of the less able boys who kept a pet snake, and conflicting views of Alice Cooper! Next the teacher introduced and read Lawrence's poem, the children had copies in front of them. After a pause, she asked if anyone had found anything difficult to understand, and several children asked about words – 'fissure', 'perversity', 'paltry' . . . 'Hens and things', one boy offered, and such was the atmosphere that teacher and children laughed together with the boy about it. Some teachers might prefer to explain some difficult words and phrases before reading a poem but then it is the teacher's selection of words of course. Next, the children, who were sitting in groups, were asked to discuss some questions written on the board, with one member of the group acting as scribe. They were told that they would have about twenty minutes, then come back together as a class, and the teacher explained that some questions would need a close look at the poem. The questions included:

Find out all you can from the poem about the place and the weather.

What words and phrases make the snake seem attractive, and show
that the poet likes it?
What do you notice about:

'He sipped with his straight mouth.
Softly drank through his straight gums, into his slack long body.
Silently.'

Why is 'Silently' on a line by itself do you think?
What do you think 'the voice of his education' is?

The questions went on to discuss the end of the poem and
Lawrence's feelings about what he had done.

While the groups were working the teacher went round from table to
table. When the class came together again, and contributed their
findings it was a boy who was in the remedial department for his other
lessons who heard the sibilants in 'He sipped with his straight mouth
. . .' and called out 'that hissing, that hissing, it *sounds* like a snake'.
Another, after much class discussion crystallized the difference
between the voice of education and instincts.

The children had confidence to venture their ideas because of the
relationships between teacher and group and within the group itself.
Although this is what one hopes for in all teaching situations, it is vital
in mixed ability teaching, and it isn't easy to build when teachers and
children are products of competitive schools and classrooms.

Some of the boys in the *Snake* lesson would not have been able to
write down their ideas in clearly readable English. A second-year girl
has just written for me a very perceptive account of an eposide in
Carrie's War (N. Bawden Penguin), but I had to guess a number of the
words. Such children must have extra help to try to overcome such
basic problems. How do we give it? One way is for children to help
each other within groups which have developed a cooperative and
understanding attitude – as the children of the School of Barbiana in
Letter to a Teacher (Penguin), did so effectively. Sixth-formers can
come into the lessons or take children out for extra attention and their
involvement builds more than the children's basic skills. English and
remedial teachers can be timetabled to give help.

Perhaps many people would be ready to teach mixed ability groups
in the first three years of the secondary school, but not in the fourth and
fifth when examination courses begin. The sixteen plus schemes make
the idea viable, and certainly some schools are teaching mixed ability
in the sixteen plus pilot schemes. I haven't had the opportunity to be
involved and my own experience has been in schools which separate an
O level group (or groups) and then have wide ability CSE
groups. With O level people and non-examinees taken off this has still
meant a cross section of between 68 per cent and 75 per cent of the
year. However, the books we use and the work we do would stretch

very able candidates too. We use the CSE Folio option of literature by course work, and novels and plays we have studied together in the fourth year include:

NOVELS

Animal Farm   Orwell   Heinemann
Lord of the Flies   Golding   Faber
Cider with Rosie   Lee   Penguin
To Sir with Love   Braithwaite   Heinemann
Jamaica Inn   Du Maurier   Penguin
Across the Barricades   Lingard   Penguin

SHORT STORIES

The Kite   Maugham   Heinemann
The Human Element   Barstow   Longman
A Sillitoe Selection   Sillitoe   Longman
Late Night on Watling Street   Naughton   Longman

PLAYS

Zigger Zagger   Terson   Penguin
Our Town   Wilder   Penguin
Pygmalion   Shaw   Penguin
Unman, Wittering and Zigo   Cooper   Macmillan
A Taste of Honey   Delaney   Methuen
Z Cars   ed. Marland   Longman
Conflicting Generations   ed. Marland   Longman
Hobson's Choice   Brighouse   Heinemann
The Importance of Being Earnest   Wilde   Heinemann

The material studied together at fifth-year level includes the following:

My Childhood   Gorky   Penguin
To Kill a Mockingbird   Harper Lee   Penguin
Go Tell it on the Mountain   Baldwin   Corgi
All Quiet on the Western Front   Remarque   Heinemann
Of Mice and Men   Steinbeck   Heinemann
The Chrysalids   Wyndham   Penguin
Golden Apples of the Sun   Bradbury   Corgi
The Caretaker   Pinter   Methuen
The Quare Fellow   Behan   Methuen
The Crucible   Miller   Penguin
A View from the Bridge
Death of a Salesman
All My Sons
Journey's End   Sheriff   Heinemann

The Long and the Short and the Tall   Hall   Penguin
Three Plays   Lawrence   Penguin
Mother Courage   Brecht   Penguin
The Caucasian Chalk Circle

We use, too, with fourth- and fifth-years, some of the excellent short stories in collections such as Penguin *Story* (Second and Third Books) (ed D. Jackson & D. Pepper) and *Spectrum I and II* (ed B. Bennett, P. Cowan, J. Hay Longman) and poetry anthologies such as *Touchstones 4 and 5, Seven Themes in Modern Verse, Tunes on a Tin Whistle* (A. Craig Pergamon).

Apart from the omission of Shakespeare I think there is material here to challenge and interest people of all abilities. Certainly there is nothing on the list inferior to some of the set books for JMB O level literature.

A much closer and more detailed study of the text is needed at this level of course, and I set essays which are much more structured. This in fact gives guidance to the less able people, and at the same time gives abler ones the opportunity to work at a more academic level. It is possible still to give a choice of work, but there are the constraints of the Board's requirements and one's self-set standards in a course which is designed and marked internally, though moderated by the Boards.

My own fifth-year CSE group in a term and a half worked around the theme of Loners or Outsiders. We read together and they wrote about: Steinbeck's *Of Mice and Men*; The Richard and Elizabeth extracts from Baldwin's *Go Tell it on the Mountain*; Dorothy Johnson's *A Man Called Horse* and two other short stories, *Flight* and *The Witness* by Doris Lessing. Poetry included Frost's *Death of a Hired Man*, Larkin's *Mr Bleaney's Room*, Betjeman's *Death in Leamington*, Thomas's *Evans*, Sansom's *Almshouses*; and we read Miller's play *A View from the Bridge*.

I had previously read the play with an A level group but had never tried it with CSE people. I had asked the group to watch *On the Waterfront* on television, and decided to use it as a launching-ground for *View from the Bridge* – the Brando-figure and Eddie Carbone share the same world and face the same dilemmas of loyalty and betrayal in family and community. The situation of Marco and Rodolpho as illegal immigrants and the Carbones' sense of responsibility for them has very immediate relevence. Of course, people in the group who entirely sympathized with illegal Italian immigrants in New York had a very different attitude to Pakistani immigrants in Birmingham – but I hope that the study of the play and the discussions arising from it led to some extension of empathy.

We read the play together, acted parts of it on stage, and discussed many of the issues, and the group wrote four pieces of work:

115

Show how in Act I Miller reveals to us Eddie's obsession with Catherine, and how he builds the tension to the confrontation between Marco and Eddie at the end of the Act.

Three views of Rodolpho: look at him through the eyes (and in the words) of Eddie; Catherine; Marco.

Watch the ending of the play again. Think yourself into the skin of Eddie and write a poem – his thoughts and feelings as he goes out to face Marco. Do the same for Marco.

Write an extra scene for the play as Miller might have written it.

Consider the relationships of Beatrice and Catherine with Eddie and Rodolpho. Why do they feel and act as they do? What do you think about their attitudes as wife, niece, girlfriend?

Some of these were very good, some poor, but the level of achievement did not always correlate with the students' ability as assumed in the school's streaming system. Examination work, of course, must be graded, and on a comparative basis, which is particularly invidious in a mixed ability group. It's possible at times to give an additional grade for effort, but most important is the comment written by the teacher. I do not give grades except in examination course work since the only meaningful grading is against a child's own standard, and a full and constructive comment seems to me to be much more valuable.

Besides literature we study together, I always include books which the children read on their own, although there isn't the time at fifth-year level for the amount of form library reading one expects from younger children. The library which linked with our theme included several copies of each of the following:

Native Son and *Black Boy*   Wright   Cape
Go Tell it on the Mountain   Baldwin   Corgi
African Child   Laye   Penguin
One Day in the Life of Ivan Denisovitch   Solzhenitsyn   Penguin
The Loneliness of the Long Distance Runner   Sillitoe   Penguin
Billy Liar   Waterhouse   Penguin
The Great Gatsby   Fitzgerald   Penguin
The Catcher in the Rye   Salinger   Penguin

There is a range of books for all but the poorest reader and I think that anyone who can't cope with Sillitoe or Waterhouse should not be entered for CSE. In fact, three of the weakest girls chose to read *Native Son* and worked valiantly, writing conscientiously and at length about it, but with very little insight. Two of the abler boys chose the Solzhenitsyn possibly because it was the shortest book. They produced very thin essays which were not accepted and they repeated the work.

The essays from the two girls and the two boys were given the same grades, but for very different reasons, as the comments made clear.

Several problems arise when the children are asked to read on their own. How much freedom of choice do we give? How much guidance? How much do we discuss, direct, structure the written work? What demands do we make? My own method is first to talk to the whole group about each book, being honest about the level of difficulty. If someone chooses a book which will be tough going for him, I have a quiet word with him and tell him so. But if one offers a choice of books, it would be quite wrong to prevent someone from reading a book he is keen to read. When everyone has chosen, I go round and talk for a while with an individual or a group who have chosen the same book, saying something about its background, and asking them to consider certain points in writing about it. If someone seems to have chosen an unsuitable book I adapt the suggested approach. Work can be made as individualized as one likes; the choice can be widened by using one's own books and library books, and it is always possible to produce a book and simply say, 'I think you'd like this one. Try it.' As with any teaching, but especially with mixed ability groups, we need to know our pupils in that way and to know their capabilities and potential and to accept nothing less than their best.

Class libraries

Although I've stressed the value of studying books together, children will only be doing so occasionally, and most of their reading will be their individual choice from class libraries. The Schools Council team investigating children's reading interests notes two points which are particularly relevant here: the immense variety of books mentioned by the children, and the fact that they 'greatly value the opportunity to exercise their own choice and to pursue highly individual interests and tastes through books' (Working Paper 52 1975 pp. 20). The authors suggest that secondary schools do not as a rule provide this opportunity; class libraries are the obvious way in which we can do so.

One method of organizing such a library is to have, say, half-a-dozen copies of each of several books linked to a theme or to a book which the group is reading together. The advantages include opportunities for small groups to cooperate and share appreciation of a book, and the wider exploration of a theme in literature. Disadvantages include the restricted choice of books, and the difficulty of catering for a wide range of abilities. In my own department we have adopted this method only for fifth-year groups, partly because at this stage, when children often use the books as part of their examination work, I prefer to keep to a few books which I know to be of quality. So that part of the library linked to the Future theme includes several copies of: Huxley's *Brave New World*, Orwell's *1984*, Wells' *War of the Worlds*, Bradbury's *Fahrenheit 451*, Pohl's *The Space Merchants*, Asimov's *I Robot*, and three anthologies of short stories: *The Stars and Under*, ed Doherty, and *World Zero Minus* and *In Time To Come*, both ed Chambers. The Asimov stories of robotics are not easy, but the last three collections, all by science-fiction writers of quality, I find are read and enjoyed across the ability range. Members of the department add their own books to augment any of the libraries and we have other libraries grouped around the themes of War, Crime and Punishment, Growing Up, and the Outsider theme already mentioned.

With the younger children we have developed miscellaneous libraries offering a wide choice, although of course some of the books link with the themes and with books which the whole class may share; for instance myths and legends, animals, the past, autobiography. There will be between one and three copies of each book – occasionally more – and each library includes between thirty-five and fifty titles at the moment. The range has to be very wide, of course; my current fourth-year library ranges from Dickens' *Great Expectations* to Joan Tate's *The Tree*, a Heinemann easy reader. The libraries circulate, each group having a new one every term, and although some of the books are duplicated, many are not.

In choosing books for the libraries I have included much children's (and adult) literature of quality, as well as books to tempt the reluctant reader – and, of course, books for less able readers. I do not belong to that school which says that it doesn't matter what they're reading as long as they're reading something. If they want to read *Dr No*, *Jaws* or *Son of Frankenstein*, they can, and will do so in their own time. I see it as part of the English teacher's job to put before children, books they might otherwise not discover. If few become keen readers, and many later reject reading altogether, at least the opportunities have been there. The children who reported to the Schools Council team on their reading at home did not mention one contemporary children's writer. The Victorian fiction they listed probably reflected their parents' or grandparents' choice of Christmas stocking-fillers or their idea of what children are officially expected ro read. It may also be a reflection on what schools are making available to them, in school libraries, for example. My own hope is that the next generation of parents will have an interest in contemporary children's fiction, having enjoyed what they've read at school.

Books for less able readers can be a problem. Often the subject-matter is unsuitable for the age-group at which the books are aimed; discos, motor-bikes, and girl- or boy-friends predominate – a limited diet at fourteen, but sadly so at eleven. Illustrations and format are often poor by contrast to the usually well-produced paperbacks for abler readers, but there are notable exceptions.

Birmingham Public Library, and I am sure many others, publishes a booklet: *Books for the Slow Reader*, with books listed under the appropriate reading age. The important thing is not to offend a child with unsuitable content or oversimple language and format, and it is necessary to get to know the books, and the children and their needs.

In any mixed-ability group there will be a range not only of 'reading ages', but of reading levels and reading interests – three separate considerations. A child in my second-year group, for instance, has a measured reading age which indicates that she is capable of reading *Tom Sawyer*, but the level at which she is reading means that she is unable to understand its subtleties, and her reading interests mean that she is unwilling to tackle anything other than books about horses. The library she has to choose from includes:

Storr   *Marianne Dreams*
Le Guin   *The Wizard of Earthsea*
L'Engle   *A Wrinkle in Time*
Pearce   *Tom's Midnight Garden*
Pearce   *A Dog so Small*
Twain   *Tom Sawyer*
Verne   *Twenty Thousand Leagues under the Sea*
Church   *The Cave*
Kastner   *Lottie and Lisa*
Smith   *The Hundred and One Dalmations*
Patchett   *The Brumby*
Sutcliff   *Brother Dusty Feet*
Sutcliff   *Knight's Fee*
Trease   *The Red Towers of Granada*
Treece   *The Dream Time*
Guillot   *Kpo the Leopard*
Sewell   *Black Beauty*
Green   *Tales of Ancient Egypt*
Alcott   *Little Women*
Bawden   *On the Run*
O'Brien   *The Silver Crown*

It also includes easier reading in Macmillan Club 75s and Cassell Solos:
Foster   *My Friend Cheryl*
Smith   *The New House*
Rowe   *Lone Wolf*
Plater   *Trouble with Abracadabra*
Chambers   *Don't forget Charlie*
Morpurgo   *It never rained*
Baudouy   *Mick and the Motorbike*
Cleary   *Ramona the Pest*
Ramsey   *Ron takes over*
Chilton   *Contact from out there*
McKinnon   *Sea Otters come Home*

McKinnon   *Spinning in Space*
Kings   *Meet Linda King*
Kings   *Leather jacket boys*
Kings   *Tests and Things*
S. Chitty and A. Parry (eds)   *The Puffin Book of Horses*
Glanville   *The Puffin Book of Football*
Milligan   *A Book of Milliganimals*
Milligan   *Silly Verse for Kids*

I would expect Angela, who is hooked on horsey books, to read *The Brumby* and *Black Beauty* if she hasn't already read them, and *The Puffin Book of Horses*. Then I would hope to edge her over to the other animal books, such as *The Hundred and One Dalmatians*, then perhaps to *Brother Dusty Feet*, where the boy first runs away because his aunt is going to put his dog to death. It is, of course, an historic novel, and might launch Angela onto a different type of fiction; and it involves some human problems which might encourage reading in a little more depth.

This is not to say that there is anything intrinsically wrong in spending a whole term reading a certain type of book, or a certain author.

Michael has a measured reading age of 9.2, and might be happier starting with Cassell books and working up to the Macmillan Club 75.

Peter, on the other hand, is quite an able reader, but a reluctant one. He might start with the Milligan poems, or *The Puffin Book of Football*, and perhaps be persuaded to try the science fiction books. I am not sure yet whether there is anyone in the group who might be ready for some more adult fiction, but if so I can lend him my own books, or send him along to the library. For all the children, one hopes that class libraries are a jumping-off ground, and that they will go on to discover more books and authors they like in school and public libraries and bookshops.

I try to include in each library some poetry and some short stories, and, especially in third- and fourth-year libraries some non-fiction. The Schools Council research has confirmed the fact that most boys in this age group read, by choice, mainly non-fiction – usually magazines connected with a hobby. I see this drift away from imaginative fiction as something to be compensated for, rather than catered for in school; it would be a pity if state schools helped to perpetuate the image of Forster's public school Englishman of the 'undeveloped heart'. While it seems sensible to provide books by writers such as Heyerdahl, Cousteau, and Durrell, it seems important to include fiction which might appeal to these boys. Books such as Hinton *The Outsiders* and *That was Then, This is Now*, (Fontana) written by a seventeen-year old American boy, and McGrath *The Green Leaves of Nottingham* (Hutchinson) written by a British teenager, can involve the most

120

reluctant reader, yet all three deal sensitively with issues of human relationships and values. McGrath's book has an introduction by Alan Sillitoe, and this is an obvious opportunity to introduce the reader to some of his stories.

Clearly all this takes time, and I think that it's essential to make time for it; a couple of lessons to launch the library, to say a little about each book, for the children to note down the ones they like the sound of, and to come and choose their first book. During the term, there is time while other work is going on to chat to people about what they are reading, to make suggestions, and to check on the amount and type of reading each person is doing. It is essential to have a reliable record scheme, and we use a system of cards on which children record the titles of books read, and the dates when they have taken and returned them. Class librarians can help to organize the library, and to check the condition of the books – mending them when necessary. Mercury-film covering and requesting that books be carried around in polythene bags help to prolong the life of paperbacks.

When one provides a wide range of reading for a group, there are bound to be people who choose books which are too easy or too difficult for them. To a certain extent this is acceptable; we all enjoy reading below our ability range at times, and we can also enjoy something which is not entirely within our grasp. What is important is to make sure that generally children are reading books which they enjoy, and which may stretch but not daunt them.

The problem arises of making sure that the children are actually reading the books. I do not belive in just providing the books and leaving it to trust. Some teachers of mixed ability classes are unhappy about the idea of reading a novel together with the whole class, and prefer not to do so, in which case the books which the children take from the form library will be the only ones they read in English. It seems to me particularly important to keep a close watch on the quantity and quality of the reading which each individual is doing. Some children undoubtedly try to pull the wool over their teachers' eyes, and there are also those children who can read a book in the technical sense, but are unable to understand what it is all about. In each case, firm or tactful intervention is called for.

The best recommendation to read a book is likely to be that of a friend or classmate, and 'book-chats' in small groups or in the whole class are useful, as are written reviews which can be 'bound' in some way and kept for the class to refer to. Another idea is a 'radio programme' on tape or cassette, including book reviews, which can also be played to other groups. It's necessary to give some guidelines for the talks and written accounts if they're to be of value. Especially if the children are otherwise doing little or no reading of complete books in English lessons, they should sometimes write in more depth about a class library book. Character studies, writing an extra chapter for the book, adapting an episode for the stage or for a television play, are some suggestions which I have found successful.

. The overall organization of class libraries for the whole school is an immense job, and involves a great deal of work, especially at the beginning and end of the year, for the two members of the department who are responsible for all stock – but we think that it is well worthwhile.

The Bullock Report points out that when people enrolling for the government's adult literacy scheme were asked why they thought they had not learned to read at school, the answer most often given was that reading had never been shown to be something one did for pleasure. The underlying aim of all that has been said in this chapter is that the children in mixed ability groups should leave school as literate young people, who have had every opportunity to see reading as a source of interest and enjoyment.

5   Drama games and simulations

Leslie Stringer

Part one
'Though drama comes by school tradition into the English field, it is a creative art embracing much more than English.'

(Newsom Report 1963)

Opinions still vary concerning the place of drama in the school timetable. Certainly the case for the teaching of drama as a specialist subject has been convincingly stated. On the other hand, I imagine there are few teachers of English or drama who do not agree that it has a part to play not only in English but also in other subject areas. I have some sympathy with a good many of the arguments on both sides, but I believe that a more basic concern should be to see that every child in the secondary school receives some experience of drama, and that all teachers, whatever their subject, are made aware of the value of dramatic activity, for its own sake, for the part that it can be made to play in the learning process, and for its role in the personal development of the individual.

A Language for Life defines drama in the school context as a 'fundamental human activity which may include such elements as play, ritual, simulations and role playing . . .' (10.31). I would readily accept this definition, as I would the distinctions made between 'theatre' and 'drama'. It is claimed that whereas 'theatre' implies a performance to an audience, generally based on some form of script, 'drama' covers an extremely wide range of activities, verbal and non-verbal, whose common feature is that they depend largely on improvisation of various sorts.

The situation is not now as serious as it once was, but, even so, as the Bullock Report suggests, there still exists a tendency for these two kinds of practice to be in sharp opposition to one another – regrettable, I believe, since both approaches have their place. The ideal situation is where the two forms of activity are complementary, but both have their strengths, so why not draw from them? My opinions here derive from my experience of teaching in a large comprehensive school, which had no separate drama department, nor even a drama specialist, as such, but which offered children a considerable range of activities. A list of some of them might indicate this range.

1 Drama, taught in mixed ability groups, was a time-tabled subject for all first- and second-year pupils.
2 Each of the twelve second-year forms, under the guidance of its English teacher performed a play in a second-year drama festival at the end of the year. These were almost invariably unscripted plays developed through improvised drama and arising from work done in English lessons.
3 Drama was used extensively for a variety of purposes in other English lessons, at all levels.
4 The annual School Play – *Noah, The Good Woman of Setzuan, Sergeant Musgrave's Dance, The Crucible* – each one directed by a different member of staff, involved children from throughout the school.
5 An active staff drama group performed plays to the public – *The Caretaker, Waiting for Godot, Black Comedy*.
6 Pupils regularly visited the theatre – the professional theatre and amateur groups, including youth groups.
7 Where opportunity arose, touring groups, such as RSC's Theatre-go-round were brought into school.
8 The English department assisted the history department in the production of historical documentaries on Education and the Navy, which involved the use of film, live drama, music and tape recorded material; the music department in the production of works by Gilbert and Sullivan; and the modern languages department in Christmas entertainments in Spanish and French.
9 The English department possessed its own 8mm camera and made films; used commercially produced films extensively in teaching; and ran a well-supported film society out of school hours.

I do not propose to give here a list of suggestions for actual drama work, since this has been done by numerous authors, including Pemberton-Billing and Clegg (1965), Brian Way (1967), Scher and Verrall (1975) and Self (1975). The specific benefits of drama have also been too fully dealt with elsewhere for me to need to repeat them in this context. We are, perhaps, only too familiar with the claims made for child drama as a 'creative' activity, providing, as with all creative activities, a medium through which the individual can express his ideas. Drama it is said, enables the child to come to terms with the world outside his own private world, and extends and deepens his understanding of himself.

My concern, however, is to consider drama from just one viewpoint, and to comment on a few of the claims made for it that seem relevant to the teaching of English in mixed ability groups, drawing attention to one area – the field of games and simulations – where, I feel that

English teachers could find a valuable, and largely untapped, source of material, and from which they could derive interesting methods of approach.

Drama and group work

For English to be taught really successfully in mixed ability groups, there are certain prerequisites: the teacher must want the system to work and there must be an atmosphere within the group that fosters a spirit of cooperation amongst the children. In many instances, in the ways indicated throughout this book, children will be called upon to work together in groups of varying sizes, so that some degree of cooperation is essential if this type of work is to stand a chance of success. There are few activities better than drama for providing opportunities for cooperation in group work and for promoting an attitude of tolerance towards the ideas of others.

Drama and the less able

One of the real problems of mixed ability teaching is catering for the needs of the weaker members of the group. Another simple but important point is that drama helps to do just this.

There is a problem of measuring 'ability' with reference to drama, for the criteria of competence are not easily defined, but clearly creative or improvised drama does not require the sort of academic abilities demanded by many subjects in the curriculum. Thus the carefully handled use of drama in an English lesson can provide a valuable boost to those who would generally be classified among the less able members of the group. The fact is hardly surprising when you consider the demands of drama in relation to the problems which must face these children for most of the time. Drama provides an activity which is relatively short-term and self-contained, with the result that a specific goal can be quite easily achieved; there is no written work, no homework, no examination to worry about; more often than not there is no teacher-intervention. In short, these children can participate on equal terms with everyone else; they can achieve success in the lesson and, in consequence, enjoy it.

I am not suggesting that all our weaker pupils are good at drama, nor that our abler ones are not successful – far from it. But, in my experience, many pupils of low academic ability have approached drama work with genuine interest, and have responded in lively, imaginative and sensitive ways. Their uninhibited enthusiasm and delight have testified to the effect that drama has had on the development of their self-confidence.

Furthermore, when the status of the activity is raised, so that pupils can see the importance which the teacher attaches to it, there is a consequent increase in its effect. I am not sure whether the question I have more than once been asked by pupils: 'Are we going to work today, or do drama?' is a mark of success or failure, but it is a reminder that as teachers we should be clear about our reasons for using drama, even if our pupils do not always see them. It is perhaps worth remembering the emphasis that such authors as Pemberton-Billing and Clegg put on the need for the teacher of drama to create a situation and atmosphere in which children will tackle the work seriously.

As a rider to this point about status, I must add that participation by less able pupils in full scale dramatic productions – the school play, for example – seems to have a whole range of beneficial effects. I do not wish to give the impression here that young Masher Snarlup – who used to be an illiterate tearaway until he played Ophelia in the school play – is now at Cambridge reading Botany. But, it is a fact that many 'unlikely' pupils have responded very well to the rigorous demands of public performance. Perhaps for the first time in their school careers they have been asked to shoulder genuine responsibilities, and they have proved to be an essential member of a team? Perhaps it is merely pride at achieving something worthwhile? The experience is certainly something that remains in the memory. The fact that many English teachers can look back at their own school careers and see drama as a highlight is evidence of the terrific hold it has on the memory.

Drama and language development
With reference to drama and English teaching it is impossible to ignore the comments made in *A Language for Life* concerning the importance of improvisation in language development. The Report makes the point that there is an important distinction between children's language in improvised drama and that of most of their written work in school. 'The one is open-ended, volatile and incremental in structure the other is relatively closed and formalistic.' (10.35) Whereas writing tends to be merely a patterning of words into which thoughts and feelings are made to fit, in drama 'an element of invention lies round every corner, and dialogue has a way of surprising itself so that nothing is predictable'. The report continues, to make these points:

An important aspect of the creativity of speech as distinct from writing is the inexhaustible fund of grammatical forms and idioms available to children from a very early age. If, as Chomsky argues, the 'normal use of language is innovative', it becomes a vital principle that the teacher should create opportunities most likely to produce innovation and general 'natural' language in all its forms. An increasing number of teachers of drama . . . do in fact see their work as productive of such language. They would add that it helps to establish confidence in social intercourse, as well as familiarity with a variety of speech forms. They devise what might be described as a concentric series of situations. These vary from the known and readily observed, such as family

situations, to a wider range of less familiar situatio
the pupils are led to resort to unfamiliar language pa
the roles they are playing. Drama thus has the
sensitizing the ear for appropriate registers and
encourages linguistic adaptability, often accustoming children to
unfamiliar modes of language. (10.36)

An account of one of my own lessons, with a socially, temperamen-
tally, academically, racially mixed group of third-year pupils, in which
I began with a 'known' situation and moved outwards from it to
increasingly less familiar situations – might illustrate some of these
points.

By way of background information I should mention that when I
used the lesson I had only recently taken over the teaching of the
group, and that they had come to me with something of a reputation for
being badly behaved. So, one of my initial general aims was to get the
class working productively in small groups, ideally to try to encourage
a little self-discipline. My object in this particular lesson was to get the
pupils to consider – and where possible explore through improvised
drama – some attitudes towards stealing.

It was obvious from the outset that the class needed to be handled
quite firmly. With this in mind I used to begin with a common drama
exercise which I call 'statues'. The object of this is to get the children to
move around the working area – in my case the school hall – and then
on a word of command or a signal such as a bang on a tambourine or
anything else handy, for each child to 'freeze' on the spot. The game
may be elaborated by asking the children to freeze into a certain shape
– a sportsman in action for example. The point is that they do not move
a muscle until instructed to do so – enabling any information to be
given quickly and without fuss.

I have used the technique often as a means of getting attention
quickly, and have found in practice that most children realize that to
stand still immediately on a word of command, listen to an instruction
and then get on with the lesson is more enjoyable – or at least less
boring – than waiting for a whole class to come to attention in its own
time.

Having used this as a warm-up exercise I began the lesson proper.
Some type of initial stimulus is always necessary in drama, and for this
reason I chose a poem – although I would not necessarily agree with
the Bullock committee's suggestion implying that the 'stimulus of good
writing . . . offered from time to time' is a panacea, and that by this
means alone improvised dialogue is to be rescued from triviality. There
is, I admit, a danger that such dialogue will often derive from
'playground scraps' and 'casual chats' – but I have found the stimulus
of, for example, a photograph, a film, a slide or set of slides, a physical
object, a piece of music, not to mention a well-told anecdote from a

￼acher or pupil to be just as useful.

However, in this instance, I used Raymond Souster's poem *The Man who finds that his Son has become a Thief* (to be found on page five of *Themes: Conflict*, edited by Rhodri Jones, published by Heinemann 1969). This twenty line poem shows the various mental stages which a father goes through, from the time he first hears the accusation against his boy of shop lifting, to the point at which he comes to believe it is true.

I read the poem to the whole class, twice, and after the briefest of discussions, to ascertain that all the pupils had at least understood the narrative of the poem, I asked them to stand up and walk around the hall, imagining they were walking round a store such as the one referred to. Here I emphasized that everyone was working on his/her own, and insisted that they were all to ignore what the others were doing. This is an injunction I often use – partly in the hope that it will help to persuade the more self-conscious members of the group that their classmates are not simply watching *them*.

I allowed a few moments for them to get used to this idea of walking round the store, and then introduced a basic mime exercise by asking the children to pause at a particular counter and have a closer look at one item they were interested in, suggesting they should pick it up and examine it, hinting that they should consider its weight, the size and shape, the texture and colour. While they were doing this I walked round the hall and asked individuals to describe to me in some detail the object they were looking at. (For the girls: rings, bracelets, various items of make-up and a football scarf. For the boys: a pocket radio, a wristwatch, football badges and scarves, a model-kit and in one case a set of pens and pencils.)

Apart from this discrete questioning, the first stage can be carried out in complete silence – so that as well as setting the scene for the rest of the lesson it can be used as a means of concentrating the attention of the individual on the task in hand.

The children having explored the store, I then asked them to become detectives following someone they suspected of shoplifting. Again this exercise was done with the pupils working entirely on their own.

A number of ways of developing the lesson from this point suggest themselves. If you are interested primarily in movement, and it is perhaps unfortunate that many English teachers see this as an area outside their concern, you could concentrate on this area alone, breaking off at this point to discuss with the pupils the way someone walks when he is wandering aimlessly round the store; the way he moves when he has stolen something; or the way detectives follow someone. The introduction of music might help here. With pupils used to this sort of work you could perhaps build up a polished dance drama, involving a chase and arrest.

My own interest, however, lay in exploring the poem in terms of the attitudes and motives of the three characters – the father, the son and the store manager.

Thus, beginning with a situation familiar to all my pupils – that of walking round a large store – I moved on to one which, in fact, *some* had experienced and others might envisage without stretching their imaginations too far – that of stealing. (Although I must add that I took great care to feign naivety by not revealing that I knew that some of my pupils had been in trouble with the police for similar offences.) I asked them, again working individually, to act out the stealing of an object from the store, including the walk to the exit.

My next step was to divide the class into groups of three – the composition of the groups being determined by the pupils themselves. My reason for asking for groups of three was primarily because of the three principal characters in the poem, but these small 'friendship' groups have always seemed to me to work successfully, in at least one respect. This is a purely subjective assessment, but it appears to me that restricting the size of the group to three tends to minimise (I don't say eliminate) one of the more serious problems of this type of activity. The problem to which I refer is that of the quiet or timid or inarticulate child being squeezed out of group drama work by the brighter, more articulate ones, who not only tend to take the 'best', the largest and most enjoyable parts in 'performance', but also tend to dominate discussions and planning sessions by their more original and/or forcefully expressed ideas. A disturbing feature for the teacher is that he is unable to protect the 'weaker' children by direct intervention.

With the class in groups of three I allocated each of them to a specific area of work, and asked them to discuss, to plan and to act out in sequence four separate scenes.

1 The boy/girl bringing home the news of the accusation to his/her parents and convincing them of his/her innocence.
2 The parent, believing the child's story, angrily confronting the store manager.
3 The manager in calmer mood slowly convincing the parent of the child's guilt.
4 The scene between parents and child *after* returning from the interview with the manager.

I allowed about five minutes for a general planning session where I insisted that the groups sat down to pool their ideas and decide upon roles, and then five minutes or so for them to act out each scene. Every five minutes I indicated to the whole class which scene they should be moving on to next, so that after twenty minutes they had all been through the full sequence once.

Thus, I had moved from situations very close to the experience of the children to those which were completely unfamiliar. The idea of the manager's controlled and reasoned argument finally overcoming the parent's indignation and instinctive loyalty to the child was difficult for many pupils to grasp – although some managed it well – and here I felt it worthwhile to interrupt a number of groups to ask them to think about this scene very carefully.

What I found most interesting, however, was the pathos of the final scene from several groups, as pupils came to realize that a parent's reaction is not always to 'rant and rave' and 'go mad' as they had first suggested, and that the deeply injured, disillusioned tone of one girl, playing a mother, who asked; 'How could you do this?' was in itself as effective as any punishment.

Drama and literature
The importance of the relationship between improvisation and work on literature should not be underestimated, particularly as both these areas can be related to the personal experience of the pupils. Shirley Hoole indicates something of the nature of the relationship by including in her assignments some suggestions for drama work. (See for example the work on *Horned Helmet* in chapter four.)

On the simplest level, improvisation can be initiated by the use of literature as a stimulus. The account of my own lesson illustrates this – the reading of a poem forming the basis for the rest of the work. I know from talking with a group of sixth-form students that Serraillier's account of the story of Beowulf remained in the memory of many of them – as it has remained with me – as a result of a series of improvisations they worked on in a first-year mixed group.

Conversely, improvised drama can provide a physical context for the printed word to come to life. Bullock quotes the amusing exchange between Antony and Enobarbus in Shakespeare's *Antony and Cleopatra*:

Ant: Fulvia is dead.
Eno: Sir?
Ant: Fulvia is dead.
Eno: Fulvia!
Ant: Dead.

The written words are dead. They need to be illuminated by being placed in a real context. Improvisation can help do this. Thus, we have a relationship between literature and improvisation. Literature initiates improvisation; improvisation illuminates literature.

But, consider at the same time the place of the child's personal experience, and the way that it would be used in practice in an English lesson. Surely, this third aspect – the child's own first-hand experience constantly intrudes into these two secondary forms. Personal experience could be used to illuminate literature which might then be used to initiate drama. (The child's own experience of lying awake at night and hearing a strange noise might be discussed first, to help him appreciate the feelings of Beowulf and his warriors as they lay waiting for the arrival of Grendel, and this in turn could be used to promote a piece of improvisation.)

Literature could equally well illuminate a child's own experience, which in its turn might initiate drama. (A first-year child reading of Tom Sawyer's attempts to avoid school by feigning illness, may come to realize that his own attempts to do the same have a precedent, and if he can then be persuaded to relate these experiences to a friend or friends we have already the basis of an improvisation.)

The astute teacher will perceive the inter-relationship of drama, literature and the child's first-hand experience and will make full use of it.

Part two

Games, simulations and simulation-games

Although the use of games and simulations in teaching appears to be increasing, I feel that, as a teaching method, it is in danger of being overlooked by English teachers, as it tends to be seen as the province of the teacher of History, Geography or Social Science. My purpose here is to examine the effectiveness of games and simulations as educational tools, and this I hope to do by illustrating their possible uses.

As a working definition, 'games' might be distinguished from 'simulations' in terms of the presence or absence of two factors: competition and realism. It has been said that a 'game' is any contest between adversaries, operating under the constraint of rules and having an objective; a 'simulation', on the other hand, has been described as a simplified slice of life – 'an operating representation of the central features of reality'. A 'simulation-game', therefore, is something which contains elements of both of these. It combines the features of a game (competition, rules, players) with those of a simulation (the incorporation of critical features of reality).

Games, simulations and simulation-games may take several forms. They may be based on a conflict situation. In this case, various groups, some or all with opposing interests, would be engaged in conflict of some kind. Another common type is the 'in-tray' simulation, where individuals are presented with problems to solve, with case histories to help them. A variant of this is the committee simulation where a group rather than an individual is given a problem. There may be conflict in this, but it is usually contributed by the character of the participants rather than the nature of the game itself. Finally there are those which involve role-playing and cooperation rather than competition. In all of these it is possible, and in most cases it is desirable, to have a post play discussion. It could be said that these feedback sessions are the most valuable part of the exercise.

There may be many reasons for using games and simulations and not all of them will be applicable to the English teacher. It is claimed, for example, that a situation or concept may be illuminated or clarified by the use of a game. The use of a game might provide an insight into quite a complex problem – hence the number of business and commercial games. In games and simulations, patterns of interpersonal behaviour may be discerned and used to compare with real life – hence their use in the training of teachers and youth leaders.

The game *Starpower* provides an excellent example of this, although I would earnestly urge the greatest caution in using it. I have heard of two accounts of the game, one from a theatre director who claims he had been hit by someone while playing, and one from a College of Education lecturer, who had played the game with his colleagues and whose telling comment was that 'the RE chap sat on the side-lines and refused to have anything to do with it!' I have used the game with a group of secondary school teachers and with two groups of fourth-year pupils. On each of the three occasions the game seems to have had such an unerring and frightening facility for engendering enmity and bringing out the very worst in people that I would be reluctant to use it again.

Despite my objection to *Starpower,* the players' emotional involvement illustrates what I believe is the greatest strength of games and simulations. Of the commonly held reasons for their use, perhaps the most readily apparent is that they stimulate interest. The promise that games and simulations offer of transforming the classroom from a collection of passive spectators into a workshop of active participants in the learning process, is probably their greatest attraction.

Tansey and Unwin (1969) comment on the uses of simulation with less academic school leavers, but make the point that: 'There does not seem to be any level of education at which simulation cannot be used'. It is precisely this breadth of application, the scope which games and simulations offer for adaptation to a variety of purposes, that makes them valuable to an English teacher with a mixed ability class. If we accept the rather loose definition of a simulation as being essentially a simplified slice of reality, then for most simulations there is an obvious advantage in having participants with a broad spread of interests, abilities and background.

It seems that English teachers in secondary schools in this country may be lagging behind their colleagues in other departments, who have long used games and simulations, in realizing the valuable potential of this type of activity. Rex Walford (1972), a geographer, wrote:

The idea of 'geographical games' is no longer the intellectual curiosity that it once was; neither has it remained the oasis of frenzied euphoria that some classroom practitioners once imagined it to be. It has already become a regular part of the curriculum for some teachers ... Current discussion about simulations focuses not so much on their justification and mechanics, as on their integration into the general syllabuses of schools.

A note of irony! In this particular essay Walford quotes a fairly lengthy extract from Brian Way (1967) in which he describes a group working in a drama lesson on a situation built up around the idea of coal mining: '. . . a coal-mine scene is built up using the whole class'. Walford makes the point that although this lesson was intended for the 'drama' period it would seem to have valuable possibilities with regard to cognitive learning, and as such would have a place in the history or geography lesson. My point is that since geographers, historians, careers teachers and economists now seem to have adopted and developed the use of games and simulations, English teachers, many of whom have never hesitated to use drama as an essential part of their teaching method, could at least examine the potential use of this type of material in the English classroom.

As an illustration of the way that simulation could be used I refer to three separate simulations; *The Parkhurst Simulation, Tenement* and one called *Forum* devised by a colleague.

The Parkhurst Simulation

My own involvement with games and simulations as a teaching method was stimulated by the centre page spread of a magazine called *Teaching London Kids* (No. 3), published by a group of teachers within the London Association for the Teaching of English.

Against the rather dramatic black background of the double page was arranged a collection of twelve documents: letters, notes – formal and informal, memoranda, and a newspaper headline. The common theme of this collection was the attempt by some pupils at 'The Parkhurst School' to organize a 'walk-out' by pupils in support of a teachers' strike, and the reaction of teachers and senior staff when this attempt was discovered.

On very realistic looking headed notepaper was a letter to parents from the headmaster, describing the effect on Parkhurst of the proposed teachers' strike:

> . . . I am pleased to be able to tell you that, since only eight teachers from this school are joining the strike we are not closing on Thursday . . .
> . . . It has come to my notice that certain subversive groups have taken advantage of the situation to urge some of our pupils to

stage a 'walk-out' . . . any unexplained absence . . . will be treated with the utmost severity.

Less formally a note from the headmaster to his deputy read:

I'm at a Rotary lunch and will be back later this afternoon – but we must do something about this . . .

There were notes from pupil to pupil:

Steve – tell the others the meeting will be Lloyd's room at dinner time but go in quietly because Grope is on the look-out. JR

Notes between members of staff:

Mike – can you please come over and take my 1st years? Gross scotched John Rhodes' plan to have a meeting in my room at dinner time . . .

There was the newspaper headline:

THREE 'WALK-OUT' KIDS EXPELLED
Parkhurst's strong line headmaster . . .

By way of explanation there was one short paragraph:

This collection of documents was duplicated on A4 sheets and used as the basis for discussion for simulated scenes with fourth and fifth-year CSE pupils. All the names and incidents are fictitious. One approach was to divide the class into four groups. One group was to become the production team of a television current affairs programme whose job was to decide how to cover the incident in a ten minute slot. The three other groups were to represent the striking pupils, the teachers and the senior members of staff; each of these had to work out what line they would take on the programme.

I tried out a simulation along almost exactly the same line. I chose a mixed ability fifth-year drama group to test reactions, and was surprised by their reception of it; surprised by their initial interest and willingness to participate, and surprised by the intensity of their involvement.

Here was, in fact, something directly relevant to the pupils' own experiences, yet sufficiently out of the ordinary to be interesting. Since it was for use in a drama lesson that I had originally used the idea, my first interest in the simulation was in the obvious possibilities it presented for role play. However, I was impressed too by the flexibility of the material. Leaving aside the value of the role play, the preliminary discussions I had with the pupils would have justified its use to me as a teacher of English.

To begin with, it was obvious that the stimulus of this material gave rise to a level of discussion far higher than that which I had come to expect with this particular group. Such discussion began with a genuine interest in the hierarchical nature of a school staff – clearly evident from the documents. Two letters, one from the headmaster and one from an obviously 'junior' member of staff, to the fourth-year Master caused some surprise, and featured later in the role play. From this point the group went on to consider the effects on the staff of the involvement of the press and television, and the influence of parents, not only in this incident, but as a whole.

After a while, however, discussion centred on the need to examine the characters and deduce the motives of the various authors of the documents, and, above all, the need to appreciate the tone of the writing. Two points which I would have been anxious to communicate in English lessons had arisen naturally and directly out of the demands of the simulation; out of the need to adopt a role.

To my regret I took the simulation very little further. When I later considered the opportunities I had missed in not following up the work, particularly in terms of written assignments which I indicate later, I realized just how superficial my start had been. It had, however, made me aware of a number of possibilities, and it was this that prompted me to look into the use of other games and simulations in the classroom, and to try them as part of my teaching method.

My first really successful use of simulation came with *Tenement,* and it is to this that I propose to refer in detail.

Tenement
There are several reasons for recommending *Tenement*. It was designed specifically for schools by the education section of Shelter, is inexpensive, easily obtainable and, having been widely used, has the advantage of having been tried and tested.

Before describing it in any detail it might be interesting to look briefly at a description by Mr Pat Tansey of the manner in which it originated. In the booklet edited by Chris Longley accompanying the BBC radio series *Games and Simulations* (1972), part of the BBC *In-Service Education Project for Teachers*, Tansey describes his involvement with the earliest stages of the development of *Tenement*:

> The first thing to do before designing a simulation is to decide on its educational objectives, and the more precise these are the better.
> The Shelter workers were concerned to expose to students

some of the problems and frustrations of the homeless. They wanted to organize a situation in which students could explore some of the attitudes commonly held about the homeless and the poorly housed. This is an 'attitude changing' simulation – designed, not to inculcate the 'right' attitude but rather to encourage participants to examine their own and other people's prejudices in the light of their simulation experience.

Two points here, I feel, have general application: the need for predetermined educational objectives, and the nature of the simulation.

In its published form the aims of *Tenement* are stated quite simply:

Tenement is a simulation concerned with the problems of a family living in a multi-occupied house in a large city. The idea of the simulation is to make people aware of some of the difficulties and frustrations of living in such a situation and to point to ways in which some of those difficulties could be solved· by the introduction of agencies concerned with such problems.

From the point of view of an English teacher the rationale for the use of *Tenement* will almost certainly involve a number of other objectives. I list a number of purposes for which the simulation could be used:

1 To stimulate the use of role play – either to put a pupil into someone else's shoes, allowing him to develop an understanding of other people's feelings, or to enable him to explore his own reactions in a previously unknown or only half-known situation.
2 To promote interesting, relevant and purposeful discussion in small groups which are not directly supervised by a teacher – offering, thereby opportunities for peer-group and cooperative learning.
3 To offer a rich source of factual information and background material for future discussions – either in small groups or with a full class.
4 To provide a stimulus for a number of different types of writing.
5 To provide a source of written material which pupils will want to read and comprehend.
6 To provide an activity which can genuinely be shared by every member of the group and which every member of the group can succeed in and enjoy.

Obviously an individual teacher could have one specific aim in mind, and aims differ according to circumstances. Opinions of the importance of Shelter's stated objectives will differ. What I hope to indicate,

136

however, is that the methods adopted to achieve those ends are relevant to an English teacher in other respects.

To be more explicit about the simulation, the kit contains a number of A4-size sheets of information.

One sheet, headed 'The landlord' has a brief description of the owner of the property.

> You own the multi-occupied house, a drawing of which is on this sheet. You bought the house shortly after the war at a low price and finished paying for it ten years ago. The house is giving you an income of about £43 per week . . .

It describes the condition of the house.

> The house is not in a very good condition. It has not been properly converted into flats to enable a large number of people to live comfortably in it . . .

There is also a description of the tenants; a brief description of each family unit, including details of how long they have lived in the house, the amount of rent each pays, the conditions of the rooms and other salient background information.

The next set of sheets describes the families in more detail – one sheet per family. There are seven families. There are, for example, the Campbells, a West Indian couple with three young children, living in four basement rooms, two of which are uninhabitable due to dampness and dangerous electrical wiring.

> . . . You live and cook in one room and sleep in the other. All the children have to sleep together in one bed as the room is very small. You have separated the bedroom with a curtain. The dampness puts up your heating bills. The rooms have very poor ventilation.

The family is charged £8.50 per week – a pound a week more than the family on the floor above, with better rooms – because the landlord knows the Campbells will have difficulty finding accommodation elsewhere. There are details of the family's income and basic expenses and a paragraph of other information which hints at the effects on the members of the family of living in these conditions.

There is a similarly detailed account of each of the other families – including Mr White, a sixty-eight year old pensioner, and Emily Brown, an unmarried mother with a nine month old daughter.

The next set of sheets has information about six local and government agencies from whom the families can obtain help. Full details of the services these agencies can offer including council or housing association property available, are described on the appropriate sheet. The agencies are: Citizen's Advice Bureau, Local Authority Housing Department, Voluntary Housing Aid Centre, Rent Tribunal, Department of Health and Social Security and the Department of Employment.

There is a series of 'chance-cards', which may be used at the discretion of the controller (usually the teacher). These contain such pieces of informations as: 'Your ceiling has just fallen in', or 'You have been made redundant'.

Finally, there are notes for the controller which introduce the simulation, explain the parts, describe the methods of playing and give suggestions for post play discussion.

Materials and preliminary organization

In addition to the actual *Tenement* kit, very little else is needed by way of materials. I find it helpful to have large notices to identify the various agencies. I usually pin these to the walls at intervals around the room – although they would serve the same purpose standing on tables. It is useful, though again not essential to have badges to identify the families. These are not supplied with the kit.

There are fourteen parts altogether, so that you really need at least fourteen pupils to play the simulation. However between twenty and thirty players are preferable, as more than one person can 'man' an agency, and families can be played by more than one person, depending on the size of the family and the age of the children.

I would say that the material is best suited to fourth- and fifth-year pupils, although it has been used very successfully with children in the third year.

The simulation is best carried out in a large area, such as the school hall, although it is possible to use a classroom. An often much neglected area in schools is the canteen, or dining room – especially if it is permanently set out with tables and chairs, making it useless for more traditional 'drama'. This type of area is ideal for *Tenement*, not only because of its size, but because the furniture can be so easily rearranged to form offices and waiting rooms, adding that extra little touch of verisimilitude.

Operating

The first task is for the controller to allocate the parts, to issue the information sheets and make sure that each participant has details of his role. A word of warning here: it is advisable for the controller to know the pupils and the information on the sheets fairly well, for it is useful to some extent to fit the players' interests and abilities to the requirements of the parts. For instance, the Department of Health and Social Security requires someone who is reasonably adept at arithmetic. I would say, too, that the landlord, since he will probably have to withstand much criticism, needs to be played by someone who is reasonably extrovert and uninhibited, with a fairly resilient and forceful personality – although to typecast him as a sort of villain of Victorian melodrama is not necessarily helpful or accurate.

When you are allocating the families, if you can persuade pupils to pair off into 'mums and dads' so much the better, although I am aware that this is not always an easy task with pupils of this age. I have found it useful to emphasize constantly the fact that from the start of the exercise pupils should try to identify with the role they are playing. The success of the simulation depends largely on how well the controller managers to do this.

Having assigned the roles and given out the information sheets – and I also give the pupils a sheet of paper to record useful information – I send them either to their places of employment (in the case of the agencies) or to sit in family groups, to read and digest the information on their sheets. Obviously, then, at this stage pupils could be working on their own, in pairs or in groups of three or four.

If you were looking for a justification for using *Tenement* in an English lesson you might offer the fact that at this point in the simulation the pupils are provided with an excellent test of comprehension – with a built-in motivation. Unless participants comprehend the information on the sheet they are unable to progress. It also has the added advantage, in a mixed ability group, that it provides an excellent means for more able pupils to help the poorer readers, in a natural way, that causes no embarrassment. It has been my experience that pupils scarcely able to read at all for themselves, once they have had the sheet explained to them by a classmate, are quite able to adopt their role – and have often been very good indeed at the actual role-playing.

I usually allow ten to fifteen minutes for this stage, where I insist that each pupil sits down and reads and takes in the information. At the end of this time I remind them again that they have adopted a role and that they should stay in character from this point onwards. My own method of actually starting play is to ask the families if they are satisfied with their living conditions. The inevitable chorus of 'no' in response, is the cue to tell them to go and do something about it, and that from this point onwards they are on their own. My final request as a 'teacher' before allowing the simulation to follow its own course, is to ask the families to record details of where they go and what sort of response they get, and the agencies to make a note of the people who come to see them and what, if anything, they have been able to do for them, as an aid to the post play discussion.

In classes not too used to this sort of activity there could well be a few moments of puzzled silence. But, normally, with very little further prompting the families will get up and go off to see the landlord to complain, to the Housing Authority to try to get a council house or the

Citizens' Advice Bureau to ask what to do next. What happens in practice, initially, is that pupils will begin by working in friendship groups. Rarely is the adopted role strong enough to overcome the natural preferences of the pupil to work within the relatively safe framework of a group of friends. At first, anyway, a family with a problem will tend to seek advice from an agency staffed by friends – whatever the agency! This is not really a drawback, as it provides a not too disturbing beginning for those who may have difficulty relating to others and need the security of friends. Having made this 'easy' start such pupils are more ready to move on to another agency for reasons prompted by the simulation.

It is usually best if the controller stays out of things completely from this stage onwards, except maybe to give out a few 'chance' cards to families who look as if they might need a little added motivation, for with any luck the simulation will begin to snowball from this stage.

The notes to the controller supplied with the kit suggest:

Unless absolutely necessary players should not be led by the controller to the agencies. In a real life situation a family in need of advice has to discover for itself where it can get the help or advice. *Tenement* is an attempt to simulate that situation.

There are positive benefits for the teacher too. Mr. Tansey, in his account of the pilot scheme, describes the advantages for a teacher of using simulation:

He can step out from behind his desk – he is no longer required out in front ordering and directing his class. He can move freely amongst his students observing what's going on. He can observe the learning process.

This role of 'observer' may be a new one to some teachers, but in this instance – and I am sure many other similar instances arise teaching a mixed ability group – it is an essential one. It *is* difficult for a teacher to simply stand back and let children get on with things; he feels he is abrogating his responsibility. But, to a large extent, the point of the simulation is destroyed if the teacher is too intrusive once it is under way.

Assuming that things are running smoothly, the pupils are all actively engaged in discussions, there is a general buzz of chatter and excitement in the room – when do you stop the simulation? A time limit can be imposed at the outset, but I have found that it is far better for the controller to make the decision to stop at his own discretion. It should be pointed out that in a real-life situation, offices tend to close at a stipulated time each day, and if a family still has not sorted out its problems at that time they will have to wait until the following day. So, stopping the simulation before all families have solved their problems is a true-to-life situation.

Concerning time-limits, I have had a group of fifth-year pupils of very different abilities – ranging from those considered unable to take external examinations (and those merely waiting for their sixteenth birthday!) to good O level candidates – work on this simulation for over an hour with remarkable enthusiasm and enjoyment. That a group like this should be able to share the experience of working on such a project and enjoy the activity could be considered a recommendation in itself. Normally I find that about forty minutes is ample for the actual playing out of the simulation, and at this stage I stop all activity and prepare the group for a discussion. The 'Notes for Controller' are useful in suggesting points that could be taken up and discussed, and as these are questions directed at each family and agency, it is possible for the pupils to stay in their roles. Addressing them by the names of the parts they take will help them to do this.

The whole exercise, including the post-play discussion should take just over an hour, but I have found that pupils enjoy the activity sufficiently to make it worthwhile repeating the simulation in a subsequent lesson, changing the roles, so that the families play the agencies and vice versa. This serves to give the pupils a more rounded picture of what is actually happening.

The value of the dramatic activity involved in the exercise I hope is self-evident; so too, I think is the social value of learning something of the Department of Employment or the Department of Health and Social Security. However, these are not my prime concerns, and I should like to consider the numerous 'spin-offs'. I have mentioned already the importance of the need for pupils to read and understand the written material contained in the information sheets. Consider, too, the possible writing tasks arising from this activity. To assist a pupil to use the information given on a particular sheet, he could be asked to extract and note down the essential points; if he is to remember what has happened to him over a period of forty minutes, he could be asked to record the events he considered important or significant. What better way is there of introducing the notion or explaining the technique of 'summarizing'? Along similar lines pupils could be asked to assess the characters of the people with whom they came into contact.

As a follow-up activity, the writing of letters is an obvious example. Pupils who have played through the simulation could be asked at a later stage to write a letter they might have had to write in the role which they played. Writing letters would be a normal part of the daily duties of the staff of the various agencies and the participants readily recognize this fact. Tenants could easily be called upon to write to the landlord or one of the agencies; they might be moved to write a personal letter to a friend, commenting on their situation, describing their feelings of frustration, disappointment, helplessness or whatever. One only has to take note of the comments recently of CSE examiners to realize that fifth-year pupils often experience difficulty finding adequate material for letter writing. *Tenement* not only supplies pupils with material and background information but, if it is successfully played creates feelings and attitudes which they want to express.

A letter which a fourth-year pupil in the role of Albert White wrote to the landlord is not only an improvement on anything else he had previously written, but it is a forceful and effective letter in its own right, despite its obvious technical weaknesses.

Dear Sir,

I am complianing about the condistion I live in this is my last warning before I go to the rent Turbulal (Tribunal) I have had enoff you have muck me about in the past. I am feed up the conditions are that the room is cold and damp and the window does not open. Plaster is falling of the wall and rain often comes through the ceiling and my bed is affected by damp I am socold at night I want you to put New Slates on the roof and the ceiling fixed. I want the hole room fixed. I am old and can no longer fix it myself so if you do not fix it I will go to the rent tribunar and let them lower the rent as well. I have to share the kitchen with other people and it semells of bad food. And I have to share the Tolet with all the people in the house I can not keep food in the kitchen with out coming back and find it all gone. I am 68 years old and it is all bad for me so I want something to be don to it. the whole house is rotting away slowly so if you do not do something about it you shall be one tenant less than before.

Yours faithfully,

Albert White

An assignment sheet to be given to a fourth- or fifth-year group, involving a series of further writing tasks arising directly from the simulation could include the following choices:

1 Describe factually the condition of either the basement or one of the attic rooms.
2 Find out about and write an account of how you would deal with rising damp or dry rot.
3 Imagine your are the mother of three children living in the basement. Write an account of a typical day.
4 Choose any of the tenants you have played or come into contact with, and write a diary of a week's events in his/her life.
5 What would be the thoughts of a mother having to bring up a family in this house? Write these in free verse if you wish.

6 Write a story called 'The day the ceiling fell in'.
7 Imagine you work at one of the agencies. Write an account of a typical working day.
8 As a member of the staff of one of the agencies write a detailed account of an interview with one of the families.
9 Write a short play, a scene from a play, or a story based on any of your experiences in the simulation.
10 Find out about and write an account of the work of Shelter.
11 Find out about and write an account of any of the agencies involved in the simulation.
12 Why do certain urban areas become so seriously over-populated? What do sociologists claim are the effects on the inhabitants of such areas?

A group of fourth-year girls tackled question 3 on the assignment sheet. I include here some extracts from their work to illustrate their understanding of the condition of the house and their sympathy with the occupants.

Jane went home and wrote a twelve-page account of the day in the life of a mother. When I asked her for permission to quote her work in this chapter, she chose these extracts from her writing to give a flavour of the whole:

A day in the life of Mrs Anne Ward
I woke up feeling very cold and tired. I pulled what few blankets I had up around my neck and turned over to lie on my back. As I lay there looking up at the ceiling, which had plaster hanging from it I remember thinking 'Oh God, not another day to face. I don't think I'll be able to face it, not living here, not in all this filth and dampness. I can't let my children grow up in a place like this...

I've often thought of taking the kids and going to live in a hostel, but I don't like those places much...

I hadn't been silly at all in thinking that Jean was dead. It could easily happen with all the dangerous loose electrical fittings around.

It takes me much longer than it does anybody else to do the washing. For a start I have to do it all by hand, and secondly there isn't any hot water. The house is a very old one and I have to heat the water on the cooker . . .

I didn't like going into the shops. The assistants could tell that we didn't have much money and they used to watch us like hawks, even the children, just to make sure we didn't steal anything.

I used to watch their eyes light up as they pressed noses flat against the windows, longing for all the different toys. I'd have given anything to have walked into the shop and bought them something, but I knew I just couldn't afford it.

It's funny, but sometimes, living in those two rooms really got me down and made me depressed. Thats why I was so jumpy and irritable and why I was always shouting at the kids. Other times it didn't seem so bad really. At least we did have somewhere to live. Somewhere private.

I wondered what mood I'd be in tomorrow, hoping I wouldn't feel depressed. That's bad for all of us.

Along the same lines Alison writes:

... We usually spend the afternoon at the group organized for mothers and their children. There are a lot of unmarried mothers in the same situation as me, and we are all sympathetic to each other. The other mothers are kind to us, and do not scorn us because we are poor. The children all mix and play together. I like going there because I get away from the depressing atmosphere of our house, and the scorning eyes of other people. I like to see the children laughing. The usually solemn faces crack and break into wide smiles, and the usually old looking, dull eyes, spectacled by dark lines, change into gleeful, dancing, children's eyes ...

Alison had worked with Joanne on this exercise so I imagine that it was not coincidental that Joanne too had been struck by the idea of poverty being reflected in the eyes of the children.
She writes:

I turned round to see three little white faces looking up at me, their eyes hollow and circled by big black lines. Their cheeks are sunken in, and their hair is grubby and un-brushed ...

The concern for the effects on the children of living in this type of house was evident from much of the writing.
Tracy writes:

Every day is the same old routine, I get up out of my springless bed at around 6.30 am. The children are already up waiting patiently at the breakfast table, hoping that this morning will be lucky for them. But no it is Friday morning Tuesday's allowance has already been swallowed up...

The walls are black, the cooker has broken down, the rooms are a disgrace, and the children get the worst end of the stick...I really wanted to be out of here before Christmas so the children could have a better one for once. But there seems no chance of that now.

144

Lorraine is more explicit:

> I got up at about 6.00 to get my husband John off to work, I made
> him some breakfast and then he went. After he had gone I sat
> down and had a drink and a smoke. The children didn't get up till
> about 11.0 and they did nothing but moan, I hit Jane the eldest,
> and sent her to bed for the rest of the day, sometimes it is the only
> way to keep her quiet. Susan the youngest went with me to do a
> bit of shopping and I mean a bit. When we got back home I made
> the children something to eat then Jane went back to bed.
>
> When John came home he wasn't in a very good mood and
> when I told him Jane had been playing up he hit her very hard.
> After I had told Susan to go to bed I started to do some washing,
> while John went down the pub, he came back in a stinking mood
> and started to knock me about. The kids woke up and came to see
> what the matter was. He started belting the kids and there was a
> big row. I took the kids and walked out. We walked round for a
> while and when we come back John was in bed so I put the kids to
> bed and went myself.

It is my practice to ask children to read and comment on each other's
work. An unsolicited and unsigned comment on one piece read: 'a very
descriptive paragraph showing the *real* things she had to put up with'.

If you work on a thematic basis, along the lines that Judith Atkinson
describes in chapter three, the simulation could well provide an
excellent starting point for a theme called *Homes and Families*. The
possibilities of follow-up work based on literature for this age group
are extensive: the effects of environment (even specifically this type of
urban home background) on the individual are amply illustrated:

Hines *Kes* Penguin
Braithwaite *To Sir with Love* Heinemann
Barstow *Joby* Heinemann
Barstow *A Kind of Loving* Penguin
Sherry *A Pair of Jesus Boots* Heinemann
Causley *Timothy Winters*
Spender *My Parents kept me from Children who were Rough*
Delaney *A Taste of Honey* Methuen
Terson *Zigger Zagger* Penguin
Hopkins *A Game-like-only a Game* Longman
Brecht *The Good Woman of Setzuan* Penguin

To conclude, may I offer a few pieces of advice to an English teacher
using *Tenement* for the first time.

1 Make sure you are aware of the contents of the information sheets,
  so that you can advise on the choice of roles.

2 A good way of finding out about the problems involved is to try the material out on your colleagues before using it with your pupils.
3 Don't spend too much time at the beginning of the session explaining principles and objectives. Let the pupils participate.
4 Don't push unwilling participants too hard at first. *Tenement* allows you to cater for this type of child very well. As an additional member of staff at one of the agencies or as a son/daughter of one of the families a reluctant pupil can coast along, being part of the exercise but without being overburdened with responsibility, until he/she discovers that it is not too difficult to participate, and that involvement is actually enjoyable.
5 Be prepared for the simulation to begin slowly. Don't get too anxious if nothing happens at first.
6 Be prepared for a noisy session once it does get under way.

Forum
The logical progression from using commercially produced material is to develop your own for a specific purpose. (The two papers *Six ways to design a bad simulation game* and *How to design a simulation game* by Samuel A. Livingston offer very sound advice on doing this.)

Forum was named after the Youth and Community Centre at the school at which I teach and was first developed for use with a Drama Club, run after school hours for first-and-second-year pupils. The prime educational objective in this instance was to involve a group in an activity they would find enjoyable and which, since attendance was purely voluntary, would sustain interest for a number of sessions. Previously the group had tended to concentrate on activities which lasted only for a single session.

The simulation is set in a youth club with some space 'outside'. It is helpful if music is provided and one corner is set aside for a coffee bar. No elaborate props are needed but the coffee bar, disco unit, entrance and 'outside' area must be clearly defined and recognizable to the participants.

The children are then separated into three groups. At this point it may be useful to consider the methods which could be used to group the participants in a simulation, since nearly all simulations need some group work.

Basically there are two different approaches: child-determined grouping and teacher-determined grouping. Where grouping is determined by the children, groups build up almost invariably on the basis of friendship sets. Where much teaching depends on small group work, this is often, of course, a familiar and easy method for the children to cope with. Groups like this have the obvious advantage that the children know each other and mix together socially. There are however, several disadvantages. One group, for instance, may be particularly disruptive, or withdrawn, or talented.

Children may miss some of the broad social experience that simulations provide. Ideas may stagnate.

In the area of teacher-determined grouping two chief possibilities are open. Firstly, the teacher may be able to eliminate some of the disadvantages mentioned above by carefully deciding in advance who will work with whom. The alternative is to group children using some method of random selection. The unique advantages of this method are that over a period of time, each child will probably work with everyone else in the class, and that the grouping process itself can be made to be 'dramatic'. For example, where a teacher wishes to divide a class of thirty-two into eight groups of four, each child could be given a number between one and eight and the class could then be told to break up into their own groups without speaking or using their fingers to indicate a number. The thoughts and processes involved in solving the problem nearly always succeed in stretching the imagination and providing a useful 'warm-up' before the simulation proper begins.

To return to *Forum*, the three groups required are:

1 The 'good' members (Group A) – These people are members of the youth club and they are the ones who are always prepared to help at the coffee bar, sweep up afterwards etc.
2 The 'bad' members (Group B) – Although members of the youth club these people are not really prepared to help in its running. They are rowdy, uncooperative etc.
3 The 'outsiders' (Group C) – These are not members of the club, don't want to be, and spend club evenings trying to spoil the enjoyment of the members. The club leader (the teacher) refuses admittance to this group.

The simulation begins at the beginning of an ordinary evening at the club. The members arrive and take part in whatever activity suits the role they have been given. The outsiders of course, remain outside. After a somewhat truncated club evening, the club-leader steps in to announce that due to complaints from local residents about rowdyism and damage after meetings at the club the Council has decided that the club will have to close.

What happens from this point onwards depends on the group, but the club leader should attempt to stay out of the way after closing up the club. Some possibilities that have been observed are:

1 group A turns on groups B and C
2 groups A and B turn on group C
3 various courses of action are suggested: petitions, marches, starting another club
4 mayhem

Whatever happens it is unlikely that anything will finally be resolved in the first session, so that a second session can be begun at a later date with the participants having had time to think about the problems that face them.

The second part of the simulation begins at school the next day at breaktime. The closure of the youth club is the main topic of conversation, at least amongst the members of groups A and B. Again several different reactions are possible. One of the advantages of the new situation is that if chaos threatens or if the problems quickly come to seem insoluble, the teacher, in the guise of the teacher on playground duty, can intervene and if necessary offer suggestions and advice.

From now onwards there are numerous possibilities for further development, not only in dramatic activities but also in other fields. A post play discussion could be the next step, where pupils no longer in role, could view the simulation objectively, offer comments on it, and compare it with reality.

In an English lesson an assignment sheet, similar to that suggested for *Tenement*, for example, offering a choice of writing tasks could be provided to follow the practical sessions. These tasks would obviously bear in mind the age of the participants, but they might include, say, the writing of letters to the council asking for a reprieve, to the youth leader asking for advice, or to a local newspaper commenting on the situation, perhaps hoping to change local opinion. They would include writing expressing personal reactions or narrative writing relating to the final outcome envisaged. They would also include such tasks as the wording of petitions, the design and making of banners and posters of protest, or even composing the words of a song or chant to be used on a 'demonstration' march.

'Creative' drama can be made to play a most valuable part in the social education of all children, particularly when they are taught in mixed ability groups. The very nature of drama is such that it enables children to respond to its demands on their own level. It has, too, a vital part to play in the language development of the child. Its uses with regard to literature are many and varied. But, in all this, a flexible approach is essential if the full benefits are to be derived.

With the more specialised form of dramatic activity involved in games and simulations, I have tried to offer several reasons why their use might be contemplated. Of these perhaps the most important is that a game or simulation can offer the child insight, interest and involvement – a chance to participate in the learning process. It is a tool which can offer the teacher the opportunity to invigorate and revitalise his approach to many of the more traditional aspects of his work. Use of simulation is one strategy which I have found useful and which English teachers may wish to try. As Tansey points out: 'A tool which motivates and involves children, persuades them towards cooperative effort and shapes attitudes in such a way that they are their own attitudes, reached by them and not forced on them, must be a powerful tool'.

APPENDIX ONE

Games and simulations – materials and sources

A guide to most of the games and simulations available in this country may be obtained from the Secretary, *Society for Academic Gaming and Simulation in Education and Training*, 5, Errington, Moreton-in-the-Marsh, Glos. (£3.75)

Two valuable sources of information about games and simulations are: *Youth Service Information Centre*, 37, Belvoir Street, Leicester, LE1 6sc and *National Youth Bureau*, 17-23 Albion Street, Leicester, LE1 6GD.

There are many games available from the USA. Some of them could be useful – if only as a source of ideas – but since not all of them travel well I have deliberately omitted mentioning them.

In addition to *Tenement* which I have described in detail, available in revised form (October 1976) from Shelter Youth Education Programme, 157 Waterloo Road, London SE1, (£1.50), the following are easily obtainable:

Man in his environment (1971)
Widely used in schools and colleges, the kit consists of a magnetised board which simulates a geographical area containing forests, farms, rivers and a small urban development. The kit also contains ten 'projects' such as an Airport, a Motorway and a Shopping Centre – each with its own merits and drawbacks. The class is divided into teams representing the various interests, including non-human and through argument and debate decides whether or not to accept each project. The wisdom or otherwise of the decisions is decided as the game progresses. (£6.00)
The Coca Cola Export Corporation, Atlantic House, Rockley Road, London W14 0DH.

The Spring Green motorway (1972)
A role-playing game for up to thirty. A simulation exercise on the advantages and disadvantages of building a motorway. (40p)

Resettlement (1973)
A board game about the problems faced by Ugandan-Asian families as they went through the process of finding a house, getting a job and placing their children in schools. (80p)

149

South Street Hostel Storm
A role-playing game for up to thirty. Some of the members of South Street Residents' Association feel very strongly about the Social Services Department's plan to locate a hostel for the mentally handicapped in South Street. (40p)

Greenham District Council (1974, 1975, 1976)
A role-playing game for eight to fifteen players. A simulation of a council meeting which aims to make the players more aware of how councils work and how decisions are made. The players take on the roles of councillors and discuss the seven items on the agenda, all concerned with the development of Greenham, and ranging from the shopping facilities to the provision of a site for Gypsies. (£1.00)

Spring Green Motorway, Resettlement, South Street Hostel Storm and *Greenham District Council* are all available from The Advisory Centre, Community Service Volunteers, 237 Pentonville Road, London N1 9NG.

In addition to these the CSV Publications List 1976 gives details of six other games and simulations.

Growing up
One of the twelve units in the Schools Council General Studies Project, this contains a simulation with four case studies called *Control in school*.
The Publishing Manager, Longman Group Ltd., Resources Unit, 35 Tanner Row, York.

There is a considerable range of material published by the Longman Group, including history games, geography games, science games. Some of the material could be adapted for use in an English classroom.

Streets ahead
A game designed to help children face and understand the problems of city life.
Priority, Harrison Jones School, West Derby Street, Liverpool 7.

The poverty game
A game for eight to thirty players from thirteen years old upwards. A game demonstrating the vulnerability of people who are poor and who live in a difficult climate. Participants play the roles of subsistence farmers in the savannah region of Africa. Dice, chance and disease cards to a great extent control their fate. (40p.) Oxfam.

The aid committee game
A game for players of fourteen years old and upwards. Participants study one developing country and its problems and decide what projects they would help if they had the money. Oxfam.

The trade game
A game for players of fourteen years old and upwards. People play the parts of consumers, traders and retailers of a commodity such as bananas, sugar and coffee. (Free)
Oxfam Education Department, 274 Banbury Road, Oxford OX2 7DZ.

Nine graded simulations (1975)
This series, published by ILEA Media Resources Centre, aims to develop communication skills of all kinds; discussion, argument, reporting, interviewing and presenting a case, among others. The nine individual packs contain documentary information, controller's notes and notes for the participants. (Units 1, 2, 3 – £3.00; 4, 5, 6 – £3.00; 7, 8, 9 – £4.00).
The Media Resources Centre ILEA, Highbury Station Road, Islington, London N1 1SB.

Passport (1976)
Originally designed for sixth-formers but used very successfully with twelve year olds. Designed by Keith Bradford, Community Relations Officer in Coventry, to give participants some sort of personal experience of the realities of racial discrimination . . . 'a kind of giant Monopoly set, with the dice loaded against the black players' (£7.00 plus 65p. postage).
Passport Production, Coventry, C.R.C. 14 Spon Street, Coventry.

The Careers Research and Advisory Centre, besides marketing the Esso games: *The star river project, The Esso students' business game* and *The Esso service station game* (£16.00 each and suitable for sixth form and above) advertise: *Work experience projects* – six units containing material for a classroom simulation of a variety of real work situations. (Units 1-5 £5.00 per unit; Unit 6 £2.50; complete set £25.00) and *Speedcop* a careers simulation using techniques common to most family board games. It can be played by groups of all abilities and ages. (£4.50 plus VAT for a six-player set; £12.50 plus VAT for eighteen player set. Hobsons Press (Cambridge) Ltd., Bateman Street, Cambridge, CB2 1LZ.

APPENDIX TWO

Bibliography

Drama
BULLOCK REPORT (1975) *A Language for Life* HMSO
DODD, N. and HICKSON, W. (1973) *Drama and Theatre in Education* Heinemann
HODGSON, J. and RICHARDS, E. (1968) *Improvisation* Methuen
LEACH, R. (1970) *Theatre for Youth* Pergamon
PEMBERTON-BILLING, R. N. and CLEGG, J. (1965) *Teaching Drama* ULP
SCHER, A. and VERRALL, C. (1975) *100+ Ideas for Drama* Heinemann
SELF, D. (1975) *A Practical Guide to Drama in the Secondary School,* Ward Lock Educational
WAY, B. (1967) *Development through Drama* Longman

Games and simulations
ELLIOTT, G. et al (1975) *Games and Simulations in the Classroom* Booklet accompanying Schools Council project *History, Geography and Social Science* Collins 1975
LONGLEY, C. (ed) (1972) *Games and Simulations* BBC
MEEK, R. L. (1972) *Figuring out Society* Fontana
POSTMAN, N. and WEINGARTEN, C. (1969) *Teaching as a Subversive Activity* Penguin
TANSEY, P. and UNWIN, D. (1969) *Simulation and Gaming in Education* Methuen
WALFORD, R. A. (1970) *Games in Geography* Longman
WALFORD, R. A. (1972) 'Games and Simulations', *New Movements in the Study and Teaching of Geography* ed. N. Graves, Temple Smith
WALFORD, R. A. (1971) *Simulation and Gaming in the Classroom* Penguin
WILSON, A. (1970) *War Gaming* Penguin

6 Visual stimuli

Gordon Taylor

The use of visual materials in English teaching has developed rapidly in recent years, because teachers have seen in them new and exciting ways of working. It's my belief that such developments have a valuable part to play in streamed, setted and mixed ability teaching.

The last situation makes exacting demands on us. We can no longer rely solely on conventional teaching methods and materials. Mixed ability emphasizes the needs of the individual, and in order to fulfil these needs we must have as wide a range of teaching strategies as possible; we need a diversity of approach, a wide range of activities, and flexible classroom organization. The use of visual materials helps us to achieve this. They extend the range of resources and activities available, and these activities lend themselves to a variety of ways of working: individual, group and class-based work are all possible.

Before considering the benefits of visual materials in more specific terms, I would like to make clear what material I'm referring to and what activities I have in mind. For the sake of clarity I've divided them into materials that the teacher brings into the classroom, and the practical activities that the students can undertake and which centre on the production of visual materials themselves.

First, then, the materials – among these I include:

1 a variety of evocative objects that can be brought into the classroom, i.e. bones, seashore debris, food, masks etc.
2 still photographs, colour slides, postcards, reproductions of paintings covering a wide variety of subjects, i.e. people, scenes, shapes, animals etc.
3 16 mm film including shorts, extracts, and full length feature films.

Secondly, the activities; apart from the central activities of writing and discussion these include:

(a) drama, painting, collage etc.
(b) producing sequences of photographs or colour slides accompanied by tape recordings or writing.
(c) making 8 mm movie films.

What part, then, can such materials and activities play in the mixed ability situation, and what specific benefits are there in terms of our students' English? They provide extremely powerful stimuli for a variety of tasks in the classroom. Their impact is immediate and creates a high motivation for learning. Above all, though, they are accessible to the whole range of ability.

An object brought into the classroom, for instance, is not an abstract system like the written word with rules and perhaps associations which may create problems for the less able. It can be touched, felt, smelt, tasted and closely examined, and such immediate sense responses generate a flow of language and anecdotes in students of all abilities. If these objects are a focus of a class or group discussion, this talk will form the basis for valuable processes and activities: students will be developing their language resources; they will be re-examining the familiar and the unfamiliar; they will be developing accuracy of observation. They can also be led to look at the language they use and see how it works as a tool to express their understanding, and as an object in itself with qualities such as sound, rhythm and 'feel'. They are, therefore, encouraged to make a deeper imaginative response to the world and have a new interest in the vitality of language that leads to accurate, fresh writing, drama, role play and story telling.

What I have outlined above about real objects is equally true of photographs and 16 mm film. They offer us an immediate, concrete experience that is a familiar aspect of life and as such, one that is readily acceptable to our students. Good photographs and films, like some poetry, crystallize moments of experience and offer us insights into our lives and the lives of others. They therefore, give students the scope for deep and rewarding study. Groups of students can talk about them, argue about them, discover more and more about them until they perhaps reach some conclusions, and ultimately learn something new from the experience they capture. Photographs present themselves as a whole to the imagination and don't have to be built up detail by detail, painstakingly in some cases, as in reading. That is not to say that reading isn't important but we have to build up confidence in some students by getting them to work with a more accessible medium. By doing so, we can encourage them to enter willingly into the processes of talking, writing and reading and stimulate them into producing something of value on which they can build. In short, visual materials such as these, provide a bridge to the verbal and, for the less able, an essential bridge.

Photographs and films, of course, have an advantage over real objects in that they considerably widen the range of appropriate material. They can present people in a variety of situations and places, from cities to deserts. They offer us an opportunity to examine the relationships between people, and the way language is governed by such relationships. Much interesting work on story and dialogue is possible, therefore, both in writing and improvised drama. Students' responses are not, of course, limited to imaginative work. Photographs, films and paintings can sometimes present aspects of modern life more graphically than through other media. I'm thinking of scenes of pollution and the suffering of human beings which have powerfully stimulated discussion and discursive writing.

Photographs, films and paintings are art forms and as such have their own perspective on experience and their own way of expressing it. They have structure and tone which is peculiar to themselves in some respects but in others is comparable to some aspects of writing. I'm thinking here, for example, of the way the visual can focus on detail, of the relationship between various elements in a photograph, between the central figure and its background or other figures, and the force of juxtaposition and contrast; equally, the idea of sequence in a film, the building up to a particular climax. Exploring these with students, I've found, has helped them to become aware of techniques they can use to add power to their writing and to understand the writing process more consciously. On one level, this has simply consisted in exploring the amount of detail that goes to make up a scene, a person and an incident. On another level, the medium's power of suggesting meaning without actually stating anything, has allowed us to explore how detail can be selected to express character, or create a particular mood, and from there to move on to the qualities of language which heighten the effect. Similarly, we've explored the way the relationship between people can be suggested through their physical position and mannerisms, the way mood can be suggested by background and the enormous power that comes from simply placing one picture next to another and, by extension, one idea next to another. The narrative sequence of film has enabled us to explore what makes an effective sequence, why one scene is better next to another, and the idea of speed in building up to a climax. Even a form such as the ballad can be powerfully illuminated by seeing the film *Ballad of Crowfoot*. This may sound a little beyond the range of some students in a mixed ability group, and if we were dealing with such techniques without the use of photographs and film, it could be. However, given suitable concrete examples in visual materials, such discussions become not only possible, but fruitful.

Consideration of technique in film is, of course, valuable in itself. Film is a powerful medium and the discussion of its techniques provides a basis for discrimination. Moreover, I've found comments on the effectiveness or otherwise of particular techniques have been spontaneously offered by students of all levels of ability which has led me to believe that we shouldn't underestimate their ability to understand what appear to us to be sophisticated ideas.

I've made some comment above on the way photographs and films are related to writing. It doesn't end with the students' own writing, however. Through the visual we can introduce a particular area of experience, and provide a framework of discussion and writing that will enable students to understand more clearly what professional writers are saying. For instance, I have used the film *Dream of Wild Horses* (See Appendix Two) to precede a reading of Ted Hughes' enigmatic poem *A Dream of Horses*. Not that seeing the film is the only way of dealing with such a poem, but seeing the film and discussing it allows us to feel that the introduction of such a poem would not be out of place in a wide ability situation. Even the weak reader will find such difficult material more accessible. Following literature with film or photographs on a similar theme is equally valid.

Practical activities, such as making films and slide sequences, are also of great benefit. On the one hand students are learning the purely technical processes involved in taking a photograph, from the need to focus, to the complexities of continuity and editing. All this again provides some basis for reasoned discrimination. More important, these activities are a stimulating framework within which talking, writing and drama can take place.

The idea of making a film or taking photographs is usually sufficient to arouse interest in the most apathetic student. It provides an alternative to the pen as a means of responding and perhaps a more congenial one; not so flexible, perhaps, but at least one that isn't associated with failure. Students write stories and convert them into scripts; this, in itself, provides valuable opportunities for structured group work in which all can participate. Students will need to use language to cooperate and organize themselves, whether it be simply ordering a sequence of events, writing a story, or converting it into a script. They will be forming concepts of structure in this process as the need arises to decide which event comes where, how much emphasis needs to be put on a particular event, which dwelt on etc.

I've talked here in terms of making films from scratch, but this isn't the only way of working. Literature can provide the starting point for such activities, though these activities in themselves are a means of re-examining that literature and expressing a response to it. This applies as much to the simpler process of making a collage or drawing, as to the more complex processes of making animated cartoons, slide/tape sequences, or films using actors. Students involved in this have to consider the meaning of the original. This means understanding the text and its implications. For instance, anyone working on the opening scene from *Of Mice and Men* would first of all have to examine the text to find out what happened and where it happened. Then, since it is an opening, they would need to consider how to establish the sense of place and the character in visual terms. This means a return to the text to examine its mood, to come to some understanding of the characters of Lennie and George and their relationship. Then they will have to make an attempt to translate these into visual terms through camera position, angle, movement and so on. The ending of the novel presents similar problems; you cannot make an attempt to translate it into visual terms without fully understanding its meaning and implications and that means a close examination of the text.

These, then, are the reasons why I feel visual materials can play an important part in mixed ability teaching. I would like, at this point, to emphasize that this is only a part of English teaching and one that must take its place alongside others of equal importance. Visual materials have their place, and provided they are used with specific objectives in mind, rather than as a means of occupying time or providing entertainment, can be of real benefit to the English teacher in a mixed ability situation.

Having outlined the reasons for my belief in the benefits of visual materials I shall now consider how such ideas can work in practice. What follows is not intended to be exhaustive; in most areas the possibilities are endless. I've simply tried to suggest something of the range of these possibilities based on my experiences in the classroom. I've dealt with the materials in different areas, though I'm aware that in certain cases there is some overlap in the type of work generated by them. I have, therefore, tended to concentrate in each section on the work that is particularly relevant to the material under consideration in that section, and have pointed out when the work is relevant to other materials. Similarly, the reader should bear in mind a point I made above, that all these materials lend themselves to different kinds of classroom organization; they can be used for individual or group work, but they can also, in some instances, form the basis of whole class work even in the mixed ability situation.

Objects

The range of objects I've found useful in teaching at all ages is very wide. Some I've used because, in themselves, they are worthy of close examination; some because they relate directly to students' experience; others because they are particularly evocative. Ideally, they should combine all three aspects.

Occasionally I've used objects to stimulate accurate and fresh descriptive writing. For instance, I ask students to bring in, or I provide them with, oranges, apples, or some seasonal fruit, and explore their shape and texture and find words that describe their feel, taste, smell etc. We make a collection of these words and discuss their merits in terms of appropriateness and accuracy. In this situation, I concentrate the initial reaction on a personal response and collection of words and phrases by individuals or pairs of students. But some items, when a variety of objects is under scrutiny (autumn debris, for instance), can be dealt with in groups of five or six students, exchanging words or phrases amongst themselves and compiling a group list. The discussion that follows the initial reaction often includes comparisons which arise spontaneously and their merits as a means of self expression, has formed the basis of further class or group discussion, as have sound or other word qualities. One of the responses to this initial work is personal writing in either free verse or prose, though it need not necessarily be confined to these. Students with severe writing difficulties may feel more at ease and be more encouraged to produce a fluent response using a tape recorder, and perhaps later making a transcript of the tape, or having it made for them by another student or the teacher in the way that Richard Mills illustrates in chapter 1. Alternatively, some students could make a display of the objects, if this is appropriate, with written information. This work needn't be confined to what can be brought into the classroom. Visits, either simply to the school grounds or the local park, museum or other places of interest can provide a great deal of accurate observation to work on.

In some instances, objects stimulate an exploration of personal experience. This can be deliberate as when students and I have brought in objects of personal value and have in turn explained what value they have for us and why. This offers an insight into each other and mutual understanding in the group can be built up. The discussion can move out to a consideration of other personal possessions, people's rooms, and what a person's individual possessions and the way they live tell us about them. This in turn can lead to writing about personal possessions and rooms, and later to groups of students examining writing which deals with this aspect of experience such as extracts from Muriel Spark's *You Should Have Seen the Mess* and Philip Larkin's *Mr Bleaney*. Other groups have written autobiographies, and others have seen short films such as *The Visit* or *Paul Tomkowicz* (see Appendix Two). They consider the lives of these people and answer such questions as: 'What do we learn about these people from the way they live?' and 'What do they value?'

In other circumstances, objects spontaneously generate discussion of personal experience as an off-shoot of other activities. Apples, for instance, apart from being useful in descriptive writing as outlined above, have sparked off talk of 'scrumping', and through anecdotes to related areas of experience such as fear, daring and heroes. Following this, groups have discussed the section in Stan Barstow's *Joby* where Joby is caught shoplifting (a passage that seems popular with Judith Atkinson, I notice). Questions like: 'Why does Joby steal?' and 'Could either Gus, Joby or the shopkeeper be described as heroes?' have provided small group discussion with some direction. Similarly, an examination of bones and skulls has led to a discussion of dead animals that students have found, and pets they have lost; and later to an examination of Ted Hughes' *View of a Pig* and Seamus Heaney's *The Early Purges*.

Alternatively, I have found concentration on the shape, texture and colour of objects has been a powerful stimulus to the imagination of

158

students. Bones or driftwood are useful for this, as are bottled biological 'horrors'. The latter have proved particularly powerful in stimulating work on fear or monsters. The initial reaction can be a class sharing their personal fears if the right atmosphere making mutual confidences possible exists. Or the class can work in groups and individually on a variety of tasks: drawing pictures of monsters and writing descriptions of them; reading poems like *Beowulf* or short stories like Ray Bradbury's *One Who Waits* and tape recording them with suitable sound effects; or writing similar stories and plays of their own and tape recording them; making lists of reasons for and against a belief in the existence of life on other planets and presenting the evidence with conclusions to the rest of the class, and perhaps writing essays on the subject. Any one or all of these options could be suitable follow-up work to the original stimulus.

I have listed below objects that I've found useful which can be treated in the ways I've suggested:

Driftwood
Spring buds and leaves
Pets
Live laboratory animals
Items of personal value to
    students
Fossils
Masks
African or Eastern curios
Skulls and bones
Autumn leaves and twigs
Bottled biological specimens
Seasonal fruit
Scientific or medical
    instruments

Rocks and coloured stones
Ornaments
Flowers
Insects
Stuffed animals
Shells
Old farm implements e.g.
    scythes
Hunting traps
Brass rubbings
Old books e.g. family Bibles
Ships in bottles
Oddly shaped coloured bottles
Sweets

Photographs and colour slides

Photographs on a wide variety of subjects are now a common feature of many anthologies of prose and poetry. Such photographs often include reproductions of paintings which are equally useful to the English teacher. Some publishers are also producing colour slides to accompany their printed materials (such as those with *Occasions*, R.W. Mills, Longman), though these are still comparatively rare. You can, of course, produce slides yourself without too much difficulty, and then you're able to include features of local life and the local environment, as well as particular subjects and treatments of subjects which may not otherwise be available.

Photographs and colour slides can be used as a stimulus in a way similar to objects. They can generate exploration and experience, stimulate the imagination, as well as provide discussion of language itself. For instance, good still photographs or reproductions of paintings, or scenes such as building sites, city centres, and factories and of a variety of interesting people, such as old people, children, and tramps provide an excellent stimuli for discussion, and personal and descriptive writing. If you are dealing with the theme of childhood, for instance, one group could examine some of the excellent photographs of children that are available. A series of questions can direct their attention to the essential qualities of childhood that are revealed in the photograph. After the discussion, various tasks can be attempted in groups or as individuals: imaginative writing based on the picture; lists of children's games with rules; childhood memories; autobiographies; descriptions of younger brothers or sisters; the examination of Dylan Thomas's short stories and poems; writing children's short stories etc. The photographs need not always be provided by the teacher. I have had many successful discussions on people and places based on photographs of students' relatives and places they have visited.

Colour slides provide an interesting variation on stills. A series of slides on a particular theme backed by appropriate music and readings can create a powerful impact. A series of slides of coastal scenery backed by Debussy's *La Mer*, for instance, can open up this whole area in an original way. As a starter to a theme it's surprising how effective slides taken with a simple camera can be. A department interested in this work will, of course, build up its own collection of slides, together with the appropriate tapes. Photographs can be used to focus on techniques of writing and explore some of the ways we can make language work for us. I have indicated some of the possibilities here in the opening section, and I shall now elaborate on these, and provide some specific examples.

Accurate observation
Students' writing can lack detail because they have not been able to visualise clearly what they are describing. Concentration on individual photographs or slides can increase their powers of observation so that they eventually develop an 'inner eye' and can imagine more fully when no visual stimuli are present.

To this end, small groups of students closely examine photographs of people or places, picking out all the details and as a group build up a word picture of them. Faces are particularly good for this, being followed by word portraits or, if appropriate, wanted posters.

You can go on to look at the way *selecting* details can create a particular effect; for instance the way a person's character and way of life can be suggested through concentrating on details of appearance. Again, concentration on photographs of people is valuable here. Imagine a group has a picture of an old man rummaging through a

160

dustbin in an alley of a large city. He's untidy, unshaven and wears old clothes. The group could be asked:

1 What do you learn about this man and his way of life from the picture?
2 Pick out particular details that support your ideas.

Each group then reports back to the class and selected detail is discussed. Students can go on to speculate on the lives of people in various pictures, where they live, their jobs, and build up case histories, stories, diaries, or monologues.

Similarly, work can be done on examining the mood of a particular photograph. Pictures of bleak landscapes or bright Spring mornings can be studied with the object of choosing detail that establishes their mood or atmosphere. Much interesting work can be done on Haiku here with groups examining the way Haiku poets choose detail to create a word picture or establish a mood. The students can then go on to write their own from appropriate photographs.

None of this, of course, is inseparable from the language used to express this detail, and I've found examining this can be valuable. Students consider the way we express our attitudes towards people or things not only by the *detail* we choose to describe, but by the language we use. For example, they could consider the implications of words like: fat, well-built, tubby, greasy, sallow, pale, florid etc. as they examine specific photographs of people.

Likewise, students can examine the mood of advertising photographs and how the advertisement language itself describes the mood or reinforces it. This work can serve as an introduction to the language of persuasion.

As I suggested in the opening section, people reveal their relationships by their physical positions and mannerisms. Individual photographs can generate discussion of this, but so too can 16mm shorts and extracts. For instance, there is an extract from *A Kind of Loving* (available from BFI, see Appendix one) which shows Victor and Ingrid in a cafe. Victor is obviously not interested in Ingrid and what she is saying; this is not only suggested by the fact that he doesn't speak or listen to her, but also by his slouched position and his turning away from her, to examine other couples in the cafe. Ingrid, on the other hand, is bent towards him, eager to attract his attention and tell him her news. A great deal can be got out of simply examining this aspect of the visual image, and seeing that we can add details like this to descriptive writing.

Sequence
Series of photographs that can be put together to form stories can offer work on narrative and sequence. These consist of between six and ten

photographs which can be made with cut-outs from magazines, or photographs you have taken yourself, or packs of such series which can be purchased. Students can build up narrative sequences by simply putting the photographs into an order and writing the story they tell. The better series will allow for a variety of arrangements within a specific sequence by the judicious choice of photographs. Students who have produced different stories from the same sequence could compare each other's work and discuss why they chose their particular sequence.

Similar work is possible with 16mm film. Students could consider the effectiveness of the sequencing of a film. Take for example *Incident at Owl Creek* which is about a man who is hanged in the American Civil War. We see him escaping but it is not until the end of the film that we realize this was imaginary – his last living thoughts. The question that could be discussed is how effective is this sequence of shots. *The Boy Next Door* is a film about two boys exploring an empty house. It builds up to a climax with the caretaker frightening them away. Again, the class could explore how effective the film is in building up to this climax. Following discussions like these, classes could write their own stories with a twist or a climax, or perhaps examine other stories with these qualities.

The force of juxtaposition and contrast can be illustrated by putting two still photographs together; for instance, a new car next to a scrap heap. A film that uses this technique particularly effectively is *Very Nice, Very Nice*, made entirely of stills which juxtapose many images of modern society. Literature which explores contrasts, like Ted Hughes' *Pike* or *To Paint a Water Lily* could be usefully discussed here. (See Appendix Two for details of the films just mentioned.)

Photographs and abstract paintings which do not depict real scenes or people can be used to evoke personal imaginative writing without the help of guidance from the teacher, apart from: 'Let the shape work on your imagination and write freely from your thoughts'. The subject need not necessarily be abstract, but might simply explore the symmetry and beauty of the shapes of natural objects. In this case they could provide the basis for work on concrete poems, or shape poems which explore the relationship between shape and word.

Apart from leading to writing, photographs, or films for that matter, can also be the stimuli for role play and work on dialogue. Here I've chosen photographs that simply show interesting places, such as an old house, a cave; or one depicting a mysterious or interesting object; or photographs that show a particular relationship between people, or that highlight a dramatic situation. In the case of the places or objects, small groups of students dramatize an incident in the place or make up a play centred around the object. In the case of photographs of people, the possibilities are wider. Apart from enacting the scene that is suggested by the photograph, for example an argument, or a thief discovered, the group could examine how people in different social situations might talk. Does the boy in the photograph speaking to his teacher express himself in the same way when he's talking to his friends? Students could try out these differences in role play.

I have dealt in general here with photographs and slides that the teacher can provide for the students. However, a great deal of interesting work can be done with groups of students making their own photographs and slides. The following are some suggestions:

1 A group of students working on a theme can produce a series of slides on the theme and a tape recording of appropriate music and readings of poetry and prose that they have chosen (see the earlier suggestion on coastal scenery).
2 A story written by students or a suitable story or part of a story they have read can be illustrated by slides they have taken of themselves acting it out. The finished product is shown with the story as a tape recorded background. An alternative to this is to use a polaroid camera, which has the advantage of instant results. The photographs are mounted with the story either as a wall display or as a book. Poetry that students have written can also be illustrated by suitable photographs, thus producing their own poetry cards.
3 Visits that might be part of a theme in progress can be recorded either by slides or stills. Still photographs can be mounted with an account of what happened, and slides can be shown with a tape recorded commentary. Individual photographs can also be used as the stimulus for writing.
4 Students can make a documentary on a subject connected with a theme using slides and tape recordings of music, songs, poetry and interviews. Subjects such as the impact on an area of a motorway, or first-year impressions of school provide good material for these activities.
5 A series of slides as advertisements with a tape recording of music and advertising language, or photographs and written accounts, are also possible. I have had some success here with students advertising the school under such headings as: 'Send your child to . . . school – the chance of a lifetime', or advertising the local area: 'Visit . . ., the world's most fascinating place!'

Film – 16mm
The possibilities created by the use of film in English teaching are great, whether you are dealing with full length feature films or shorts and extracts. Their accessibility makes them a powerful tool for work with mixed ability classes and they are flexible enough to be used with one class or several classes together.

Anyone wishing to use films will soon realize that they create the need for careful planning. You will need a selection of distributors' catalogues from whom you can hire suitable films (see Appendix One). Films need to be ordered one or two months in advance and, if you are working thematically, programmes of work have to be planned with this in mind and sometimes adjusted to fit in with their arrival. You also should be sure a room with blackout and screen is available, as well as a projector in working order. This may seem daunting, but once your department has established a routine the administrative details pose no real problem. I have included as an appendix a list of films that I have found useful together with a brief synopsis of each. This should be referred to for further details of films mentioned below. Having ordered and received the film there are many possible ways of using them. I offer here some of the more important of these.

1 Some films are particularly useful as a one-off experience as a stimulus for imaginative writing. You can show *A Dream of Wild Horses* or *Snow* to a mixed ability class and simply ask them to write an individual response to it in any form they wish. On the other hand, you can structure the work in a way similar to that outlined in the section on still photographs.

2 Having seen the film, the group (it could be a class or several classes) breaks up into small groups for discussion of their initial response. These groups could operate alone, or with staff, students in training, and possibly with sixth formers where appropriate. The discussions could be free or structured by questions intended to focus attention on important aspects of the film or related personal experience. Some of these discussions could be taped for further consideration later. Students could then pursue one of a variety of activities arising from the film: different types of writing – personal, stories, plays etc; role play; making collages or posters to advertise the film. This could follow immediately after the discussion or after a re-run of the film where this has been planned.

3 Much can be done by using poems and written extracts which are on the same theme as the film. The approach outlined in the previous section could be followed by examination of related literature in subsequent English lessons. Such literature can help to illuminate the key themes of the film from a different angle. Alternatively, the viewing of the film and the initial work can be used as a means of illuminating literature or related themes. For example, *I Think They Call Him John* could lead into a study of Philip Larkin's *Mr Bleaney* and other literature on the theme of people who are alone. In this way the whole subject of people can be set in motion. The film *Snow* can be followed by Auden's *Night Mail* and work on onomatopeia, rhythm and alliteration can be begun. *Morning on the Lièvre* could lead into Haiku or other writing expressing mood. A study of related literature could, of course, precede the film. Individual pieces can be studied and

related to each other and their common theme. By this means the students' attention is directed to certain significant issues. They then watch the film approaching it via this background of initial discussion of written material. Their focus has been sharpened by the time they reach the film itself. The movement of a series of lessons may be:

students' real experience → film → support material

or any one of the other five permutations of this formula, providing that the permutation chosen is appropriate for the film. For example, *Incident at Owl Creek* should be shown without preliminary discussion.

4 If the class is working on a particular theme or topic they will have read or studied various pieces of prose and poetry; discussed visual material; listened to tape recordings and records; perhaps made a visit or had a visiting speaker. They can now go through all the stages of planning to make a film and this activity either culminates in actually making this film or it stops just before the last stage. At this point a film on the same subject, which the teacher had already planned for, is hired and, after seeing it, students discuss the professional film in relation to the one they might have made. Each film may be measured against the other in terms of content, attitude and visual impact. With some projectors it is possible to stop the film in order to concentrate attention for a few moments on a particular frame.

5 Sometimes the sound track of the film can be tape recorded for later consideration, provided you have made the appropriate arrangements. This would be, perhaps, particularly relevant where the support material contains dialogue, or where work on the music and sound effects of the film might be relevant.

Making 8mm film

Making 8mm film with students has all the glamour of the professional world of cinema, reinforced by the excitement of using the equipment. It is therefore taken up with much enthusiasm by the majority of students. It has, of course, its own problems. It demands reasonably good lighting conditions which limit you in general to outdoor subjects unless you can arrange sophisticated lighting. There is also a time lag between shooting the film and getting it developed. Most classes, however, are prepared to accept this as inevitable, and continue with other work while they are waiting. Some people may be put off by the apparent need for some kind of photographic expertise, but not a great deal is required as most cameras these days are fully automatic. Though we are obviously concerned with producing a film that is reasonably successful, what is important are the processes that have gone into the making of the film, rather than the end product. Film work, like other visual materials can lend itself to small group work or whole class involvement depending on the subject and its treatment. Whole-class work can present problems of involving everyone, unless the subject uses crowds of people for long periods of time. However, whether working with a small group or the whole class, I have found the following sequence a useful guide for organizing the work:

1 Each member of the group writes a story, one of which will be chosen by them as a basis for the film. Some of those chosen will sometimes be rather ambitious and you will need to tactfully suggest some alterations. Alternatively, literature can form the basis of the film.

2 The group then needs to consider the problems they are likely to encounter in making the film: the location, costume, camera positions etc. I favour here the group producing a shooting script. This is a writing of the script with notes on matters such as length of shot, camera angle etc. Again one is not looking for a professional product, merely encouraging the group to consider the problems they will meet when they begin shooting.

3 The actual making of the film can now begin. Without doubt this is best done in one session, though this is not always possible and it is surprising how enthusiasm can be maintained. I favour students taking it in turns to operate the camera and a group responsibility for directing, though it is possible to delegate these jobs to individuals.

The actual subjects for the films are as varied as those outlined for use with photographs and slides: the documentary, students' original stories, plays, short stories and poems, visits and advertisements – all can be equally rewarding subjects for films. I've made films from students' ideas and from literature with whole classes. One based on students' ideas was with a group of third years and was about a delicate old man who was set upon by a gang of ruffians. The old man, however, had a wonder pill which, true to the tradition of such films, gave him immense strength and enabled him to rout the ruffians. The film ended with him walking into the setting sun surrounded by an admiring group of girls, the one-time girl friends of his attackers. The finished product was no technical masterpiece, but it brought this group together in a joint venture that had tremendous vitality.

Another film I made, this time based on literature, was with a second-year group. We used *The Wierdstone of Brisingamen* by Alan Garner. They first worked to adapt the story which involved closely examining the original and considerably abridging it for their own purposes. The film required exotic costumes and masks, some of which we got from the school costume cupboard, others the students made

166

themselves. We used special effects to make objects appear and disappear and to allow the forces of evil to materialize. Again, the important feature of the venture was the renewed sense of purpose within the group, and the fact that talking and writing became a natural and necessary part of the work.

Animated Cartoons
A very different approach to film making is that offered by animated cartoons. There are two basic approaches:

1 One method uses two dimensional cut-outs. These are placed on a flat surface and filmed from above. The figures and settings can be drawn and painted by the students or cut out from magazines. Figures can be articulated by joining the limbs to the body with pins, which saves the necessity of having to draw separate figures for each movement. Special effects are easily achieved with these: they can fly or sink, appear or disappear.
2 The other method uses three dimensional figures (made from plasticine, for example) or manufactured toys. Again the figures and settings can be made by the students. Special effects are more difficult here as the figures are subject to the laws of gravity.

The basic principle of animation is the same in both cases. Each movement in the cartoon picture must be filmed separately. This is done with the camera on single exposure setting and allowing between four to eight shots per part of a movement, depending on the speed of the action. This is best illustrated for students by drawing a series of stick men on flexible cards so that when they are flicked the figure executes a movement. In order to reinforce this idea, students then make their own.

All this may sound rather complicated, but the techniques are easily mastered, and animations have certain advantages over conventional film making. Stories and scripts which are unsuitable for conventional films can be made into animations. Stories with exotic settings and characters requiring special effects, like costume and the ability to fly, are possible. You don't even have to be bound by conventional ideas of character and plot; films can explore movement of patterns. Animated cartoons also solve the problem of having to film outside, since they can be filmed indoors using an angle poised light. They don't require a great deal of space and acting ability, of course, is not a consideration.

I've found these cartoons work best with small groups, either as one activity amongst many, or when the whole class has divided into groups for a cartoon-making session. When I was working on the theme of monsters, the following ideas cropped up. Some people centred on monsters from outer space who landed on earth and ate the entire population of the world and then the earth itself, before they exploded;

others created much nicer monsters, but they were destroyed by evil men; some based their film on the story of Frankenstein. On a more abstract plane, small yellow blobs escaped from mysterious packets and dropped into inkwells then climbed out, leaving a trail of footprints behind; balls of plasticine rolled around forming themselves into strange shapes and doing untold damage until they were trodden on by a boot which suddenly appeared from nowhere; mysterious houses had faces which appeared and disappeared at their windows until the houses collapsed in a heap, and so on.

Both animations and conventional films provide further work for students in the form of tape recorded speech, sound effects, and music to accompany them. Students can best work on this by using an editor. This is a simple machine with a small screen which allows you to inspect the film frame by frame, or continuously. By using this you can inspect the film without the need for blackout and can easily find appropriate points for cutting and deciding where sound effects should be. This work can be slow and I've found it best completed as an out-of-class activity for a group of enthusiasts.

These, then, are some of the possibilities open to you when working with visual materials. In order to take full advantage of them a department needs to build up a large stock of objects, photographs, photo essays, series of slides, poem cards, useful films etc., and make them easily available to staff and students. With the possible exception of 16mm film, they perhaps flourish best as part of a workshop approach to mixed ability teaching, where students can move easily between the visual and the literary, benefiting from what each has to offer their developing language potential.

APPENDIX ONE: Address of distributors

BBC Television Enterprises Film Hire Department, Woodston House, Oundle Road, Peterborough PE2 9PZ. Peterborough (0733) 52257

British Film Institute, 81 Dean Street, London W1V 6AA. 01-437 4355. BFI Distribution Library, 42 Lower Marsh, London SE1 7RG. 01-928 4742

British Transport Films, Melbury House, Melbury Terrace, London NW1 6LP. 01-262 3232

Canada High Commissioner's Office, Canada House, Trafalgar Square, London SW1. 01-930 9741

Canadian Government Travel Film Library, 1 Grosvenor Square, London W1X 0AB. 01-629 9492

Central Film Library, Government Building, Bromyard Avenue, Acton, London W3. 01-743 5555

Columbia-Warner Distributors Ltd, 16mm Booking Department, Film House, 142 Wardour Street, London W1V 4AH. 01-437 4321

Concord Films Council Ltd, Nacton, Ipswich, Suffolk 1P10 0JZ. Ipswich 76012

Connoisseur Films Ltd, 167 Oxford Street, London w1R 2DX. 01-734 6555

Contemporary Films Ltd, 55 Greek Street, London w1V 6DB. 01-734 4901

Darvill Associates Ltd, 280 Chartridge Lane, Chesham, Bucks. Chesham 3643

Educational and Television Films Ltd., 2 Doughty Street, London wc1N 2PJ. 01-405 0395

Film Distributors Associated, 16mm Ltd, Building 9, GEC Estate, East Lane, Wembley, Middlesex HA9 7QB. 01-908 2366

Gateway Educational Media, Waverley Road, Yate, Bristol BS17 5RB. Chipping Sodbury (0454) 316774

Golden Films, Stewart House, 23 Francis Road, Windsor, Berks. Windsor 69566

Guild Sound & Vision Ltd, Woodston House, Oundle Road, Woodston, Peterborough PE2 9PZ. Peterborough (0733) 63122

Robert Kingston Films Ltd, 645/7 Uxbridge Road, Hayes End, Middlesex. 01-573 2940

National Association for Film in Education (NAFE), Honorary Secretary, 3 The Croft, Wall Street, London N1 3NB

National Audio-Visual Aids Library, Paxton Place, Gipsy Road, London SE27 9SR. 01-670 4247

National Film Board of Canada, 1 Grosvenor Square, London w1x 0AB. 01-629 9492

Rank Film Library, PO Box 20, Great West Road, Brentford, Middlesex TW8 9HR. 01-568 9222

Ron Harris Cinema Services Ltd, Glenbuck House, Glenbuck Road, Surbiton, Surrey. 01-399 0022

Scottish Central Film Library, 16-17 Woodside Terrace, Charing Cross, Glasgow G3 7XN. 041-332 9988

United Artists Corporation Ltd, Mortimer House, Mortimer Street, London w1. 01-636 1655

Visual Programme Systems Ltd, 21 Great Titchfield Street, London w1. 01-573 2940

APPENDIX TWO: Useful films

The following information on films which may confidently be used with mixed ability classes is reproduced by kind permission of Harrap from *Look-Out* by Richard W. Mills and Gordon T. Taylor (1974) a package of materials designed to be used with the twenty-two films here listed.

Film index

1	The Boy Next Door	11–12 years
2	Un Enfant Un Pays	11–12 years
3	Johnny	11–12 years

4 Snow	11–13 years
5 One Potato, Two Potato . . .	11–16 years
6 Sunday Lark	11–15 years
7 Terminus	11–16 years
8 The Red Balloon	11–16 years
9 Morning on the Lièvre	12–13 years
10 Dream of Wild Horses	13–15 years
11 La Première Nuit	13–16 years
12 The Visit	14–15 years
13 I think they call him John	14–16 years
14 Have I Told You Lately That I Love you?	14–16 years
15 Now	14–16 years
16 Very Nice, Very Nice	14–16 years
17 Young Offenders	14–16 years
18 Incident at Owl Creek	14–16 years
19 Culloden	14–16 years
20 Phoebe	14–16 years
21 Children of Hiroshima	15–16 years
22 Paul Tomkowicz	15–16 years

The Boy Next Door
Available from: Canada House Film Library. Canada, 1962.
Colour. 18 minutes. Free.
Age range: 11–12 years.
Themes: Childhood; fear; adventure.

Synopsis
The film traces the developing relationship between a ten-year-old Canadian boy and his new next-door neighbour, a French-speaking boy of the same age. After initial encounters with a dog and a horse they explore an old house together and, in doing so, are frightened by an old man who contrives some Hitchcock-type situations for them. They are relieved to make their escape back home, firmer friends than ever.

ADDITIONAL FILMS
The Summer we moved to Elm Street: Concord. Canada, 1966.
Colour. 28 mins. £4.40.
Friends for Life: Contemporary. Italy; 1957 (English sub-titles). 95 mins. £9.00.

Un Enfant Un Pays
Available from: Canada House Film Library. Canada, 1967.
Colour. 13 minutes. Free. Also available from Guild Sound & Vision Ltd, listed under the title *A Child in His Country*. £3.80.

Age range: 11–12 years.
Themes: Fantasy; adventure; growing up.

Synopsis
The film is an animated childhood fantasy of a boy who, by turns, becomes an eskimo bear hunter; an expert ice hockey player; a red Indian hunting deer; a cowboy; a swimmer. We first see him on an ocean liner and we leave him back home in the big city.

The visual and sound effects are very skilfully done and provide a number of useful talking points. Since the film is not easy to appreciate immediately we would recommend an introductory explanation by the teacher.

ADDITIONAL FILMS
The Dreamer: Concord. Yugoslavia. Colour. 12 mins. £2.00.

Johnny
Available from: Contemporary Films Ltd. Germany. Black and white. 14 minutes. £1.25.
Age range: 11–12 years.
Themes: Outsider; home and family; games.

Synopsis
This film was made in Germany but, since it has no dialogue of importance, no subtitles are needed and there is little difficulty in understanding.

It concerns a young boy of poor background who is sent on a shopping errand by his mother. We follow him to the shops, noting the things he amuses himself with and the games he plays. On the way he meets a group of children who snub him. Undeterred, he shows them his prowess on the climbing bars before continuing on his way. Nearer the shops he sees a marble that he would like to buy. He decides to get cheaper eggs for his mother and is, therefore, able to buy his marble.

Returning home he again meets the group of children and in a tussle the eggs are broken, for which he is soundly punished by his mother. He comes out of the caravan where he lives and, to his surprise, sees one of the little girls from the play school. She has come to give him his marble which he had left behind. The film ends with them walking away, hand in hand.

Snow
Available from: British Transport Films. Britain, 1963. Colour. 8 minutes. £2.00.
Age range: 11–13 years.
Themes: Winter; travel.

Synopsis
This film follows the progress of a train as it starts from a station and moves across country in winter. We see shots of winter landscape from the moving train, men clearing snow from the tracks, and the train ploughing into snow, sweeping it aside. The film has no commentary but is backed by music which follows the rhythm of the wheels.

ADDITIONAL FILMS
Snow. BFI. Canada, 1961. B/w, 13 mins. £1.50.
Night Mail: Central Film Library. Britain, 1936. B/w. 25 mins. £1.80. (This film was made by the GPO with Auden's poem as commentary.)
Daybreak Express: Contemporary. 1963. Colour. 5 mins. £0.87.

One Potato, Two Potato . . .
Available from: British Film Institute. Britain, 1957. Black and white. 18 minutes. £1.50.
Age range: 11–16 years.
Themes: Children's games; growing up; play.

Synopsis
This delightful film is a study of children playing games in the streets and waste grounds of London. It shows a wide variety of games from the most robust boys' games like 'King of the Castle' to the more poetic girls' games involving story, song and mime. The dated appearance of the children and the setting brings home the way these games and traditions are passed on from generation to generation.

ADDITIONAL FILMS
Buckets and Spades and Hand Grenades: Concord. Britain. Colour. 52 mins. £7.00.

Sunday Lark
Available from: Contemporary Films Ltd. USA. Black and white. 10 minutes. £2.00.
Age range: 11–15 years.
Themes: Humour; childhood; machines.

Synopsis
This film follows the amusing exploits of a charming little Chinese girl of about seven years of age, who strays into a multi-storey office block on a Sunday and proceeds to enjoy herself by playing inventively with any of the office equipment that appeals to her, from staplers to computers.
   A frightened policeman, investigating suspicious noises, overhears a dictaphone which the little girl has turned on, and immediately 'phones

for vast reinforcements. Seconds later several police cars scream to a halt, sirens blaring, and surround the building. Our heroine, unaware of this chain of events, skips away unobserved, and the police prepare to investigate.

ADDITIONAL FILMS
Sandcastles: Contemporary (cinemascope). USSR. 1968. B/w. 17 mins. £2.75.
The Key: Contemporary. Netherlands. 1961. Colour. 11 mins. £2.50.
Les Jojos: Connoisseur. France. B/w. 12 mins. £2.00.

Terminus

Available from: British Transport Films. Britain. 1961. Black and white. 33 minutes. £3.00.
Age range: 11–16 years.
Themes: People; loneliness; getting lost.

Synopsis
The film shows Waterloo Station from rush hour in the morning until late at night, when most activity ceases. Shots of employees at work are juxtaposed with glimpses of a wide variety of travellers in different situations: people in a hurry, or taking life easily: meeting, or saying goodbye; looking assured or bewildered; inquiring, booking, drinking. There are soldiers; prisoners in custody; tramps; famous people; a group of West Indians; a funeral cortège – to name but a few of the centres of interest, and an outstanding sequence in which a little boy who is lost slowly but inevitably gives way to tears.

ADDITIONAL FILMS
Everyday Occurrence: Contemporary. Colour. 10 mins. £2.00.
Multiple Man: Contemporary. Canada, 1967. Colour. 16 mins. £3.50.

The Red Balloon

Available from: Connoisseur Films Ltd. France, 1956. Colour. 35 mins. £5.00.
Age range: 11–16 years.
Theme: Childhood.

Synopsis
A French schoolboy finds a balloon caught on a lampost. On release it begins to follow him everywhere and they become good friends. The boy is heartbroken when a gang of hooligans steals the balloon, 'tortures' it, and eventually bursts it. At this point, all the balloons in Paris escape from their owners and come flying to comfort the boy.

Ballon Vole: Connoisseur. France, 1960. B/w. 12 mins. £2.00.

Morning on the Lièvre
Available from: Canadian Government Travel Film Library. Canada, 1961. Colour. 15 mins. Free.
Age range: 13 years.
Themes: Autumn/nature – but more appropriately used as a stimulus for descriptive writing.

Synopsis
The scene is set on the River Lièvre which runs in all for two hundred miles through Quebec Province. We follow the progress of two men as they paddle a canoe in the early dawn. As the sun rises the beauty of the mist-covered river and the surrounding hills and woodland is revealed in all its autumn splendour.

There is no dialogue but the journey mirrors the spoken words of a poem by the Canadian writer Archibald Lampman (1861-99) on the same subject.

ADDITIONAL FILMS
(Useful as visual stimuli for descriptive writing.)
Errigal: Contemporary. Eire, 1968. Colour. 14 mins. £2.50.
One by One: Contemporary. USA, 1960. Colour. 10 mins. £2.00.
November: Canada House. Canada, 1970. Colour. 9 mins. Free.

A Dream of Wild Horses
Available from: Connoisseur Films Ltd. France, 1960. Colour. 9 mins. £2.50.
Age range: 13–16 years.
Themes: Power and savagery in nature.

Synopsis
Set in the Camargue, this film shows a series of wild horses seen galloping across open plains, plunging through fire and into water. A dreamlike quality is created by using slow motion throughout and sustaining a rhythm through repetition and juxtaposition that makes it a form of filmic ballet.

A very evocative film that captures the essential beauty and power of wild horses.

ADDITIONAL FILMS
Araby: Contemporary. Poland. B/w. 12 mins. £2.00.
The Wild Stallion: (Directed by Albert Lamorisse, who also directed *The Red Balloon.*) Connoisseur. France, 1962. B/w. 3 mins. £4.50.

La Première Nuit
Available from: Contemporary Films Ltd. France, 1957 (directed by
Georges Franju). Black and white. 20 mins. £2.10.
Age range: 13–16 years.
Themes: The outsider; loneliness; growing up; sexual attraction.

Synopsis
A small boy of about eleven arrives at school in Paris in a
chauffeur-driven car. He is infatuated with a young girl whom he sees
but does not speak to. In the evening he escapes from the car and
pursues the girl down the Métro but is just too late to catch her. He
wanders around without finding her until, exhausted, he falls asleep on
an escalator after the station has closed. He dreams of the girl but still
does not communicate with her. He wakes in the morning and walks
out of the station into the fresh air.

ADDITIONAL FILMS
Les Mistons: Visual Programme Systems Ltd. France, 1957. (English
narration). 26 mins. £5.00.

The Visit
Available from: Contemporary Films Ltd. Britain, 1959 (directed by
Jack Gold). Black and white. 34 mins. £3.50.
Age range: 14–15 years.
Themes: Old age; personal relationships; loneliness; personal respon-
sibility.

Synopsis
The film shows a day in the life of a woman approaching thirty who is
tied to her dull and ageing parents. Rising early, she mechanically goes
through a routine accepted unthinkingly by her parents. The tedium of
her home life is unrelieved by noisy, boring (and, to the viewer,
incomprehensible) factory work.
   On this occasion the evening's routine is interrupted by a visit from
the woman's nephew and his fiancée, a situation which only serves to
highlight her own unhappiness and frustration, heightening her
awareness of the poverty of her relationship with her parents.
   The film is slow moving. However, if you are prepared to accept its
faults, it does offer a valuable insight into a relationship which is,
perhaps, not often thought about.

ADDITIONAL FILMS
Bleak Moments: Contemporary. Britain, 1971. Colour. 110 mins.
£17.00.

The entire film of *Rachel, Rachel,* starring Joanne Woodward and directed by Paul Newman, is available from Columbia-Warner for £12.50. It is in colour and lasts 101 mins. (This film relates to the prose extract in the leaflet.)

I think they call him John
Available from: Contemporary Films Ltd. Britain, 1964. Black and white. 28 mins. £2.50.
Age range: 14–16 years.
Themes: Old age; loneliness.

Synopsis
This is a slow moving film which captures the pace of, and offers insight into, the life of an old man who has lived on his own in a block of flats since the death of his wife. John Ronson's typical Sunday consists only of household chores, frugal meals and memories, all of which he faces with resignation and even courage.

ADDITIONAL FILMS
The Golden Age: Concord. Canada, 1958. B/w. 30 mins. £3.00.
Legault's Place: Concord. Canada, 1964. B/w. 11 mins. £1.40.
Application: Concord. Holland (English commentary). Colour. 10 mins. £1.50.

Have I Told You Lately That I Love You?
Available from: Contemporary Films Ltd. USA, 1960. Black and white. 12 mins. £2.00.
Age range: 14–16 years.
Themes: Personal relationships (or lack of); modern life; machines.

Synopsis
Gadgets and machines dominate this average day in the life of an average American family. There appears to be little need or desire to communicate with, or respond to, each other, or act for themselves, as the cogs turn, the switches click, and the labour-saving devices save labour.
 The film perhaps tends to exaggerate the non-communicative style of life but serves as a useful starting point for a discussion of personal relationships and the quality of existence.

ADDITIONAL FILMS
The Commuter: Contemporary. Britain. B/w. 16 mins. £2.25.
Little Man, Big City: Concord. Hungary. Col. cartoon. 10 mins. £2.00.
Modern Times: Darvill Associates Ltd. USA, 1937. B/w. 89 mins. £13.50.

Now
Available from: Contemporary Films Ltd. USA, 1960. Black and white. 6 mins. £2.00.
Age range: 14–16 years.
Themes: Racial conflict; law and order; the outsider; the negro in the States.
Note. For those with sophisticated projectors, this film is ideal for pauses during projection in order to permit concentration on single shots.

Synopsis
The film opens with the credits superimposed on a photograph of American Civil Rights leaders in discussion with President Johnson. It presents, through a series of stills and moving sequences, an impression of the Civil Rights movement and the opposition it meets. The film incorporates a number of emotive scenes from the past and, with many shots of violence and terror, builds up a powerful case for the negro cause.

ADDITIONAL FILMS
Sunday: Contemporary. USA, 1961. B/w. 20 mins. £2.00.
Now is the Time: Concord. USA. B/w. 36 mins. £3.40.
Ivanhoe Donaldson: Concord. USA. B/w. 55 mins. £3.00.
Far from Vietnam: Contemporary. France, 1967. Colour. 10 mins. (extract). £1.00.

Very Nice, Very Nice
Available from: Concord Films Council Ltd. Canada, 1961. Black and white. 7 mins. £1.40.
Age range: 14–16 years.
Themes: Modern life; people; communications.
Note: We strongly recommend a second showing of this film after initial discussion.

Synopsis
Through a fast-moving series of stills from modern life, backed by snatches of speech, this short conveys something of the pace and multi-faceted aspect of twentieth-century living. By judicious selection and juxtaposition of shots and words the film encourages you to examine your values and personal relationships.

ADDITIONAL FILMS
Tilt: Concord. Canada, 1972. Col. cartoon. 14 mins. (Overpopulation). £2.60.

Grapes of Wrath, starring Henry Fonda, is available from Columbia-Warner for £11.50. It is in black and white and lasts 130 mins. (This film relates to the prose extract in the leaflet.)

Young Offenders
Available from: British Film Institute. Britain, 1965. Black and white. 32 mins. £3.00.
Age range: 14–16 years.
Themes: Crime and punishment; the rebel and outsider.

Synopsis
This excellent documentary gives an insight into life in detention centres in Britain. The attitudes of the officials and of the young offenders themselves to these institutions and to the people in them are revealed through striking visuals and through recorded statements, which provide the only commentary.

ADDITIONAL FILMS
Men in Prison: BFI. Britain, 1965. B/w. 32 mins. £3.00.
Women in Prison: BFI. Britain, 1965. B/w. 32 mins. £3.00.
Women in Prison: (from BBC 'Man Alive' Series) Concord. Britain, 1971. B/w. 70 mins. £6.00.
Prison Officer: Central Film Library. Britain, 1960. B/w. 56 mins. £3.60.
A Good and Useful Life?: (BBC) Concord. Britain, 1969. B/w. 50 mins. £4.40.

Incident at Owl Creek
Available from: Connoisseur Films Ltd. France, 1961. Black and white. 27 mins. £4.50.
Age range: 14–16 years.
Themes: Death; war; capital punishment; time.

Synopsis
The scene is set during the American Civil War. A suspected saboteur is about to face execution by hanging. As the plank on which he is standing is withdrawn the rope around his neck breaks and he drops into the Owl Creek river. He frees himself of the rope and swims downstream, under heavy fire from the soldiers. After running through a forest he reaches home and sees his wife waiting to welcome him. He embraces her but the rope suddenly tightens on his neck.
This excellent short brilliantly depicts the turbulence of thought in the man's mind as he waits to fall to his death on the end of the rope.

Falls the Shadow: Contemporary. Britain, 1957. B/w. 14 mins. (Exploration of death.) £2.50.

Culloden
Available from: British Film Institute. Britain, 1964. Black and white. 11 mins. (extract). £0.75.
Age range: 14–16 years.
Theme: War.

Synopsis
This extract is taken from a documentary reconstruction of the battle of Culloden made by Peter Watkins for television. The extract concerns the events immediately after the battle. It opens with shots of the weary foot soldiers, and we learn, through interviews, their reactions to, and opinions of, the fighting that took place. The soldiers go through the battle field mercilessly slaughtering any survivors. The people around the area of Inverness, many of them innocent of any crime, suffer terrible brutalities at the hands of Cumberland's troops as they roam the area afterwards. Cumberland himself is seen dining in the mess, and the dead and wounded on the moor are visited during the night by people looking for relatives. The documentary style of the film does much to emphasize the horror of war.

The War Game: (regarded as too horrifying for television transmission) BFI. Britain, 1966. B/w. 47 mins. (Also directed by Peter Watkins.) £7.50.
Hotel des Invalides: BFI. France, 1952. B/w. 23 mins. (French commentary without sub-titles. Written translation supplied.) £1.50.

The entire film *Culloden*, 1964, is available from Concord Films Council for £5.60. It was directed by Peter Watkins for the BBC from the book by John Prebble. It is in black and white and lasts 70 mins.

Phoebe
Available from: Concord Films Council Ltd. Canada, 1964. Black and white. 30 mins. £3.00.
Age range: 15 years.
Themes: Family/personal relationships; people; communication.

Synopsis
The film concerns a young girl who finds she is pregnant. Both her parents and boyfriend are unaware of her condition, and we witness the tension created in her by this situation as she struggles to tell them.

The film portrays her thoughts as she goes back over the events leading up to her pregnancy, and also as she examines the different reactions of people, (i.e., her parents, headmistress, boyfriend) when they learn the truth.

It ends as she finally tells her boyfriend over the telephone.

ADDITIONAL FILMS
Il Posto: BFI. Italy, 1961. 10 mins. (extract). (Boy-girl relationships.) £1.50.
A Kind of Loving: (with Alan Bates and Thora Hird) Rank. Britain. B/w. 112 mins. £8.50.
Family: (from BBC 'Space Between Words' Series) BBC. B/w. 75 mins. (Difficulty of communicating within a family.) £6.00.
Who is Sylvia?: Central Film Library. Canada, 1957. B/w. 29 mins. £1.80.
Let's Have a Party: Contemporary. Netherlands. B/w. 28 mins. £3.50.

Children of Hiroshima
Available from: Contemporary Films Ltd. Japan, 1952. Black and white. 10 mins. (extract). £0.75.
Age range: 15–16 years.
Theme: War.

Synopsis
This is a short extract from the opening of a Japanese film which deals with the situation in Hiroshima after the dropping of the atom bomb. It begins with shots of a young girl returning to the city as it is at the time this film was made, but then we move back in time to the moments immediately before and after the disaster. We see adults and children rising one morning and setting out for work and school. The tension rises rapidly as shots of the bomb-carrying plane are juxtaposed with glimpses of babies playing and men working. The actual explosion is frighteningly realistic. The camera then shows the horrific devastation that has been caused and the girl wanders amongst the ruins which remain to tell the story seven years after.

ADDITIONAL FILMS
Children of the Ashes: Concord. 1961. B/w. 40 mins. £2.80.
Hiroshima, Nagasaki: August 1945: Concord. USA, 1970. B/w. 15 mins. £1.40.

FOR INFORMATION
The entire film *Children of Hiroshima* is available from Contemporary for £7.50. It is in black and white and lasts 85 mins.

Paul Tomkowicz
Available from: British Film Institute. Canada, 1954. Black and white.
10 mins. £0.75.
Age range: 15–16 years.
Themes: People; work.

Synopsis
The film portrays something of the life of a Polish crossing-sweeper,
nearing retirement, who lives in Winnipeg. We see him at work
clearing snow from the tracks one night in winter. An impression of his
life and character is built up through his own reflections which are
concerned with memories from the past, his life now and ideas for the
future.

   This high quality, naturalistic film offers a superb insight into the
character and temperament of one man.

ADDITIONAL FILMS
The Gentle Corsican: Contemporary. Britain, 1956. Colour. 25 mins.
£3.00.
Work: (from BBC 'Space Between Words' Series) BBC. B/w. 55 mins.
£6.00.

7 Small group work

Richard Mills

The stance which each contributor to this book has taken on the matter of pupil grouping within a mixed ability structure is pragmatic and flexible. The kind of grouping adopted is dependent on the nature of the task, the objectives being pursued and the numbers you are dealing with. Sometimes pupils will work alone (and often in a class much of the activity is of an isolated kind); sometimes in pairs and small groups of four or five; sometimes as a class of thirty; occasionally in a group of a hundred. Variety, consistent with good organization and clear aims, is to be encouraged, so that all may benefit from the linguistic, social, and ritualistic demands and experiences of each different method of grouping. No single way of organizing children is the panacea for mixed ability teaching but, since we believe children should often be encouraged to operate in small groups, some justification for this view, and some analysis of appropriate tasks, may be helpful.

As a way into this discussion, let us first consider some of the characteristics of the traditional class teaching structure in order to highlight some of its virtues and some of its limitations. I've labelled this method the *Shooting Star Model*. Choose your own interpretation of that metaphor: teacher as attractive source of energy whose power burns brightly and momentarily as it lands on two or three areas and is remembered briefly for its impact; or teacher as extra-terrestrial phenomenon, incomprehensible to earthlings who merely stare at the performance. Clearly both these are caricatures but they possess elements of truth.

The teaching situation represented by the diagram is unambiguous. The teacher is the focal point and can be seen more or less by everyone. The physical layout of the room testifies both to the status of knowledge and to some of its apparent characteristics. The teacher possesses that knowledge and information to impart to recipients who are intended to be fairly passive overtly as they sit isolated from each other in their separate desks. They may be note-taking or merely listening, but they are not entering into discussion, although there may be two or three questions. The teacher teaches and the pupils learn. That is what the structure of the room is saying and there are

Shooting star model

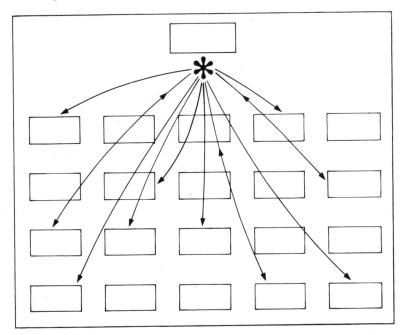

many occasions when this is perfectly appropriate. I don't wish for a moment to decry a method of organization for learning which, in many circumstances, is quite acceptable and should be encouraged, particularly where there is factual information to be conveyed, or a process explained.

However, as I indicated in an earlier chapter, a so-called class discussion lesson held in this kind of setting may often become something of an interrogation, with the teacher asking the questions; giving or withholding approval; judging guiding and controlling; selecting the speaker, and acting as mediator. The language required of the pupils is generally that of performance rather than exploration. As teachers , we've all held this kind of discussion many times and no doubt will continue to do so, since it is often a very satisfying activity for us. The fact that it serves to emphasize the corporateness of the class seems to be a positive gain and, provided we recognize its language constraints, and constantly make other additional arrangements to compensate for them, there is less of a problem. However, in this traditional class structure the pupils' language potential is so limited. They rarely ask searching questions of each other; rarely speculate or make hypotheses, using such phrases as: 'What if...' 'I wonder if...' 'Possibly...' 'It might be that...'; are rarely able to exercise initiative and control; can rarely respond genuinely to what other pupils say, since the attention is more often on the teacher as focal point than the item under consideration. In addition to all this, the teacher's own language, intonation and expectations will have their effects, and many pupils merely try to please by telling their teacher what they think he wants to hear. There may be barriers, too, thrown up by one's method of speaking. I sometimes wonder whether my own habit of asking a question, giving praise, then asking for further elaboration, doesn't in fact deter pupils. On the one hand, I'm trying to stretch them to articulate their thoughts in more detail; on the other, I'm aware of the danger of the predictability of supplementary questions, but some teaching habits are as tenacious as rust and keep breaking through despite efforts to eradicate them.   What this adds up to is one of the major justifications for organizing children to work in small groups. Under such a system they have the opportunity to use different kinds of language and develop skills in questioning, speculation, exploration, initiation, and participation. As eleven year old Trevor says:

> Sir, when you're in er smaller groups you've got more chance to say what you want to, but when you, when there's a teacher out the front, you know, you have you have you have to wait and then er, the next thing you know the bell's gone and, you know, you have to wait until the next lesson. So it's better to work in groups so you can say what you like quicker.

This is supported by Andrew:

> When you're erm, oh yeah, when you're in a mixed, you don't you you talk louder usually, when you've got about four or five people all talking at once, but you don't start going all over the room to find someone to talk about what you're doing cos you're next to someone. You've got about four other people right there.

Incidentally, these two boys were in the same mixed ability class. One was a very weak reader, and the other a highly intelligent, very good reader. Perhaps you'd like to speculate on which is which.

With regard to the physical layout, small groups should be conveniently arranged, with chairs or desks close together, for virtual face-to-face discussion. By this means, no one is forced to talk to the back of someone else's head or respond to a disembodied voice. It's a structure as appropriate for eleven year olds as for sixth formers. The following diagram may suggest other benefits too. I'll call this the *Measles Model* on the the grounds that it's what I imagined, probably erroneously, a measles germ would look like under a microscope. Further justification occurred to me later. Measles are contagious; people are affected by being in close proximity with others and catch

184

something from them. The fact that it's an illness is unfortunate for the development of my metaphor but one might even, I suppose, make capital out of that, on the grounds that many teachers are wary of small group work and endeavour to avoid it, as they would disease. That's quite enough commentary for one metaphor and the fact that I've made it may testify to the inherent weakness of the image. Let's return to the major arguments.

In this kind of structure, with which pupils are familiar from their primary school days, there is often greater involvement, even by the shy boys and girls who may feel less overawed. It should be a cooperative enterprise, with useful social skills encouraged, where pupils may learn from each other, with everyone, hopefully, able to contribute something, and the weak ones able to hear the language of the strong and perhaps in a better position to respond to it since the danger of being exposed is less. Pupils will get to know each other much better and the fact that some of them don't regard group activity as 'real work' may be a positive advantage. The teacher will learn a lot more about individuals and, perhaps, be better able to diagnose problems and weaknesses. A teacher unsure of himself may even use small groups as a disciplinary aid, on the grounds of 'divide and rule'.

Above all, the structure is saying that pupils are, in themselves,

Measles model

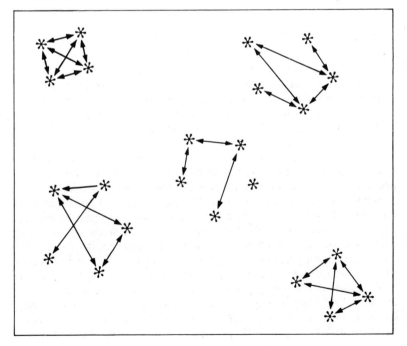

learning resources, and have a contribution to make to each other; they can, at times, assume responsibility for their own learning and that of their peers and be trusted to operate independently. A sense of commitment, a reasonable level of motivation and a willingness to persevere in a task seem to me to be of more significance for the success of this kind of operation than above average intelligence or high reading age.

Naturally, there will be difficulties. Nothing is ever all sweetness and light. There are organizational problems in constituting viable groups, often in small rooms with unhelpful furniture. A quick thinking pupil may be exasperated by a slow group member and the latter may hear language and ideas which are incomprehensible to him. There is, inevitably, a higher noise level and there is the teacher's professional fear that he may be presiding over a situation in which much irrelevant discussion may occur. There may also be the clash of incompatible personalities, as eleven year old Lynn observes;

> You know, if I was in Lesley, Lesley's form and erm, she was erm, in the group with I am and we was working in two's, she might, I'd just say to her something like this: 'Eh, Lesley, ooh, erm, what's this answer?' or something like that, 'What's this question?' or someat, but she'd say, 'Oh shurrup, I'm doing me own.' (*Lesley laughs.*)

What, then, is the teacher's role? Perhaps the phrase 'peripatetic adviser' best describes it. Once the structure has been determined and the tasks decided, the teacher should, I believe, move from group to group, in an *apparently* haphazard sequence, sometimes asking a searching and specific question in order to focus attention; sometimes giving a summary of points made and thereby indicating one of the functions of a chairman; sometimes exercising a disciplinary function; sometimes giving information; often just remaining silent, listening and storing away in his head all kinds of thoughts and impressions for later use.

When a teacher joins a small group he automatically becomes a focal point, a point of reference, and can, in a matter of seconds, dominate the group and deprive it of its independence, initiative and autonomy. He must be sensitive to this danger. There are occasions when a catalyst is needed but often a teacher may wish to be merely as a fly on the wall and a group will not easily permit him to play that role. In any event, unlike a fly, his presence will, inevitably, modify the language used, at least initially.

Whether active or passive, the teacher as overall coordinator is always present within the structure he has designed and the tasks being pursued. He is initially responsible for the way in which the groups are composed. This way may be random or intentional. If random, the teacher may organize the groups according to previous classroom seating: or by arbitrary alphabetical selection or from a class list. If the grouping is intentional then, according to selection either by the children – on the grounds of mixing abilities; giving variety of experience, of task; ensuring compatibility of personality or deliberately engineering introverts to work with extroverts; or ringing the changes on previous groupings.

What of the tasks which he sets? They seem, to me, to be of three kinds; Exploration; Production; Analysis – and I'd like to spend the greater part of this chapter considering each of these in turn.

Exploration
Here the aim of the small group of four or five boys and girls is to open up or 'explore' some topic or area which it is felt is relevant to their needs and interests. These could include the following, although they are obviously not in watertight compartments:

first year:	bullying; adventures; being frightened; brothers and sisters
second year:	ideal school; cruelty to animals; neighbours; fashions
third year:	parents; superstitions; gangs; cruelty to children; cowardice and heroism
fourth year:	authority; pollution; war; outsiders; town and country; marriage
fifth year:	minority groups; youth clubs; old people; work; crime and punishment.

Such an exploration is often the preliminary to some other activity – perhaps whole-class consideration or investigation of relevant prose or poetry text or film. Sometimes it may follow a whole-class stimulus of some kind. The intention is to involve the pupils and permit discussion to proceed in a fairly intimate setting so that all kinds of initial ideas may be agitated. Often this kind of exploration may have no clear objectives and no clear end, other than that signified by the bell or the teacher. It may only rarely stimulate real challenge and incisive debate, unless presented in some polarized form.

However, within these blanket themes or topics an issue may be presented in such a way as to force the small group participants to become decision makers. Here the exploration may have more of a cutting edge to it and I've found that children often respond well to 'problem cards' such as the following:

Mary is a fourteen year old girl who has run away from school many times, threatened her mother with a carving knife, and has now taken to staying out all hours. Her mother, with two younger children to look after, can do nothing with her. A psychiatrist's report states that Mary is of above average intelligence, alert and interested, but has never really recovered from the death of her father ten months previously.

What advice would you give the mother?

Lennie, aged thirteen years, has come before the magistrate's court as being 'in need of care and protection'. He has five brothers and sisters and lives with them and his mother in a two-roomed flat. Father has gone off with another woman. Lennie has recently stolen some torch batteries and an alarm clock from Woolworths.

What should be done?

Other interesting material which calls for a group decision on the basis of discussion is to be found in the Schools Council *Moral Education* Sensitivity packs as is well worth investigating. More detail is given in the chapter on the Schools Council Projects.

Sometimes a quotation may help to initiate a discussion. In the example which follows I was working with some eighty mixed ability fifth-year pupils who considered in their groups certain questions set out on cards and then came together for a plenary session at which a spokesman for each group reported on points made. The activity lasted the whole afternoon, with a break of some twenty minutes, and the cards, with quotations from an *Observer* competition on 'The Ideal School', and to be found in *The School That I'd Like* by Edward Blishen (Penguin) were as follows:

Card one

'Because I think the eleven-plus is very unfair and I am all for everyone having the same chances of education, streaming would be necessary. But it should be arranged in such a way that each child would be in good streams for good subjects and bad streams for bad subjects, and not in a bad stream for every subject if they were not very academic.'

Girl, 14

Which are the 'good' and 'bad' streams? Why?
Do you prefer streaming or mixed ability grouping? Why?

Card two

'At present our entire secondary educational system is geared to the GCE examinations. Eleven plus mincemeat is fed in at one end and 'O' and 'A' Level sausages emerge at the other.'

Boy, 13

Would you abolish exams? Why?
What do you think teachers feel about exams?

Card three

'History and geography are dealt with adequately, but psychology and politics, drug-taking and smoking and love and death are not mentioned in the school syllabus at all.'

Girl, 13

What subjects would you like to see excluded from your time-table? Why?
What subjects/topics should be covered which are omitted at present? Why?

Card four

'One has to learn sometime that life is not all sweetness and light and school is the best place for discovering this. I would not abolish rules or strict teachers.

Girl, 14

Which are the sensible rules? Why? How would you enforce them?
Which are the silly rules? Why are they silly?
Should teachers observe the same rules as pupils? Why? Why not?

Card five

'School should be a place where the literature teachers are poets, the history teachers political advisers, the geography teachers explorers . . . a place where literature is discussed in the geography class.'

Boy, 14

Should the curriculum be divided up into separate subjects? Why? Why not?
What do you think of this boy's views?
What do you look for in a teacher?

Card six

'The child is obsessed with the fearful 11+ exam that to pass is your ticket to happiness, to fail you might as well not continue being.'

Boy, 15

Do you agree or disagree with a fully comprehensive system of education? Why?
What can you remember about your own attitude towards the 11+ exam?

Card seven

'My idea of a school I'd like would have understanding teachers (who are few and far between at present) who would try to understand the pupils' difficulties and not look upon pupils as illiterate sub-humans. The pupils would also be treated as individuals and not as a flock of sheep all with the same purpose in life . . . The teachers would work in unison and not think that the maths teacher was aloof from the PE teacher or too proud to mix with the laboratory assistants.

The pupils would be of all nationalities and creeds: boys and girls, Jews and Moslems. This would help them in later life to have no colour prejudice and to know that one nationality or creed is no better than another.

The school (and beyond) would be a one-class society; nobody rich, nobody poor . . .'

Boy, 13

What is your idea of the ideal school?

I've also worked with a similar group of ninety fifth-years for a similar period of time on the subject of education in a Design for Living course and this time gave a forty-minute illustrated talk on the aims of education and followed this with a question sheet from which each group selected a topic of interest. In this instance there was no plenary session; we'd had enough of education for one half-day. The sheet read as follows:

Design for living course – aims of education.

Choose any *one* of these topics for your group discussion:

1 If what I've said about education is correct, then a school aims to:
   (a) prepare its pupils for society outside school
   (b) prepare for job selection (via exams)
   (c) foster the full development of each individual person.

How far has your own education met, or failed to meet, these demands?

2 Think of the nine children you saw on the slides and discuss what could be done in school to help any one of them over his/her problems.
   Should a school be so concerned about the personal problems and backgrounds of its pupils?

3 In some areas of the country the education service is divided into three parts:
   (a) infants (5-7 years)
   (b) juniors (8-10 years)
   (c) secondary (11-16/18 years).
   Suppose we became so bankrupt that one of these parts had to be abolished. Which should it be?

4 Imagine you are dictator of an under-developed country. Your national budget has to be spent on:
   (a) housing
   (b) transport systems
   (c) medical services
   (d) education
   (e) defence
   (f) industrialization (i.e. developing factories and businesses).

Which, in your view, is the most important?
Which the least?
Where does education come in the list?

Production
With the second of the three kinds of small group task originally identified, I am thinking of the kind of group activity which leads to a recognizable end product of some sort. To begin with, the group meets to plan a subsequent way of working and to divide up the tasks. They are about to initiate work on a new project or theme and the group

must first consider the options at its disposal. They are not concerned, as yet, with content, but with structure and *modus operandi*.

Their topic is, say, marriage. One individual undertakes to collect examples of marriage ceremonies from prayer books and individual wedding programmes from friends and relatives. Two others, working as a pair, decide to try two tape-recorded interviews, one with a newly married couple and one with an old couple married for many years; they discuss what questions they will ask. A fourth member of the group undertakes to do some research into the attitudes of one or two eastern cultures and to find suitable illustrations. The last pair will find examples of descriptions of weddings in novels and plays and poems. The topic has been imposed by the teacher but the pupils are free to respond to it individually. They have planned their approach for the next few days and will meet together as a group when they have something to report and when the next stage of the project needs to be planned. They have adopted a loose structure for the present but this may need to be modified later. Discussion on marriage itself will, at least in the early stages, be incidental but they will, at some point, present their findings to others.

Such a way of working, to produce a collection of written and audio-visual material, is popular, provided it's not overdone, and it gives opportunity for children of varying abilities to make full use of such talents as they possess and to develop others. As with any other activity, the teacher must monitor what is happening so that, for example, the weak reader doesn't spend all his time illustrating other people's texts, or the average pupil all his energy with the tape recorder. Moreover, the teacher needs to be clear in his mind of the value of *group* interaction. Otherwise, each 'group' could merely be composed of isolated individuals each going his own way. A useful analogy is that of the building site where each craftsman contributes his skill and must do so in concert with everyone else, and the end product is the result of team work. There is satisfaction for the pupils in being able to identify a clearly recognizable finish for their efforts – perhaps a display, or exhibition, a play or film, or happening of some sort.

Here are some more examples of group work leading to Production. Gordon Taylor suggests others in chapter six.

1 a miscellany of material on tape, e.g. for a radio programme i.e. music, sound effects, readings, interviews; slide-tape sequences on specific topics can be highly effective

2 production of a film, i.e. careful preliminary planning of plot, characters, movements, dress, location, dialogue, followed by actual shooting

3 writing of plays – highly popular even if time consuming; this could include the occasional scripting of an episode for a current radio or

television series as, for example, *Dad's Army*, where characterization is so well developed that a group could first make a transcript of part of an episode and consider the language habits of the characters involved before producing their own episode and then reading it to the rest of the class. Incidentally, not quite in the category of production, but well worth inclusion at this point is group reading of plays and short stories as a variation on silent reading. Certainly, the ability to read a character part well, in addition to merely being able to distinguish dialogue in type, from stage directions in italics, (no mean feat for some pupils) is a sophisticated and praiseworthy attribute, as well as being very enjoyable to most children.

4 Putting in rank order photocopies of four anonymous essays written by other pupils in the school but younger than those in the group. It's a useful exercise in practical criticism and the fact that the pieces under consideration are examples of pupils' work should increase motivation within the small group.

5 Group observation of a process with a written report at the end. This could be a process within the school (e.g. the making of jewelry in Metalwork; a curry in Domestic Science; a clay figure in Pottery; a hydrogen balloon in Science) or in the neighbourhood (e.g. demolition; motorway building; sheep shearing; unloading of fish; milking of cows). I recall seeing three ten-year old boys recording, at different times over a period of three days, the movements of marked wood lice in a kind of home-built adventure playground for wood lice inside the classroom. It seemed to me excellent training in observational skills which underpins so much activity, not merely scientific. I'm sorry to report that all the wood lice died. Either the public scrutiny, or the gentle prodding with pencils to get them to perform, proved too much.

So much, then, for an indication of some kinds of group production. I've omitted drama and simulations since these activities are dealt with elsewhere and my colleagues give many other examples of how children may be encouraged successfully to operate in small groups with a clear end product in view.

Analysis
The third kind of small group activity which may be identified is that geared to analysis, by which I mean that the group has, as its focal point, a text of some kind. It may be a poem, a short story, an extract from a novel, a television programme, a film, or a tape. The task of the group is either to thrash out the answers to certain questions which have been set by the teacher – in other words, a kind of corporate comprehension exercise – or to use the text as the focal point of the

discussion and to follow wherever that discussion might lead. As I stated in chapter one, I favour a firm structure early on (i.e. for several months initially and later at periodic intervals) with questions designed to take the participants into a text and help them to concentrate on specific words, phrases, ideas, characters, relationships, and often to be followed by a reporting back of some kind. Having had thorough training in how to approach the data in front of them, they should then be in a position later to be given texts without questions, for them to get to grips with the experience presented and be able to link their own world with that of the poem or story.

Here's an example (not a model) of a set of questions given to third year small groups after I had read aloud to them D. H. Lawrence's short story *Adolf,* about the effect on a family and on itself of a rabbit brought out of the wild into human civilization. Each boy and girl, in six groups of five in the dining hall, had copies of the story and each group a set of questions. The whole activity lasted sixty-five minutes and no group finished all the questions to its satisfaction. However, my own observations suggested that a good deal of learning of all kinds took place.

'Adolf' by D. H. Lawrence

1 Read the first three paragraphs again and think carefully about what sort of man the father is.
Try to discover as much as you can about him.
What appears to be the relationship between the children and their father?
What is your own attitude towards him?

2 Look carefully at how the mother reacts to the arrival of the rabbit. Look at the different ways in which she makes her comments. (One member of the group could read them out.)
What do you notice about them?
Do you think she has had any previous experience of this sort of thing?

3 Judging her on what she says and does, what sort of person does the mother appear to be?
Have you ever met anyone who is like this?

4 How do mother and father get on with each other?

5 Trace carefully the way in which the rabbit becomes acclimatized (i.e. gets used to the household).
What effects does he have on those who live in the house?

6 In what ways is it possible to compare the way of life of the father and of the rabbit?

7 What do the children feel about the departure of Adolf?
Talk about any pets you've lost and how you felt about it.

8 Using the story and your discussion as a basis, try to consider and
analyse your own attitude towards pet animals or wild animals.
Has this attitude changed over the last few years?
Are girls different from boys in this respect?
What are the attitudes of your parents?

9 You might like to act out the short story, with each member of the
group playing the part of one of the characters.

In my experience, a teacher-less small group operating in this
manner can often achieve a high degree of understanding if the
participants attend closely to the text and work in a mutually
supportive way. This won't always happen but it should happen often
enough for the method to be used without undue anxiety.

I want to end this chapter with two examples of different groups of
fifth year pupils, all subsequently CSE candidates, grappling with data
unaided by either teacher or questions. The first group, consisting of
Colin, Jane, William and Kay, had, along with sixty other pupils, seen a
thirty minute Canadian film, *Phoebe* (see chapter six, Appendix Two)
which is concerned with the breakdown in communication which
occurs when Phoebe, an American teenager, discovers she is pregnant
by her boyfriend, Paul. The group's twenty minute discussion, which
followed their viewing of the film, and was monitored only by the tape
recorder, fell into the following divisions:

1 parental attitudes towards pregnancy
2 Paul's maturity
3 an analysis of a surrealist part of the film
4 an attempt to understand Phoebe's situation
5 the problem of communication
6 consideration of what Paul would have done when he learnt the
ne·.s and of whether boys should marry their pregnant girl friends
7 parental attitude and behaviour
8 Paul's sense of responsibility
9 relationship between Paul and Phoebe
10 the problem of whether Phoebe should tell her parents
immediately
11 consideration of one scene in the film which the group found
baffling.

The transcript which follows is of section 7, 'Parental attitude and
behaviour.' I've added punctuation so as to make reading easier. The
numbers refer to the sequence of comments made.

159 J. I think if our mom told me not to hitch-hike, I wouldn't hitch-hike.

160 K. No. I wouldn't.

161 J. Because your mom and dad know best.

162 C. Mind you, they probably in the situation, that it's perhaps the only thing to do.

163 W. That's . . . that's another reason though, isn't it? Sp . . . spoilt children. They all, you know, people of our . . . they don't really really take much notice of their mother. They think, 'Oh, I'm old enough. I can do what I like.' (C. don't you do that?) But if . . .

164 C. Don't you think, 'I'm in a, I'm old enough to look after myself', and do things against your mom's word or . . .

165 K. No, not usually. You know, I always, I think I (C. If she said, say . . . J. if I strongly . . .)

166 C. If she says, 'Now be back at half-past ten, because it's school tomorrow', and you were out with all your friends and that, wouldn't you, would you make sure you went off at the right time and, you know, not be in after your mom told you to be in and, you know . . .

167 K. I think I would go back (J. yeah). I mean, when I was on me holidays, you know, I met this kid and, er, we goes out, we went out, erm, about fifteen miles to this place, you know, inn, and, like, there was these mates and they got a car. They was ever so nice, you know (C. yeah), very friendly like. Anyway, we went out and, on the way back, we ran out of petrol (C. *laughs*). Oh! I could have died (*laughing*) and I was really worried about what our mom and dad would say, you know, and I was thinking, 'Oh, I bet our mom and dad are ever so worried' like (C. yeah . . . J. yeah) and, er, I was expecting me dad to punch Pete on the nose (*laughing*) or something, you know, and, er, when we get back our dad says, 'Oh, that's alright' you know and er . . .

168 W. I bet . . . I bet . . .

169 J. They'd think it was an excuse wouldn't they?

170 K. No. And I realized, you know, I think it made me realize, you know, I was thinking over all these things about what mom and dad would say and do, you know, and . . .

171 J. Really, parents are very understanding, aren't they? (K. yeah). Even though they might not show it all the time.

172 K. I think, like er, you feel at this age, like we are, you think that they're nagging at you (J. yeah) because they're making . . .

173 C. You tend to feel, you know, some people with, perhaps, older parents, they don't understand you and they don't understand the way you think and the way you dress and

174 J. Although other parents aren't always like . . . (*inaudible*) . . .

196

your parents, because my friend, she's got some horrible parents. They really keep on at her.

175 W. And does she go out, stay out of a night longer than . . .

176 J. No. She doesn't stay out.

177 W. But (J. She likes) she's not spoilt, is she? (J. She likes . . .)

178 J. She likes other people to be with her all the time because she doesn't like to be in the house on her own with them, you know. Arguments set in (K. No . . .) and that.

179 W. That's what I was saying.

180 K. Staying with our mom and day, you know, I I don't think I'd swop, I wouldn't swop my parents for the world, you know. I really love them like.

181 J. I wouldn't either.

182 K. No. I think with our mom and dad you can talk about anything with them (C. mm).

183 J. Oh! I don't know about me dad. I couldn't talk about anything to me dad.

184 K. Erm . . .

185 J. To me mom, yeah, but not me dad.

186 W. I think if my sister got in a situation like that I'd think my mom would fall down on her, you know, and give her as much love as she could, but I think dad would act a bit ashamed, something like that.

187 C. You know, when our Rob, you know, put his wife in it, like, our mom went, er, you know, she went a bit, er, mad at him cos she didn't want him to get married at nineteen, like, and, er, of course, he did it on purpose so that they'd have to get married. And our mom went furious but, and our dad just said his bit and left it at that and helped them out, you know, and our mom kept nagging (W. It's alright, it's alright) for a bit. She got to understand (W. if they want to get married isn't it?)

188 W. But in that film, there was no thoughts of marriage. It's just like a normal boy and girl relationship, wasn't it?

189 K. Yeah. Just like, you know, just a little courtship that you get when you're about our age, you know. I mean, you don't think about usually landing up marrying them, do you, (C. laughs) you know?

190 C. Seems a bit far fetched, don't it, when you think of, 'Well, wouldn't mind marrying her', you know.

191 J. Didn't seem all that strong, you know, you know what I mean?

192 K. No.

193 C. What, the love for each other?

194 J. Yeah. Oh, I think they had love for each other, but it wasn't, you know, absolute dire love really, you know what I mean?

In this short extract we see features which occur constantly throughout the discussion. Particularly interesting is the use of expressive, informal language, often of great honesty, (notice that remarkable contribution 187) to interweave personal anecdote and experience on the one hand, with the experience which the film offers on the other. The group is successful in analysing personal relationships – their own and other people's – and I believe they are brought to a greater depth of realization (See 170, 171, 180, 186, 194) of their own relationship with their parents than would have been achieved in other ways. Moreover, they manage to sustain exchanges of this kind throughout the whole twenty minutes, never flagging, and returning time and again to different parts of the film.

In my second example of what may be achieved by pupils operating without the teacher I want to cite the work of two fifth year pupils, Christopher and Adrian. Christopher has read Philip Larkin's poem, *Mr Bleaney,* on his own and written about it. Then, after a discussion with Sandra, Ann and David, but without teacher or questions, has written a second time, thereby indicating his increase in understanding, particularly of the poem's structure. In an identical manner, Adrian has written about Yevtushenko's poem, *Schoolmaster,* and then written again after a discussion with Linda, Jayne and Malcolm, and testifies to the value of the intervening discussion although, as you will see from his first piece, he had achieved considerable understanding on his own. So much so that I was originally sceptical that he would have more to say. Hence my increased delight with what he produced. All four pieces are printed exactly as they were written and they speak for themselves without a commentary from me, showing that quite considerable learning can occur in small group *analysis* of the kind outlined.

Christopher's first piece on 'Mr Bleaney'

This poem is about a man moving into a room previously taken by a Mr Bleaney. But it concentrates far more on Mr Bleaney than the man. It discribes the room, probably in some city suburb, as an ill equiped and bare.

His second piece

This poem seems to be told by two people. Firstly the man who is coming to stay in Mr Bleaney's room and also the landlady who used to look after Mr Bleaney. The difficulty in understanding this poem is seeing who is speaking.

My impression of Mr Bleaney is an ageing man living on his own. It seems that he continually moved around, living off four groups of people untill they can take him no longer. Yet, the poet thinks that this small ill-equiped room is Mr Bleaney's home and that it show's how this man lives.

Adrian's first piece on 'Schoolmaster'

The powet is trying to portray the schoolmaster as a rarther lonely lost kind of man wandering about in a dream. The schoolmaster has lost all his charecter his vigor for life. All the indiviguality has gone from the schoolmaster his mind has broken down murging with the background. The schoolmaster fails to stand out as he used to. He not only accepts his faults but worse still play them up. The schoolmaster feels lost he has been deserted by his wife he has lost confidence in his abbillity to teach. He is seen as a old and lonely figure fadeing into obscurity as so many have before him. While seeing his world colapsing around him he cannot think why, why he's forgot about long division, why his wife has left him, why he has forgot the ticket and worst of all why he lives at all. He is a man left without a perpose without a perpose or life to defend. Soon the schoolmaster will have faded further untill neither he or anyone else shall be able to pick him out of his obscure background. It is at this point the schoolmasters mind will die compleatly.

His second piece

The poet I think is still trying to put over the idea of the schoolmasters mind having to accept a reality he did not realise had existed. One appresiated the physical side of the poem more. In that less of it seems to be taken from the mind of the schoolmaster but more from the thoughts of the children. The children and the school have become more real after disscussion they become more important and not so much reference points for the schoolmasters mind. It has become clearer that he realy did get down and feel for his ticket rarther than just a way of expressing how the schoolmaster sees himself as a stupid forgetfull man. Now it seems clearer that the schoolmaster is not only becoming obscurer himself but also as seen by the children (his pupils) It seems more that not only the schoolmasters mind is becoming old and worn out but his body itself this is shown by the reference to the clumsey walk of the schoolmaster. Everything has become more real the trees and the snow. The schoolmaster not only fades into obscurity but his physical person his body also clearly becomes covered with snow and intermingles with the white background. It seems that not only the mans mind is dying but his body also it is obvious what a poor, sick lonely figure this man is. The poem makes you more awear and feel more say for him.

APPENDIX

In order to measure my own views on small group work, having written this chapter, against some kind of yardstick, I carried out a small survey of the views of some other English teachers. One hundred and fifty questionnaires were sent out and replies received from seventy-seven teachers, representing urban and rural coeducational comprehensive schools varying in size from 500-1700, in six LEAS spread over the country. Thirty-five men and forty-two women, from 21-65, were good enough to make their views known.

I don't claim for a moment that the survey could be regarded as statistically valid. It was merely a general impression of opinion and, as such, confirmed the views expressed in the chapter regarding the composition of small groups; *modus operandi;* advantages and problems; teacher's role etc. My purpose in adding this list is not to give sets of statistics but rather to list the kinds of task which respondents felt appropriate for small groups. Such a list may prove helpful to new teachers. The tasks are numbered but the order is random.

1 discussion of ideas, topics, books, plays, poems, short stories, television and radio programmes, films, photographs
2 preparation of improvisation/scripted plays to be acted. Other drama work, including dramatization of a passage or short story
3 writing of group play/dialogue/article/summary/television or radio serial episode
4 preliminary discussion (possibly including note-making) before class discussion/writing
5 intensive study of texts
6 group reading of a play, short story, parts of a novel
7 project/theme work including research into, and production of, for example, a group newspaper, comic, magazine, advertisements, anthology; parts of these on paper; parts on tape
8 recounting a story and teaching one another in pairs
9 grammar exercises
10 compiling collections of personal and professional prose and poetry, factual and visual material, on particular themes and topics
11 word game exercises (e.g. of the Schools Council *Concept 7-9* variety) and crosswords
12 film and slide and photograph-essay production
13 decision making, including games and simulations
14 story making (possibly with pictures)
15 sharing work cards
16 marking/discussion of pupils' written work
17 reading to each other and questioning each other on what has been read
18 planning for, and follow-up from, visits
19 preparing and executing surveys/questionnaires, including making use of tape recorders
20 presentation/display/exhibition.

Part Three:

Materials

The intention in this last part of the book is to list, in what I hope is a convenient form, some of the books, and other materials which I believe worth considering by English teachers. While some will be well known, others may be brought to your attention for the first time. This latter point could apply especially to chapter 8, which departs, perhaps, from normal convention, by considering the output of one particular agency.

8   Schools Council projects

Richard Mills

A good deal of interesting and high quality material has been produced by Schools' Council project teams over the last decade or so and much of it is of considerable relevance for English teachers. In some cases the project materials can only be bought *en masse;* in other cases, inspection samples may be hard to come by. Whereas the Schools Council itself doesn't distribute materials, since this is done by individual publishers, it readily provides information and may be contacted at: Schools' Council Project Information Centre, 160 Great Portland Street, London W1N 6LL. Tel. 01-580 0352. Other sources for information include:

1 Schools' Council Liaison Officers at Colleges of Education, University Departments of Education and Polytechnics. Often such institutions possess many of the project materials and would doubtless welcome requests to inspect them.
2 Teachers' Centre Wardens, each of whom has a copy of the Project Profiles and Index.
3 LEA Advisers and Inspectors.
4 Regional Field Officers; a current list of these, with addresses and phone numbers is available from the Schools Council.
5 Publishers. (See chapter ten, section 1.)

What follows now are brief notes on specific project materials relevant to our present purposes. Even a project which would not be taken in totality might be used partially and might also throw up ideas which could be pursued. Many of the project packs are especially appropriate for mixed ability work in that they offer a very wide range of written and audio-visual material suitable across an age and ability band and are often very attractively presented. Many positively encourage or even demand pair and small group work, and all offer considerable choice to pupils – sometimes bewilderingly so. Moreover, one may discern in many of the projects a common methodology where the stress falls on concept and approach rather than on content. I hope to develop this last point in my notes on each project. Not all of them will be equally popular, of course, and teachers, by nature or nurture critical, may reject some of them on several grounds. But they should command careful scrutiny as the products of several years' work by teams of educationists on secondment from their posts in teaching and lecturing. Even if you inspect only to reject, you're sure to meet some new ideas which could be developed for your own pupils. I've included in my survey, materials from several different subject disciplines on the grounds that I consider them to be intrinsically interesting; that they give insight into work in subjects other than English; that they should offer ideas to all, and particularly those who advocate a measure of integrated study. An English teacher wouldn't generally buy material for Geography, History, or Science, but he could learn from it and, if aware of its existence, might discuss it with school colleagues from those disciplines. Good materials don't necessarily make for good teaching, but they help.

Let's now consider sixteen projects, in alphabetical order of title. I've taken some of the specific detail from the *Project Profiles* and I would refer the interested reader to this loose leaf file, available from the Schools Council at small cost, for further information. The value judgements are my own.

Communication skills in early childhood

Director: Dr Joan Tough
Duration: 1973–1976
Age range: 3–6 years

Originally aimed at helping nursery teachers to appreciate the stages of language development and to promote acquisition of language skills, much of the work of ninety teacher groups under Joan Tough's guidance has relevance for all teachers and the last part of the project will focus attention on the needs of young children for whom English is a second language. A teachers' guide *Listening to Children Talking,* Ward Lock, 1976, is extremely interesting and offers the discerning teacher of any range of children – advice, ideas, strategies and good sense. The topics covered by this guide and also by the videotapes (for hire) of teacher–pupil talk are listed in the *Project Profile* as:

1 the development of language
2 observation of children in the classroom
3 children with difficulties in communication
4 the uses of language
5 appraisal using a picture book
6 appraisal of children's use of language in different classroom situations
7 methods of keeping continuous records.

A further book, *Guide to Fostering Communication Skills,* with videotapes, will be published by Ward Lock this year, and deal with areas such as:

1 interaction in the classroom: teacher, child and situation, and the aims and methods of early childhood education
2 objectives and strategies for talking with children
3 the potential of play for promoting dialogue
4 dialogue and the curriculum: the potential of classroom activities
5 classroom interaction and the disadvantaged child
6 towards the extension of communication skills – a basis for reading and writing.

Much recent language research has brought us to the same kind of realization reached in psychology decades ago, that early experience in the handling of concepts via language is vitally important and we can't know enough about strategies to assist the process. Any teacher, like any good computer programmer, needs to know the full sequence in order to be able to play his part adequately. Hence the relevance to secondary teachers of work with infants.

English for immigrant children

Director: J. Ridge
Duration: 1966-1971
Age range: 5-16 years

In 1965 it was estimated that the normal school progress of some 44,000 children was hampered through an insufficient command of English. Accordingly, this project attempts to provide materials for teachers of pupils whose first language is not English. Full details of the materials, published by Longman, are given in the *Project Profile.* Briefly they consist of:

Scope: stage 1   aimed at teaching children of 8-13 years first to speak English and then begin reading and writing. The structural/situational course is built around fourteen topics of relevance to children and the pack includes wall pictures, flash cards, work cards, books, readers, magnet board figures etc. and a very helpful teachers' book.

Scope: stage 2   based on a study of the three themes of 'homes', 'water', and 'travel' and again employing work cards and pupil books and an essential teachers' guide which sets out particularly to provide suggestions for work within the normal class situation and to help with class organization where there is a considerable spread of language ability and development.

Scope: senior course books, pictures, tapes, designed for recently arrived non-English-speakers aged fourteen plus and with particular stress on the problems of leaving school and getting a job (discounting general economic climate!) In addition, there are further handbooks, readers, tapes etc. and films and a tape-slide sequence for hire.

English 16-19

Director: John Dixon
Duration: 1975-1979
Age range: 16-19 years

This project arose from an apparent dissatisfaction, expressed at a national conference in York, with traditional approaches to English at 16+. The aim of the project is to clarify the theory of English teaching between 16 and 19 years and to survey interesting practices in teaching English to this age range in schools and further education colleges. To this end, a number of local or regional study groups have been set up and their detailed reports will be part of the materials eventually produced by the project team, along with a statement on language functions being mastered by students at this level, samples of students' work, and an appraisal of the trials.

General studies

Director: R. Irvine Smith
Duration: 1968-1974
Age range: 15-18 years

Considerable material, of fairly basic presentation, has been produced for the general education of 15+ pupils and, although most of it is only applicable at this level, some has been successfully adapted by teachers for use with younger and less academic pupils. The units are very wordy indeed, from the pupils' point of view, but well worth investigation by teachers, if only for their own personal education and interest. Thematic collections are available from Longman on:

Religion
Politics
Nazi Germany
Genetics and evolution
World studies
Modern Britain
Crime
Science and society
Townscape
Growing up.

Geography for the young school leaver

Directors: R.A. Beddis and T.H. Dalton
Duration: 1970-1976
Age range: 14-16 years

This project was initiated as part of a programme of material for pupils of average and below average ability and one of its intentions is to make clear the distinctive contribution which the geographer can make towards the understanding of some contemporary issues relating to society and the individual. Accordingly, it is one of those projects which, as I explained to begin with, has a heavy concentration on methodology and pupils are encouraged to apply appropriate techniques to the study of their own localities. Objectives are defined in the areas of knowledge (i.e. concepts and ideas), personal attitudes, skills and creative activities.

Three packs have been published to date by Nelson on Man, Land and Leisure; Cities; and People, Place and Work, and each pack contains resource sheets, worksheets for duplication, filmstrips, slides, overhead transparencies, tapes and a teachers' guide. Much of this attractive material could be used by English teachers working on a relevant theme or participating in a scheme of integrated studies. In any event, as I indicated earlier, it's useful for any teacher of any subject to be aware of developments in the disciplines of his colleagues.

Health education

Director: Trefor Williams
Duration: 1973-1976
Age range: 5-13 years

The title may be misleading, with its connotations of PE, Sex Education and Hygiene. Certainly those elements are involved, but the material has much wider application and a lot of its ideas could be used by the English teacher who puts particular stress on the personal development and sociological models of English teaching. Writing groups from three LEAS composed of infant, junior, middle and secondary teachers, are at present preparing materials on growth, relationships, safety, human emotions, groups, disease, self-concept. Reactions I've had from practising teachers inspecting trial materials have been very favourable.

History, geography and social science

Honorary Director: Prof. W.A.L. Blyth
Associate Director: R. Derricott
Duration: 1971-1975

Age range: 8-13 years

More material here to extend the education of the English teacher, particularly in the area of teaching for concepts. The project team recognize the impossibility of producing materials which will succeed with any teacher in any situation and has concentrated on identifying specific objectives (i.e. certain skills and attitudes) and key concepts (e.g. conflict, communication, values and beliefs, continuity and change), and also providing example units and outlines which practising teachers may build on and adapt to their own circumstances. Units so far published, or shortly to be published by Collins, include:

Shops
Clues, clues, clues
Money
Floods
Life in the 1930s
People on the move
Ceremonies
Village and town
The Victorians
Growing up
Going to school.

May I particularly recommend three excellent little booklets which illustrate the project team's thinking. These are:

1 *Teaching for Concepts* Gordon Elliott
2 *Evaluation, Assessment and Record Keeping in History, Geography and Social Science* Keith Cooper (taken in conjunction with David Mears' comments on record keeping, this offers many useful ideas.)
3 *Games and Simulations in the Classroom* Gordon Elliott, Hazel Sumner, Allan Waplington.

History 13-16

Director: A.J. Boddington
Duration: 1972-1976
Age range: 13-16 years

The introductory unit of five attractive booklets and loose leaf materials, with three filmstrips and very useful teachers' guides, all entitled *What is History?* (Holmes McDougall), will interest any English teacher who not only wants an answer to that question but who is also looking for links within the curriculum and is especially concerned with the skills of analysis, informed judgement, and interpretation, which are used in many areas. The stress of these materials is on methodology and getting children to become actively involved in grappling with primary and secondary sources. There is a clear link here between judgment based on historical evidence and that part of English studies caught in the Bullock phrase of 'active interrogation of the text'. Certainly, no teacher of English would feel at all guilty about using the small pack in this project called *The Mystery of Mark Pullen* and getting his third-year pupils to work in small groups and, using the contents of Mark's wallet, trying to trace the movements of this young University of Kent student just prior to his death in a road accident. The skills involved here are evident: interpretation of evidence; sequencing of information; an awareness of the tentative nature of many conclusions – and these skills are employed on informative material not often encountered by pupils in English lessons, such as: a police report; an NUS membership card; a bus time-table; a memo; a party invitation; a tutorial notice. In other words, material in a range of registers and styles which, in addition to its stated purpose, would also offer some scope for consideration of a variety of written forms.

Humanities curriculum project

Director: L. A. Stenhouse
Duration: 1967-1972
Age range: 14-16 plus

This is one of the biggest and most well known of the Schools Council projects. Aimed at the young school leaver, the materials offered and methods proposed cut across subject boundaries between English, History, Geography, RE and Social Studies. A tremendous range of sources has been culled for a vast amount of visual material and written matter, including extracts from novels, drama, history, biography, social sciences, poems and songs, letters, reports, newspaper articles, maps, cartoons, questionnaires, graphs, statistics, photographs, advertisements. Some of the written material is well outside the comprehension range of many pupils but the HCP (Heinemann) is a kind of supermarket project and there's something for everyone on the themes of:
Education
War and Society
Family
Relations between the sexes
People and work
Poverty
Law and order
Living in cities.

The stress is on small group discussion, with the teacher as a neutral chairman, but many other activities are appropriate, as the *Project Profile* points out:

1 research into problems thrown up by the evidence, issues not fully covered, or a local study, e.g. a study of wartime bombing in the locality, or a visit to a local playgroup.
2 personal work, such as writing, painting, role-play and drama.
3 work which draws together the inquiry, e.g. the making of a film, the production of additional materials, an exhibition of work.

Teachers' Packs may be bought at a third of the cost of pupil sets and the handbooks alone are excellent reference books.

Integrated studies project

Director:	D. Bolam
Deputy Director:	D. Jenkins
Duration:	1968-1972
Age range:	11-15 years

As is often the case with schemes for integrated studies, this project is by no means easy to grasp and only substantial study of the teachers handbook (OUP), along with the material itself, will help to crack the code. The following outline may be helpful.

Alongside this packaged material there are ten 16 mm colour films which may be hired from Rank Film Library, P.O. Box 70, Great West Road, Brentford, Middlesex. An ATV booklet by David Bolam gives many follow-up suggestions for the use of the films and includes this chart linking film with subject area:

Introduction		1 *First impressions*
Social studies	Anthropology	2 *Party time*
studying	Social science	3 *All together now*
(a) present	Geography	4 *Out and about*
(b) past	Archaeology	5 *Digging up man*
	History	6 *Only yesterday*
Sciences	Biology	7 *Body power*
Arts	Drama	8 *Playing a part*
	Visual arts	9 *Clapperboard*
Values and beliefs	Mythology	10 *The Making of Hatupatu*

Topic Work in
Primary Schools

EXPLORATION MAN

Middle Schools	1	2	3	4	5	6	7	
	Getting to know you	Silent language	Myth and meaning	The remote past	The recent past	The community	Belonging to groups	Plastic packs of pupil material. 8 copies of between 5 and 8 sheets. Slides and tape available for some packs.

SOCIAL STUDIES

Living together

A Simple Societies
   (i) Tristan da Cunha
   (ii) Land Dayaks of Borneo

B Complex Society
   Imperial China

C The Manding of West Africa

Purple boxes of pupil material.

EXPRESSIVE ARTS

Communicating with others

A Making Contact
   (Communicating through language)

B Sight and Insight
   Look and Listen

C Sense of History

1st — 3rd Years

For anyone interested in how a project team functions, or doesn't function, I would strongly recommend Marten Shipman's account *Inside a Curriculum Project* (Methuen 1974). It's an exposé in the genre of the *Crossman Diaries* and is full of interesting snippets of information and insights into human nature.

Linguistics and English teaching: initial literacy project

Director: Prof. M. A. K. Halliday
Project organizer: D. Mackay
Duration: 1964-1971
Age range: 5-7 years

Better known as *Breakthrough to Literacy* (published by Longman), and a major success, materials from this project are now being used in hundreds of infant and junior classrooms and the approach, which is concerned with the initial teaching of reading and writing, and which draws for its substance on the spoken language and direct experience of pupils, could well be adapted for use with weak readers in the early years of the secondary school, as well as with illiterate adults. Details of all materials and costs are to be found in the *Project Profile*. May I repeat here my earlier recommendation in the first chapter of the *Teachers' Manual* for *Breakthrough to Literacy* by David Mackay, Brian Thompson and Pamela Schaub (Longman 1970). It's a mine of information and sound practice.

Linguistics and English teaching: language in use project

Director: Prof. M. A. K. Halliday (until December 1970)
               P. Doughty (from January 1971)
Duration: 1964-1971
Age range: 11-18 plus

There are enough ideas and suggestions in this material to keep any secondary school English class usefully occupied for months and the *Language in Use* loose leaf folder (published by Edward Arnold) may either be used almost as a course on the nature and function of language (although very different from old style analysis), or as a store of possibilities to be taken up when appropriate.

There are 110 units, each giving the outline for a sequence of between three and five lessons, and ten overall language themes (e.g. 'Language in Social Organizations'; 'Using Language to Convey Information'). Teachers may use tapes provided, in addition to their own recordings from radio and television and other sources. Pupils are often encouraged to work in pairs and small groups and there are masses of useful activities for them to be involved in, as they attempt to become more sensitive to various uses of language, ranging from selling a house, to scripting a character, talking among friends, television interviews, and weather forecasting.

Moral Education 13-16

Director:	P. McPhail
Duration:	1967-1972
Age range:	13-16 plus

The project itself has a moral aim which is 'to help children in secondary school to adopt a considerate style of life, that is to adopt patterns of behaviour which take other people's needs, interests and feelings into account as well as their own. It is interested not only in attitude change, but also in behavioural change.' *(Project Profile).* By means of drama, role play and discussion, pupils are to focus on some problem or issue presented to them and develop their awareness and insight into the nature of the dilemma. The *Lifeline* materials, published by Longman, are:

1 *Sensitivity*
   Consequences
   Points of view
   Teacher's guide

   In Other People's Shoes
   (three sets of cards presenting
      problem situations as starting
      points)

2 *Rules and individuals*
   What do you expect?
   Who do you think I am?
   In whose interest?
   Why should I?

   Proving the Rule?
   (five short books presenting moral
      difficulties)

3 *Birthday, South Africa 1904*
   Solitary confinement,
      Lincolnshire 1917
   Arrest! Amsterdam 1914
   Street scene, Los Angeles 1965
   Hard luck story, South Vietnam
      1966
   Gale in hospital, London 1969

   What Would You Have Done?
   (six booklets, each based on a true
      situation and in a worldwide
      context)

Such a methodology and materials will be familiar to English teachers and is applicable, I believe, to pupils of all abilities when the situation presented is relevant to their world. Obviously there should be no easy answers and no party line, children being encouraged to make up their own minds on the basis of the evidence and their breadth of understanding of the problem.

Materials are expected shortly from the companion project *Moral Education 8-13.*

North-West regional curriculum development project

Director: Dr W.G.A. Rudd
Duration: 1967-1972
Age range: 13-16 plus

This was a kind of umbrella project under which several sets of materials in various subjects were developed at fifteen different teachers' centres throughout thirteen LEAs for use with pupils who were then designated 'early leavers'. Three of the collections are relevant for our present purposes. They are:

1 *Situations* – a two-part RSLA course in English (Blackie & Son) with Teachers' notes and guide; pupils' material; library workcards; photographs; slides and tapes, on a number of 'situations' which adolescents might well have encountered, such as, 'Conflict with parents'; 'Happy family relationships'; 'Admiration for others'; 'Other people living in the family'.

2 *Domestic Studies* (Holmes McDougall) – various units about *Myself* – Now, at Home, From Birth, Looking Ahead, In my own Home, As a Parent.
  The material is presented in rather a dull format but there are ideas which could be taken up particularly in working on an autobiographical project such as might be appropriate at first- and second-year level.

3 *Social Education* (Macmillan) – teachers' books and worksheets on the themes of Vocation; Consumer Education; Freedom and Responsibility; Conservation; Marriage and Homemaking; Towards Tomorrow; The British.
  Unfortunately, there are seemingly endless copies of the same worksheets in these boxes. Such duplication could have been avoided by merely providing stencil master copies, as is done in the *History 13-16* project.

Science 5-13

Director: L.F. Ennever
Duration: 1967-1975
Age range: 5-13 years

You might consider it strange for me to recommend science teaching materials in a book addressed to English teachers, but throughout this section my intention has been to bring to your notice material with which you may be unfamiliar and which could offer new perspectives and insights. Certainly it's difficult enough to keep abreast of developments in one's own subject, without branching out into what would have been forbidden territory for secondary teachers until fairly recently.

I'm very impressed with much of the *Science 5-13* material, with its attractive presentation and stimulating outlook, and any teacher would be enriched by glancing through some of the twenty books which compose the project, published by Macdonald. I'd particularly recommend: *Early experiences*; *Time*; *Minibeasts*; *Ourselves*; *Like and unlike*; *Trees*. The skills of accurate observation, exploration, recording, sequencing, and communication are crucial to the study of English and Science and a school curriculum is likely to be strengthened by recognition of such common ground. If you doubt what I'm saying, look at the project book entitled *With objectives in mind*, page 59, and decide which of the objectives stated there for science *wouldn't*, with only slight modification, transfer to English.

Teaching English to West Indian children

Director: J. Wight (1967-1972)
          F.J. Worsley (1972-1973)
Duration: 1967-1973
Age range: 7-9 years

Setting aside the *Dialect Kit*, the remainder of the good humoured *Concept 7-9* materials (published by E.J. Arnold) are as appropriate for developing the language abilities of young white children as for children of West Indian origin, and some of the games, to be played in pairs and small groups, are highly effective with first- and second-year secondary pupils, whether or not their command of spoken English is assured.

Unit 1 *Listening with understanding* aims to increase children's oral comprehension and depends on individual answering of questions on a graded series of cassette tapes.
Unit 2 *Concept building* focuses on the perception of similarity and difference and the language of classification, making use of matrix cards, activity books, magnet cards, missing picture books.
Unit 3 *Communication* aims to develop children's oral skills of description and inquiry, and relies on pair and small group games, thereby encouraging co-operation and social skills also.

These materials give a great opportunity for pupils of all abilities to play a number of enjoyable games in a disciplined way and for them, almost imperceptibly, to develop a range of language skills.

Apart from project materials there are many Schools Council publications which are relevant for the English teacher. These include:

Working papers
No.3   *English: a programme for research and development in English teaching* HMSO 1965

No.13 *English for the children of immigrants* HMSO 1967

No.27 *'Cross'd with adversity': the education of socially disadvantaged children in secondary schools* Evans/Methuen Educational 1970

No.29 *Teaching English to West Indian children* Evans/Methuen Educational 1970

No.43 *School resource centres* Evans/Methuen Educational 1972

No.49 *Monitoring grade standards in English* Larry S. Skurnik Evans/Methuen Educational 1974

No.50 *Multiracial education: need and innovation* H.E.R. Townsend and E.M. Brittan Evans/Methuen Educational 1973

No.52 *Children's reading interests* Frank Whitehead, A.C. Capey and Wendy Maddren Evans/Methuen Educational 1975

No.55 *The curriculum in the middle years* A.M. Ross, A.G. Razzell and E.H. Badcock Evans/Methuen Educational 1976

Research reports and studies

The Language of Primary School Children C. and H. Rosen Penguin 1973

Reading for Meaning P. D'Arcy Two vols. Hutchinson Educational 1973

Evaluation in curriculum development: twelve case studies Macmillan Education 1973

The Quality of Listening A. Wilkinson, L. Stratta and P. Dudley. Macmillan Education 1974. The Oracy Project (11-18) itself, *Learning through Listening* is composed of listening comprehension tests for ages 10+, 13+, 17+, tapes, teachers' book, pupils' answer booklets, and is published by Macmillan Education 1976

Learning Through Drama L. McGregor et al Heinemann 1977

Organizing Resources N. Beswick Heinemann Educational 1975

Education of travelling children C. Reiss, Macmillan Education 1975

Authority and Organization in the Secondary School E. Richardson Macmillan Education 1975

The Development of Writing Abilities (11-18), J. Britton, T. Burgess, N. Martin, A. McLeod, H. Rosen Macmillan Education 1975

Writing and Learning across the Curriculum 11-16 N. Martin, P. D'Arcy, B. Newton, R. Parker Ward Lock Educational 1976

Other publications

Teaching Materials for Disadvantaged Children R. Gulliford and P. Widlake Evans/Methuen Educational 1974

Assessment and Testing in the Secondary School R.N. Deale Evans/Methuen Education 1976

Examinations at 16+: proposals for the future Evans/Methuen Educational 1975

9 Plays poetry prose

Richard Mills

Section one: source material

Some of these source books are mentioned in the section on recommended poems. They are reproduced here with author and publisher for ease of reference and ordering. Others are recommended as containing a wealth of suitable material. Such a list could virtually be endless and, no doubt, experienced teachers will readily be able to supplement this section.

ABBS, P. *English Broadsheets* (3 series) *Approaches* 1-4 Heinemann
ADLAND D. *Visual Discussions* 1-3 Longman
ALDRIDGE, J. *Come Down and Startle* Oxford
ALLOTT, K. *The Penguin Book of Contemporary Verse* Penguin
ALVAREZ, A. *Penguin New Poetry* Penguin
ATKINSON, D. & DALTON, J. *The Living Tongue* A. & C. Black
BECKETT, J. *The Keen Edge* Blackie
BENTON, M. & P. *Touchstones* (5 vols.) EUP *Poetry Workshop* EUP
BLACK, E. *Nine Modern Poets* Macmillan
CASCIANI, J. *Now* Harrap
CLEMENTS, S., DIXON, J. & STRATTA, L. *Reflections* (with Teachers' Book) Oxford *Things being various* (with Teachers' Book) Oxford

Connexions series (all published by Penguin):

ALLSOP, K. *Fit to Live In?*
BARR, J. *Standards of Living*
BULMAN, C. *Teachers' Guide*
CALDER, N. *Living Tomorrow*
FAIRBROTHER, N. *Shelter*
GILLETT, C. *All in the Game*
GILLOTT, J. *For Better, For Worse*
GROOMBRIDGE, J. *His and Hers*
HOOPER, F. *The Language of Prejudice*
JENKINS, R. *The Lawbreakers*
MABEY, R. *Food*

NEWMARK, P. *Out of Your Mind?*
ROGERS, J. *Foreign Places, Foreign Faces*
RUDINGER, E. & KELLY, V. *Break for Commercials*
TIDMARSH, S. *Disaster*
WARD, C. *Violence*
WARD, C. *Work*

COPEMAN, C. & SELF, D. *Poetrycards* Macmillan
Daily Mirror Children as Writers (annually) Heinemann
ELIOT, T.S. *Old Possum's Book of Practical Cats* Faber
FINN, F. *The Albermarle Book of Modern Verse* 1,2, Murray
FOX, G. & PHYTHIAN, B. *Starting Points* EUP
GIBSON, J. & WILSON, R. *Poetry Pack* 1,2, Macmillan
GRUGEON, E. & D. *Poemcards* 1,2,3 (with *Poemsounds* recording)
    Harrap
HACKER, G., LEARMOUTH, J., ROBINSON, R. *Conflict* 1,2 Nelson
HEWETT, S. *This Day and Age* Arnold
HOLBROOK, D. *Iron, Honey, Gold* 1-4, Cambridge
HUGHES, T. *Here Today* Hutchinson
    Poetry in the Making Faber
JACKSON, D. *Springboard* Harrap
JACKSON, D. & PEPPER, D. *Story 1,2,3* Penguin
JONES, R. *Themes: Men & Beasts*; *Imagination*; *Conflict*; *Generations*;
    (with Teachers' Book) Heinemann
    Sport & Leisure; Men at Work; Town & Country
    Preludes: Families; *Work & Play*; *Weathers*; *Five Senses*; (with
    Teachers' Book) Heinemann
MACBETH, G. *The Penguin Book of Animal Verse* Penguin
MANSFIELD, R. & ARMSTRONG, I. *Every Man Will Shout* Oxford
MARLAND, E. & M. *Friends and Families* Longman
MARLAND, M. *The Experience of Colour* Longman
    Pictures for Writing Blackie
    More Pictures for Writing Blackie
MARTIN, N. *Here, Now and Beyond* Oxford
    Truth to Tell Oxford
    Half-way Oxford (all with Teachers' Books)
MAYBURY, B. *Wordscapes* Oxford
    Thoughtshapes Oxford
    Bandstand Oxford
    Bandwagon Oxford
    Images (Teachers' Book) Oxford
MILLS, R.W. *Occasions: Births*; *Weddings*; *Funerals*; *Moments of
    Truth*; (with slide sets and Pupils' Study Guide) Longman
MILLS, R.W. & TAYLOR, G.T. *Look-out* Harrap
PALMER, F. *Sequences* (sets of photographs) Heinemann

218

Penguin English Project now available from Ward Lock Educational:

BALL, D. *Other Worlds*
BARRS, M. *Identity*
BEERS, N. *Danger*
BLACKIE P. *Things Working*
D'ARCY, P. *Bonds*
HEWITT, M. *Good Time*
JACKSON, D. *Family and School*
McLEOD, A. *Openings*
MEDWAY, P. *The Receiving End*
PEPPER, D. *That Once Was Me*
ROWLANDS, E. *Ventures*
SANDERS, G. *I Took My Mind A Walk*
SUMMERFIELD, G. *Creatures Moving*

PLIMMER, F. *Impact* (workcards) Macmillan
POOLE, R. & SHEPHERD, P. *Impact One* Heinemann
   Impact Two Heinemann (with Teachers' Book)
   Young Impact One, Two, Three (with Teachers' Book) Heinemann
PROTHEROUGH, R. & SMITH, J. *Imagine* Harrap
ROWE, A. *People Like Us* Faber
SERRAILLIER, I. *The Windmill Book of Ballads* Heinemann
SUMMERFIELD, G. *Voices* (3 vols. with Teachers' Book and records) Penguin
   Junior Voices (4 vols. Teachers' Book) Penguin
   Worlds Penguin
WATTS, J. *Interplay* 1,2 (with filmstrips and records) Longman
   Encounters (7 vols.) Longman
WILLIAMS, E. *Dragonsteeth* Arnold
WOLLMAN, M. *7 Themes in Modern Verse* Harrap
WOLLMAN, M. & GRUGEON, D. *Happenings 1* Harrap
WOLLMAN, M. & AUSTIN, A. *Happenings 2* Harrap
WOLLMAN, M. *Ten Twentieth Century Poets* Harrap

Course Books
None of the contributors to this book has been in the habit of systematically working through English course books. Nevertheless, they sometimes have their uses, perhaps for new teachers who are feeling their way, or for dipping into on odd occasions for material and ideas. It is generally as single copies for the teacher, rather than class sets for the pupil, that we would recommend them.

ADAMS, R., FOSTER, J. & WILSON, R. *Explore and Express 1-4* (with Teachers' Book and tapes) Macmillan

COPEMAN, C. & BARRETT, G. *Feelings into Words, 1,2,3* Ward Lock
Educational
DRUCE, R. and TUCKER, M. *Look; Around and About;*
Project Survival; At Hazard;
On Trial; In Evidence;
On the Horizon; Perspectives EUP
HEATH, R. *Impact Assignments in English* Longman (4-5 years)
McSWEENEY, T. and DEBES, A. *Open English* Longman (4-5 years)
ROWE, A. *English Through Experience* (5 vols.) Hart-Davis (2nd
edition)
English for Living 1-4 Macmillan
WILLIAMS, E. *People* Arnold (4-5 years)
The Quest 1,2,3, Arnold
YGLESIAS, J. and SNELLGROVE, L. *Mainstream English* (6 vols.)
Longman

Section 2: scripted drama

Most children seem to enjoy reading plays in small groups, and a
number enjoy studying the texts in depth and doing a variety of
assignments on them. Many enjoy writing their own scripts, and it's a
rare boy or girl who doesn't take to improvisation. In other words, we
start with a built-in advantage; drama is one of those marvellous
activities that doesn't seem to constitute 'real work'.

We can strongly recommend the forty or so plays now listed and
have indicated the age range they might be used with. There seems
little suitable scripted drama for first- and second-year level and
perhaps this is just as well since improvisation may be more
appropriate anyway for eleven and twelve year olds. However, there
is, in our view, no weighty reason why the two activities shouldn't be
pursued side by side at any age.

Scripted drama

ADLAND, D. *Group Approach to Drama*, 1-6 Longman (11-14 years)
ALBEE, E. *The American Dream* Penguin (15-16)
ANON *The Shepherds' Play* Penguin (11-13)
(P. 137 *Voices 1*, SUMMERFIELD, G.)
ANON *Christmas Mummers' Play* Penguin (11-13)
(P. 167 *Voices II*, SUMMERFIELD, G.)
ARDEN, J. *Sergeant Musgrave's Dance* Methuen (15-16)
AYCKBOURN, A. *Ernie's Incredible Illucinations* Hutchinson (11-13)
(in *Playbill One*)
BEHAN, B. *The Hostage* Methuen (15-16)
The Quare Fellow Methuen (15-16)
BOLT, R. *The Thwarting of Baron Bolligrew* Heinemann (11-12)
A Man for All Seasons Heinemann (15-16)
BRECHT, B. *The Good Woman of Setzuan* Penguin (14-16)

Galileo Methuen (15-16)

Mother Courage Methuen (15-16)

The Caucasian Chalk Circle Penguin (14-16)

BRIGHOUSE, H. *Hobson's Choice* Heinemann (13-14)

CHAMBERS, A. *The Chicken Run* Heinemann (12-13)

Johnny Salter Heinemann (12-13)

The Car Heinemann (12-13)

COOPER, G. *Unman, Wittering and Zigo* Macmillan Dramascript (13-16)

DELANEY, S. *A Taste of Honey* Methuen (14-15)

FUGARD, A. *Sizwe Bansi is Dead* Oxford (15-16)

GALTON, R. & SIMPSON, A. *Steptoe and Son* Longman (13-16)

HALL, W. *The Long and the Short and the Tall* Penguin (15-16)

HUGHES, T. *The Coming of the Kings and Other Plays* Faber (12-14)

JENKINS, R. *Five Green Bottles* Macmillan Dramascript (12-14)

LATIMER, J. *Maria Marten* (ed. M. Slater) Heinemann (13-15)

LAWRENCE, D.H. *A Collier's Friday Night* Penguin (14-15)

The Daughter-in-Law Penguin (14-15)

The Widowing of Mrs Holroyd Penguin (14-15)

LITTLEWOOD, J. *Oh What a Lovely War* Methuen (14-15) (Theatre Workshop)

MARLAND, M. (ed.) *Conflicting Generations* (Five plays) Longman (14-15)

Scene Scripts Longman (13-14)

Z Cars (Four television scripts) Longman (14-15)

MILLER, A. *The Crucible* Penguin (15-16)

Death of a Salesman Penguin (15-16)

A View from the Bridge Penguin (15-16)

MILNE, A.A. *Toad of Toad Hall* Methuen (11-12)

NAUGHTON, B. *Spring and Port Wine* Heinemann (14-16)

NICHOLS, P. *A Day in the Death of Joe Egg* Faber (15-16)

OBEY, A. *Noah* Heinemann (12-14)

PICK, J. *Carrigan Street* Macmillan Dramascript (12-14)

PINTER, H. *A Slight Ache and Other Plays* Methuen (14-15)

A Night Out French (14-15)

PLATER, A. *Excursion* (in *Playbill Three*) Hutchinson (14-16)

SHAW, G.B. *Androcles and the Lion* (extracts) Penguin (11-12)

Pygmalion Penguin (13-14)

TERSON, P. *Zigger Zagger* Penguin (14-15)

The Apprentices Penguin (14-15)

THOMAS, D. *Under Milk Wood* Dent (13-15)

WATERHOUSE, K. & HALL, W. *Billy Liar* Blackie (14-15)

WILDE, O. *The Importance of Being Earnest* Heinemann (13-14)

WILDER, T. *Our Town* Penguin (14-15)

Section 3: Poetry

We offer now these twenty or so poems for each year, not as a 'common core', but merely as material which we have used with children and which, we feel, is particularly suitable to be read aloud, or to study, either as part of theme work or in one-off sessions. New teachers especially may find this helpful. Each of the source books mentioned has, of course, a great deal more material which could be used. Authors, editors, and publishers of these books are detailed in Section 1: Source material (pp.217-9).

Poetry 11-12 years

ANON 'Charms and Riddles' as in *Junior Voices* I p.47-9
BARRINGTON, P. 'I Had a Hippopotamus' *English Through Experience* II p.42 (1st edition)
BLAKE, W. 'The Tyger' *Touchstones* II p.66
CARROLL, L. 'Jabberwocky' *Touchstones* II p.9
GIBSON, W.W. 'Flannan Isle' *Around and About* p.49
HUGHES, T. 'My Father' *Voices* I p.58
LEE, L. 'Apples' *Dragonsteeth* p.50
LINDSAY, V. 'Daniel' *Voices* I p.39
LOGAN, J. 'A Portrait of the Foot' *Voices* I p.17
MARE, W. de la 'The Listeners' *Dragonsteeth* p.52
MASEFIELD, J. 'Cargoes' *Touchstones* I p.132
    'Reynard the Fox' *Starting Points* p.49
MORGAN, E. 'The Computer's First Christmas Card', *Touchstones* II p.34
MORLEY, C. 'Smells' *Wordscapes* p.18
NASH, O. 'Children's Party' *Starting Points* p.40
OWEN, G. 'The Fight' *Wordscapes* p.133
ROETHKE, T. 'Child on top of a greenhouse' *Themes. Conflict* p.3
    'Snake' *At Hazard* p.10
    'My Papa's Waltz' *Wordscapes* p.87
SANDBURG, C. 'Arithmetic' *At Hazard* p.53
SONG 'The Big Rock Candy Mountains' *Look-out* Leaflet 2
STONE, G. 'Snaily House' *Project Survival* p.46

Poetry 12-13 years

ANON 'Biby's Epitaph' *Voices* II p.161
ANON 'The Death of Ben Hall' *Themes Conflict* p.12
ANON Four Limericks *Touchstones* II p.118
AUDEN, W.H. 'Night Mail' *Look-out* Leaflet 4
    'The Quarry' *Nine Modern Poets* p.94
CAUSLEY, C. 'Timothy Winters' *Here Today* p.15
FIELD, H. 'Sad Story of a Motor Fan' *English Through Experience* II p.144 (1st edition)
GRAVES, R. 'The "Alice Jean"' *Dragonsteeth* p.56

Poetry 13-14 years

Poetry 14–15 years

224

THOMAS, D. 'The Hunchback in the Park' *Themes. Conflict* p.30
WEBSTER, H. 'Street Gang' *Impact* II p.152

Section 4: Teachers' books
The books in this section deal with English teaching as a whole. In order to avoid duplication, I've generally omitted any books which have already been mentioned in earlier bibliographies or in the course of different chapters. For additional material, please refer particularly to the bibliographies for chapters one, five and six, and the Schools Council chapter.

ADAMS, A. (1970) *Team Teaching and the Teaching of English* Pergamon
ADAMS, A. and PEARCE, J. *Every English Teacher* Oxford
BULMAN, C. (1974) *Themes for English* McGraw Hill
BURGESS, C. *et al* (1973) *Understanding Children Writing* Penguin
CALTHROP, K. (1971) *Reading Together* Heinemann
CLEGG, A. (1965) *The Excitement of Writing* Chatto & Windus
    Enjoying Writing Chatto & Windus (1973)
CREBER, J. W. P. (1972) *Lost for Words* Penguin
CROXSON, M. (1966) *Using the Library* Longman
DERRICK, J. (1966) *Teaching English to Immigrants* Longman
FOSTER, J. (1973) *Reading Study Units* (3 series) Heinemann
HEATH, R. *The Mass Media* 1   *Newspapers* Bodley Head 1968
    2   *Advertising* Bodley Head 1968
    3   *Radio & Television* Hamish Hamilton 1969
HILDICK, E. *A Close Look at Newspapers* Faber 1966
    A Close Look at Magazines and Comics Faber 1966
    A Close Look at Television and Sound Broadcasting Faber 1967
HOGGART, R. (1957) *The Uses of Literacy* Penguin
HOLBROOK, D. (1961) *English for Maturity* Cambridge
    English for the Rejected Cambridge 1964
HOWARD, M. (1961) *Library Assignments* Arnold
JEREMIAH, T. (1972) *A Source Book of Creative Themes* Blackwell
JONES, A. and MULFORD, J. (1971) *Children Using Language* Oxford
LYNSKEY, A. (1974) *Children and Themes* Oxford
MARSHALL, S. (1963) *An Experiment in Education* Cambridge
MARTIN, N. *et al* (1976) *Understanding Children Talking* Penguin
MOYLE, D. (1968) *The Teaching of Reading* Ward Lock Educational
OPIE, I. & P. (1959) *The Lore and Language of Schoolchildren* Oxford
OWENS, G. and MARLAND, M. (1970) *The Practice of English Teaching* Blackie
SELF, D. (1976) *Talk: A Practical Guide to Oral Work in the Secondary School* Ward Lock Educational
STRATTA, L., DIXON, J. and WILKINSON, A. (1973) *Patterns of Language* Heinemann
SUMMERFIELD, G. (1965) *Topics in English* Batsford

SUMMERFIELD, G. and TUNNICLIFFE, S. (1971) *English in Practice* Cambridge

TANSLEY, A. (1967) *Reading and Remedial Reading* Routledge & Kegan Paul

TORBE, M. and PROTHEROUGH, R. (1976) *Classroom Encounters: Language and English Teaching* Ward Lock Educational

WHITEHEAD, F. (1966) *The Disappearing Dais* Chatto & Windus

WILKINSON, A. (1971) *The Foundations of Language* Oxford *Language and Education* Oxford 1975.

Journals

Children's Literature in Education (4 issues p.a.) APS Publications Inc., 150 Fifth Avenue, New York NY10011, USA Correspondence to Geoff Fox, Secretary to the Editorial Committee, Exeter School of Education, Thornlea, New North Road, Exeter EX4 4NS

Community Relations Commission Journal (6 times p.a.) CRC, 15/16 Bedford St. London WC2E 9HX 01-836 3545

Critical Quarterly, Manchester University Press. Ed. C. B. Cox and A. E. Dyson, The University, Manchester M13 9PL 061-273 3333

Education 3–13, Collins. Ed. Colin Richards, University of Leicester, The University Centre, Barrack Road, Northampton

English in Education (3 times p.a.), NATE, Ed. Leslie Stratta, Faculty of Education, University of Birmingham, Birmingham 15 021-472 1301. Details of the National Association for the Teaching of English from 'Fernleigh', 10B Thornhill Road, Edgerton, Huddersfield HD3 3AU

Journal of Curriculum Studies (bi-annually) Taylor and Francis Ltd., 10–14 Macklin Street, London WC2B 5NF ed. P. H. Taylor, Dean of Faculty of Education, University of Birmingham

Reading (official journal of United Kingdom Reading Association). Available from the Hon. General Secretary, S. V. Heatlie, 63 Laurel Grove, Sunderland SR2 9EE

Remedial Education (Journal of the National Association for Remedial Education, published 3 times p.a.) Ed. Paul Widlake, 20 Hanbury Crescent, Penn, Wolverhampton. Subscriptions to The Subscription Manager, Longman Group Ltd., Journals Division, 43/45 Annandale Street, Edinburgh EH7 4AT

The School Librarian (Journal of the School Library Association, published 4 times p.a.) Victoria House, 29–31 George Street, Oxford OX1 2AY Tel. Oxford (0865) 722746

Speech and Drama (Journal of the Society of Teachers of Speech and Drama, published 3 times p.a.) Available from, The Editor, 205 Ashby Road, Loughborough, Leics. LE11 3AD

Spoken English (3 times p.a.) Ed. Jocelyn Bell, English Speaking Board, 32 Roe Lane, Southport, Lancashire PR9 9EA Tel. Southport (0704) 5551

Times Educational Supplement (and *Times Literary Supplement*), P.O.
Box 7, New Printing House Square, Gray's Inn Road, London
WC1X 8EZ 01-837 1234

Times Educational Supplement Scotland, 56 Hanover Street, Edinburgh EH2 2DZ 031-225 6393

The Use of English (3 times p.a.), Hart-Davis. Ed. Christopher Parry.
Available from: The Circulation Manager (U/E), Scottish
Academic Press Ltd., 25 Perth Street, Edinburgh EH7 5JX

Visual Education (11 issues p.a.) Official journal of the National
Committee for Audio-Visual Aids in Education, 33 Queen Anne
Street, London W1M 0AL 01-636 5791

Section 5: Class libraries

We hope that the following lists will be of particular use to new
teachers but also to experienced staff who may not be familiar with the
age/interest/ability ranges contemplated here.

None of the age compartments should be regarded as watertight.
They merely indicate the points at which we've found material to be
appropriate and which we would be confident in recommending to
others. Some books, as we are all aware, can span an enormous range.

Almost all the literature in our lists is modern, not because only
modern literature is accessible or appropriate for today's pupils but
because such material may be less familiar to an English teacher
trained in the discipline. Teachers who have followed College or
University courses in English literature will be well aware of the vast
riches to be mined with pupils. Certainly, none of us would wish to rule
out great literature which is part of our cultural heritage; we must first
ascertain its appropriateness for our boys and girls. I have heard the
choice of a book (*Middlemarch*, in fact) justified to a third-year class
with the words, 'You've got to do it because it's one of the classics'.
This is not sufficient, great a book as *Middlemarch* is.

Some of the material in the lists which follow would be highly
appropriate for detailed study either with the teacher or in small
groups. Shirley Hoole gives information about this in her chapter on
literature, but each teacher must decide such a matter for himself,
when he has studied the books and knows his children well. So we
haven't been prescriptive and indicated which books, in our opinion,
are suitable for detailed work. However, we have asterisked material
for weaker readers, not to determine who should read what, but to
make the teacher's initial choice a little easier.

For additional books in the easy reading range we would refer you to
the publishers' catalogues for Longman *Knockout* and *Tempo* series;
Macmillan *Topliner* and *Nippers* books and, at a higher level,
Heinemann *Windmill* series and Longman *Imprint* books. A collection
of all publishers' current catalogues is extremely useful.

Class library 11-12 years
ALEXANDER, L. *The Book of Three* Fontana
   The Black Cauldron Fontana
ANDERSON, J. *The Vikings* Penguin
BARRY, M. *Tommy Mac* Longman
   Tommy Mac Battles On Kestrel
   Tommy Mac on Safari Kestrel
BAWDEN, N. *The Witch's Daughter* Penguin
BOTTING, D. *Pirates of the Spanish Main* Penguin
BURNETT, F. *The Secret Garden* Penguin
CARR, J. **The Red Windcheater* Macmillan
COCKETT, M. **The Lost Money* Macmillan
COOPER, L. **The Strange Feathery Beast and Other French Fables*
   Carousel
CRESSWELL, H. **John's First Fish* Macmillan
   The First Lion Book of Fairy Tales Fontana
DAHL, R. *Charlie and the Chocolate Factory* Penguin
   James and the Giant Peach Penguin
DEADMAN, R. **The Pretenders* Macmillan
ENRIGHT, E. *Thimble Summer* Heinemann
FURNEAUX, R. *On Buried and Sunken Treasure* Penguin
GARNER, A. *Elidor* Fontana
   The Moon of Gomrath Fontana
GARNETT, E. *The Family from One End Street* Penguin
GILROY, B. **Knock at Mrs Herb's* Macmillan
GORDON, J. *The Giant under the Snow* Penguin
GREEN, R. *The Tale of Troy* Penguin
   Myths of the Norsemen Penguin
   Tales of the Greek Heroes Penguin
GRICE, F. *Folk Tales of the West Midlands* (8 more folk story
   anthologies in this series) Nelson
GRIFFITHS, T. **Tip's Lot* Macmillan
HESELTINE, M. **Bri's Accident* Macmillan
HUGHES, T. *The Iron Man* Faber
JACKSON, D. & PEPPER, D. *The Yellow Storyhouse* Oxford
   The Blue Storyhouse Oxford
KASTNER, E. *Emil and the Detectives* Penguin
KAYE, G. *Nowhere to Stop* Penguin
KING, C. *Stig of the Dump* Penguin
KIPLING, R. *Just So Stories* Macmillan
   The Jungle Book Macmillan
DAY LEWIS, C. *The Otterbury Incident* Heinemann
LEWIS, C.S. *The Lion, the Witch and the Wardrobe* Penguin
   The Magician's Nephew Penguin
   Prince Caspian Penguin
   The Voyage of the Dawn Treader Penguin

The Last Battle Penguin
LIVELY, P. *The Ghost of Thomas Kempe* Heinemann
McNEIL, J. *The Family Upstairs* Macmillan
MANKOWITZ, W. *A Kid for Two Farthings* Heinemann
MILLIGAN, S. *A Book of Milliganimals* Penguin
  Silly Verse for Kids Penguin
MORRIS, M. *About Dinosaurs* Penguin
OATES, A. *Meet Harry King* Macmillan
  The Bet Macmillan
  The Milk Round Macmillan
PEARCE, P. *Tom's Midnight Garden* Penguin
  Return to Air Penguin
PICKERING, P. *Uncle Norman* Macmillan
RAFTERY, G. *Snow Cloud, Stallion* Penguin
ROBERTSON, S. *The New Pet* Macmillan
SERRAILLIER, I. *I'll Tell You a Tale* Longman
  The Way of Danger Heinemann
SILVERBERG, R. *The Auk, the Dodo and the Oryx* Penguin
SLEIGH, B. *Carbonel* Penguin
  North of Nowhere Fontana
  Spin Straw to Gold Fontana
SMITH, D. *The Hundred and One Dalmatians* Heinemann
  The Starlight Barking Penguin
STORR, C. *Marianne Dreams* Penguin
STEATFEILD, N. *Ballet Shoes* Penguin
SUTCLIFF, R. *Brother Dusty-Feet* Oxford
  Dragon Slayer Penguin
TATE, J. *The Crane* Heinemann
TOWNSEND, J. *Gumble's Yard* Penguin
TREECE, H. *Viking's Dawn* Penguin
  Viking's Sunset Penguin
  The Road to Miklagard Penguin
  Horned Helmet Penguin
WARNER, R. *Men and Gods* Heinemann
WILLIAMSON, H. *Tarka the Otter* Penguin

Class library 12-13 years
ADAMSON, J. *Born Free* Fontana
ALLEN, E. *The Latchkey Children* Oxford
BACH, R. *Jonathan Livingston Seagull* Pan
BALDWIN, M. *Grandad with Snails* Hutchinson
BAWDEN, N. *Carrie's War* Penguin
  On the Run Penguin
BRENNAND, S. *Gold and Granite* Penguin
BROWN, M. *A Book of Sea Legends* Penguin
BUSH, H. *Mary Anning's Treasures* Heinemann

BUTLER, W. *The Riddles of the Yojok Rocks* Macmillan
CHRISTOPHER, J. *In the Beginning* Longman
CLEARY, B. *Ramona the Pest* Penguin
COOKSON, C. *The Nipper* Penguin
DeJONG, M. *The House of Sixty Fathers* Penguin
DICKINSON, P. *The Weathermonger* Penguin
   The Devil's Children Penguin
   Heartsease Penguin
DOORLY, E. *The Radium Woman* Heinemann
DOYLE, A.C. *Memoirs of Sherlock Holmes* Penguin
   Hound of the Baskervilles Pan
FOSTER, J. *My Friend Cheryl* Macmillan
GARNER, A. *The Owl Service* Fontana
   The Weirdstone of Brisingamen Fontana
GARFIELD, L. *Mister Corbett's Ghost and Other Stories* Penguin
GODDEN, R. *The Diddakoi* Penguin
HARNETT, C. *The Wool Pack* Penguin
KAY, S. *Digging into the Past* Penguin
LEESON, R. *Second Class Genie* Collins
LEGUIN, U. *Wizard of Earthsea* Heinemann
MARSHALL, J. *My Boy John that Went to Sea* Penguin
MONTGOMERY, L. *Anne of Green Gables* Penguin
MORPURGO, M. *It Never Rained* (short stories) Macmillan
MORROW, H. *The Splendid Journey* Heinemann
OATES, A. *Tests and Things* Macmillan
   Meet Linda King Macmillan
   The Leather Jacket Boys Macmillan
O'DELL, S. *Island of the Blue Dolphins* Penguin
PEARCE, P. *A Dog So Small* Penguin
PICARD, B. *One is One* Oxford
PLATER, A. *Trouble with Abracadabra* Macmillan
POINTON, B. *Michelle* (4 stories) Macmillan
READ, R. *The Living Sea* Penguin
ROCKET, B. *Whales and Dolphins* Penguin
ROWE, A. *Lone Wolf* Macmillan
RYAN, P. *The Ocean World* Penguin
SALKEY, A. *Earthquake* Oxford
   Hurricane Oxford
   Drought Oxford
SERRAILLIER, I. *The Clashing Rocks* Heinemann
   The Silver Sword Penguin
SMITH, L. *The New House* Macmillan
STEVENSON, R.L. *Treasure Island* Penguin
STREATFEILD, N. *Growing Summer* Penguin
STUCLEY, E. *Magnolia Buildings* Penguin
SUTCLIFF, R. *Warrior Scarlet* Oxford

230

TOLKIEN, J.R. *The Hobbit* Allen and Unwin
TREASE, G. *Cue for Treason* Penguin
TREECE, H. *The Dream Time* Heinemann
  Legions of the Eagle Penguin
TWAIN, M. *Tom Sawyer* Penguin
  Huckleberry Finn Penguin
UNDERHILL, R. *Antelope Singer* Penguin
  Beaverbird Penguin
WALSH, G. *The Dolphin Crossing* Penguin
WHITE, T. *The Sword in the Stone* Fontana

Class library 13-14 years

ADAMS, R. *Watership Down* Penguin
ARMSTRONG, W. *Sounder* Penguin
BANKS, L. *One More River* Penguin
BLISH, J. *Star Trek* Corgi
BOYERS, B. *Lost and Found* Evans
  Two Sides to Everything Evans
CARTER, B. *The Bike Racers* Longman
CATE, D. *On the Run* Macmillan
CHAMBERS, A. *Don't Forget Charlie* Macmillan
  The Vase Macmillan
  Ghosts (short stories) Macmillan
  Ghosts 2 Macmillan
CHILTON, I. *The Hundred* Macmillan
CHITTY, S. & PARRY, A. *The Puffin Book of Horses* Penguin
CHRISTOPHER, J. *The White Mountains* Hutchinson
CLARKE, A.C. *Of Time and Stars* (short stories) Penguin
COOKSON, C. *Joe and the Gladiators* Penguin
DeJONG, M. *The Tower by the Sea* Hutchinson
DICKENSON, C. *Siege at Robins Hill* Macmillan
GALLICO, P. *The Snow Goose* Penguin
GARFIELD, L. *Smith* Penguin
GLANVILLE, B. *Goalkeepers are Different* Penguin
GOODBODY, J. *Topliner Book of Football* Macmillan
GREEN, J. *The Six* (short stories and cassette) Longman
GRICE, F. *The Bonny Pit Laddie* Oxford
HILDICK, E. *Birdy Jones* (and others in the series) Macmillan
  Louie's sos Macmillan
  Louie's Lot Macmillan
HAUGAARD, E. *The Little Fishes* Heinemann
HITCHCOCK, A. *Ghostly Gallery* (short stories) Penguin
HUDDY, D. *The Mini Prize* Macmillan
KITCHING, J. *One From Three Makes None* Macmillan
  Anyway (short stories) Macmillan

LAYTON, G. *A Northern Childhood. The Balaclava Story and Other Stories* Longman
LEGUIN, U. *The Farthest Shore* Heinemann
  Tombs of Atuan Heinemann
LINGARD, J. *The Twelfth Day of July* Penguin
LONDON, J. *White Fang* Heinemann
MADDOCK, R. *Sell Out* Macmillan
  Dragon in the Garden Macmillan
MARSHALL, A. *I Can Jump Puddles* Penguin
MARSHALL, J. *Walkabout* Penguin
MAXWELL, G. *Ring of Bright Water* Methuen
MAYNE, W. *Earthfasts* Penguin
MORSE, B. *The Ring* Macmillan
NAUGHTON, B. *The Goalkeeper's Revenge* (short stories) Penguin
OWEN, E. *Freestyle Champ* Evans
POPE, R. *Is It Always Like This?* Macmillan
  The Drum Macmillan
RAWLINGS, M. *The Yearling* Heinemann
RUDGE, K. *The Mud Scene* Macmillan
RYAN, P. *Journey to the Planets* Penguin
  UFO's *and other Worlds* Penguin
  Planet Earth Penguin
SERRAILLIER, I. *Fight for Freedom* Heinemann
SCHAEFER, J. *Shane and Other Stories* Penguin
SHERMAN, D. *Old Mali and the Boy* Heinemann
SHERRY, S. *A Pair of Jesus-Boots* Heinemann
SOUTHALL, I. *Josh* Penguin
SPERRY, A. *The Boy Who Was Afraid* Heinemann
STEINBECK, J. *The Red Pony* Heinemann
STEWART, M. *Orange Wendy* Macmillan
SUTCLIFF, R. *Eagle of the Ninth* Oxford
  The Outcast Oxford
  Mark of the Horselord Oxford
TATE, J. *Tad* Heinemann
  Ginger Mick (and cassette) Longman
  The Rabbit Boy Heinemann
  The Next Doors Heinemann
TAYLOR, T. *The Cay* Heinemann
TOWNSEND, J. *Goodnight Prof. Love* Oxford
ULYATT, K. *The Day of the Cowboy* Penguin
  The Time of the Indian Penguin
WATERHOUSE, K. *There is a Happy Land* Longman
WELLS, H.G. *War of the Worlds* Heinemann
  The First Men in the Moon Longman
WILSON, R. *All for the Rovers* Macmillan
WRIGHTSON, P. *I Own the Racecourse* Hutchinson

ZINDEL, P. *The Pigman* Macmillan

Class library 14-15 years
ABSE, D. *Ash on a Young Man's Sleeve* Pergamon
ACHEBE, C. *Things Fall Apart* Heinemann
AIKEN, J. **Night Fall* Macmillan
ALLINGHAM, M. *Tiger in the Smoke* Penguin
ANDERSON, L. & SHERWIN, D. *If* (Film script) Lorrimer
ARUNDEL, H. **The Girl in the Opposite Bed* Macmillan
AVERY, V. *London Morning* Pergamon
BARSTOW, S. *Joby* Heinemann
BATES, H.E. *The Good Corn and Other Stories* (Ed. G. Halson) Longman
My Uncle Silas (short stories) Cape
BECKMAN, G. **19 is Too Young to Die* Macmillan
BLISHEN, E. *The School that I'd Like* Penguin
BOULLE, P. *The Bridge on the River Kwai* Heinemann
BRADBURY, R. *Fahrenheit 451* Hart-Davis
BRAITHWAITE, E. *To Sir, With Love* Heinemann
BRATSTROM, I. **Since That Party* Macmillan
CHAMBERS, A. **I Want to Get Out* Macmillan
CHESTERTON, G. K. *The Incredulity of Father Brown* (short stories) Penguin
The Wisdom of Father Brown Penguin
The Innocence of Father Brown Penguin
The Secret of Father Brown Penguin
CHRISTOPHER, J. *The Guardians* Heinemann
The City of Gold and Lead Hutchinson
The Pool of Fire Hutchinson
CLEARY, B. *Fifteen* Penguin
DAVIES, M. & MARLAND, M. *Breaking Away* (extracts) Longman
FRANK, A. *The Diary of Ann Frank* Pan
FOSTER, J. **That's Love* Macmillan
GARNER, A. *Red Shift* Fontana
HANLEY, C. *A Taste of Too Much* Blackie
HEMINGWAY, E. *The Old Man and the Sea* Heinemann
HERRIOT, J. *It Shouldn't Happen to a Vet* Pan
HEYERDAHL, T. *The Kon-Tiki Expedition* Penguin
HINES, B. *A Kestrel for a Knave* Penguin
HINTON, S. *That Was Then, This is Now* Fontana
The Outsiders Fontana
HITCHMAN, J. *The King of the Barbareens* Penguin
HOLM, A. *I Am David* Penguin
INNES, H. *The White South* Fontana
The Wreck of the 'Mary Deare' Fontana
KAMM, J. *Young Mother* Heinemann

Out of Step Heinemann
KAYE, G. *Marie Alone* Macmillan
KELLER, H. *The Story of My Life* Hodder
KNOWLES, J. *A Separate Peace* Heinemann
LAYE, C. *African Child* Fontana
LEACH, C. *Decision for Katie* Macmillan
   Answering Miss Roberts Macmillan
LEE, L. *Cider with Rosie* Penguin
LEGUIN, U. *Rocannon's World* Tandem
LINGARD, J. *Across the Barricades* Penguin
LIPSYTE, R. *The Contender* Macmillan
McGRATH, P. *The Green Leaves of Nottingham* Hutchinson
MADDOCK, R. *The Pit* Macmillan
MARLAND, E. & M. *Friends and Families* (extracts) Longman
MARLAND, M. *Loves, Hopes and Fears* Longman
   The Experience of Work Longman
   The Experience of Sport Longman
   (all extracts)
MARSHALL, J. *The Children* Methuen
MORPURGO, M. *Long Way Home* Macmillan
NEVILLE, E. *It's Like This Cat* Penguin
ORWELL, G. *Animal Farm* Penguin
PEYTON, K. *Flambards* Oxford
SANDFORD, J. *Cathy Come Home* Pan
SHOLOKHOV, M. *Fierce and Gentle Warriors* (short stories) Heinemann
SHUTE, N. *A Town Like Alice* Heinemann
SMITH, C. *Ten Western Stories* Longman
STEINBECK, J. *The Pearl* Heinemann
STORR, C. *Thursday* Penguin
TATE, J. *Sam and Me* Macmillan
   Clipper Macmillan
   Whizz Kid Macmillan
   The Silver Grill Heinemann
   The Tree Heinemann
TOYNBEE, P. *A Working Life* Penguin
WALSH, J. *Fireweed* Penguin
WILLIAMS, E. *The Wooden Horse* Collins
   Great Escape Stories Penguin
ZINDEL, P. *My Darling, My Hamburger* Bodley Head

Class library 15–16 years

ANTHONY, M. *Green Days By the River* Heinemann
ASIMOV, I. *I, Robot* Panther
BALDWIN, J. *Go Tell it on the Mountain* Corgi
BARSTOW, S. *A Kind of Loving* Corgi

The Human Element (short stories) Longman
A Casual Acquaintance and Other Stories (Ed. M. Davies, with cassette) Longman
BECKMAN, G. *Mia* Longman
BRADBURY, R. *Golden Apples of the Sun* (short stories) Corgi
BUCHANAN, P. *The Marco File* Longman
CHAMBERS, A. & N. *World Zero Minus* (short stories) Macmillan
 In Time to Come (short stories) Macmillan
CRISPIN, E. *The Stars and Under* (short stories) Faber
GOLDING, W. *Lord of the Flies* Heinemann
GORKI, M. *My Childhood* Penguin
GRAVES, R. *Goodbye to All That* Penguin
GREENE, G. *Brighton Rock* Penguin
 The Power and the Glory Penguin
HARTLEY, L. P. *The Go-Between* Penguin
HELLER, J. *Catch-22* Corgi
HERSEY, J. *Hiroshima* Penguin
HOLT, J. *How Children Fail* Penguin
HUGHES, R. *High Wind in Jamaica* Penguin
HUXLEY, A. *Brave New World* Penguin
JOYCE, J. *Dubliners* (short stories) Penguin
 Portrait of the Artist as a Young Man Penguin
KAFKA, F. *Metamorphosis and Other Stories* Penguin
KAMM, J. *Young Mother* Heinemann
KAUFMAN, B. *Up the Down Staircase* Pan
KOHL, H. *36 Children* Penguin
KOZOL, J. *Death at an Early Age* Penguin
LASKI, M. *Little Boy Lost* Heinemann
LAWRENCE, D. H. *Selected Tales* Heinemann
 Sons and Lovers Penguin
 The Rainbow Penguin
LAWRENCE, L. *Andra* Macmillan
LEE, H. *To Kill a Mockingbird* Heinemann
LEGUIN, U. *Lathe of Heaven* Panther
LESSING, D. *Nine African Stories* Longman
 The Habit of Loving Panther
LONDON, J. *Twelve Short Stories* (ed. J. Tillett) Arnold
McCULLERS, C. *The Heart is a Lonely Hunter* Penguin
 The Member of the Wedding Heinemann
MALAMUD, B. *The Assistant* Penguin
MEAD, M. *Growing Up in New Guinea* Penguin
NAIPAUL, V. S. *Miguel Street* (short stories) Penguin
NAUGHTON, B. *One Small Boy* Longman
 Late Night on Watling Street Longman
O'BRIEN, E. *The Country Girls* Penguin
O'CONNOR, F. *My Oedipus Complex and Other Stories* Penguin

ORWELL, G. *Nineteen Eighty-Four* Penguin
   Down and Out in Paris and London Penguin
   The Road to Wigan Pier Penguin
PATON, A. *Cry, the Beloved Country* Penguin
REMARQUE, E. *All Quiet on the Western Front* Heinemann
SALINGER, J. D. *The Catcher in the Rye* Penguin
SILLITOE, A. *A Sillitoe Selection* Longman
   Saturday Night and Sunday Morning Longman
   The Loneliness of the Long Distance Runner Longman
SOLZHENITSYN, A. *One Day in the Life of Ivan Denisovitch* Penguin
STEINBECK, J. *Of Mice and Men* Heinemann
   The Grapes of Wrath Heinemann
UPDIKE, J. *Pigeon Feathers and Other Stories* Penguin
VONNEGUTT, K. *Slaughterhouse Five* Panther
WATERHOUSE, K. *Billy Liar* Penguin
WATTS, S. *The Breaking of Arnold* Macmillan
WINDSOR, P. *The Summer Before* Macmillan
WOODHAM-SMITH, C. *The Reason Why* Penguin
WRIGHT, R. *Black Boy* Longman
   Native Sun Cape
WYNDHAM, J. *The Chrysalids* Penguin
   The Kraken Wakes Penguin
   The Day of the Triffids Penguin

10 Useful addresses

Publishers

It's useful to have in each school an up-to-date collection of catalogues from the main educational suppliers. Most publishers will provide free catalogues on request and many include Heads of English Departments in schools on their regular mailing lists. In addition, the majority offer an inspection copy service which permits books to be assessed for a limited period on a sale/return/retain and requisition basis. Some beginning teachers may be unaware of this facility, and the following addresses may prove helpful not only to them but to all staff.

Allen (George) & Unwin Ltd., Ruskin House, 40 Museum Street, London wc1a 1lu Tel. 01-405 8577

Arnold (E. J.) & Sons Ltd., Butterley Street, Leeds ls10 1ax Tel. Leeds 442944

Arnold (Edward) (Publishers) Ltd., 25 Hill Street, London w1x 8ll Tel. 01-493 8511

Associated Book Publishers Ltd., 11, New Fetter Lane, London ec4p 4ee Tel. 01-583 9855

Batsford (B.T.) Ltd., 4 Fitzhardinge Street, Portman Square, London w1h 0ah Tel. 01-486 8484

Bell (G.) & Sons Ltd., York House, Portugal Street, London wc2a 2hl Tel. 01-405 0805

Benn (Ernest) Ltd., Sovereign Way, Tonbridge, Kent tn9 1rw Tel. Tonbridge (073-22) 64422

Black (A. & C.) Ltd., 4, 5 and 6 Soho Square, London w1v 6ad Tel. 01-734 0845

Blackie & Son Ltd., Bishopsbriggs, Glasgow g64 2nz Tel. 041-772 2311

Blackwell (Basil) & Mott Ltd., 5 Alfred Street, Oxford ox1 4hb Tel. Oxford 22146

Bodley Head Ltd., 9 Bow Street, London wc2e 7al Tel. 01-836 9081

Brodie (James) Ltd., 15 Queen Square, Bath ba1 2hw Tel. 22110

Cambridge University Press, The Pitt Building, Trumpington Street, Cambridge cb2 1rp Tel. Cambridge (0223) 58331

Cape (Jonathan) Ltd., 30 Bedford Square, London WC1B 3EL Tel. 01-636 5764

Cassell & Co. Ltd., 35 Red Lion Square, London WC1R 4SG Tel. 01-242 6281

Chambers (W. and R.) Ltd., 11 Thistle Street, Edinburgh EH2 1DG Tel. 031-225 4463

Chatto & Windus Ltd., 40-42 William IV Street, London WC2N 4DF Tel. 01-836 0127

Collins (William) Sons & Co. Ltd., 14 St. James's Place, London SW1A 1PS Tel. 01-493 5321

David & Charles (Holdings) Ltd., South Devon House, Newton Abbot, Devon TQ12 2DW Tel. Newton Abbot 3521-6

Dent (J. M.) & Sons Ltd., Aldine House, 26 Albermarle Street, London W1X 4QY Tel. 01-491 2970

Deutsch, André, Ltd., 105 Great Russell Street, London WC1B 3LJ Tel. 01-580 2746

Educational Explorers Ltd., 40 Silver Street, Reading RG1 2SU Tel. 0734-83103

Educational Productions Ltd., East Ardsley, Wakefield, Yorkshire WF3 2JN Tel. Wakefield 823971

English Universities Press Ltd., St. Paul's House, London EC4P 4AH Tel. 01-248 5797

Evans Brothers Ltd., Montague House, Russell Square, London WC1B 5BX Tel. 01-636 8521

Faber & Faber Ltd., 3 Queen Square, London WC1N 3AU Tel. 01-278 6881

French (Samuel) Ltd., 26 Southampton Street, Strand, London WC2E 7JE Tel. 01-836 7513

Ginn & Company Ltd., Elsinore House, Buckingham Street, Aylesbury, Bucks HP20 2NQ Tel. Aylesbury (0296) 88411

Gollancz (Victor) Ltd., 14 Henrietta Street, London WC2E 8QJ Tel. 01-836 2006

Hamilton (Hamish) Ltd., 90 Great Russell Street, London WC1B 3PT Tel. 01-580 4621

Harper & Row Ltd., 28 Tavistock Street, London WC2E 7PN Tel. 01-836 4635

Harrap (George G.) & Co. Ltd., P.O. Box 70, 182-4 High Holborn, London WC1V 7AX Tel. 01-405 9935

Hart-Davis Educational Ltd., (incorporating Chatto & Windus Educational Ltd., and Blond Educational Ltd.,) Frogmore, St. Albans, Herts AL2 2NF Tel. St. Albans 59101

Heinemann Educational Books Ltd., 48 Charles Street, London W1X 8AH Tel. 01-493 9103

Her Majesty's Stationery Office, Atlantic House, Holborn Viaduct, London EC1P 1BN Tel. 01-248 9876

Holmes McDougall Ltd., Allander House, 137-141 Leith Walk,

Edinburgh EH6 8NS Tel. 031-554 9444

Hutchinson Educational Ltd., 3 Fitzroy Square, London W1P 6JD Tel. 01-387 2888

Jackdaw Publications Ltd., 30 Bedford Square, London WC1B 3EL Tel. 01-636 5764

Ladybird Books Ltd., P.O. Box 12, Beeches Road, Loughborough, Leicestershire LE11 2NQ Tel. Loughborough 68021

Longman Group Ltd., Longman House, Burnt Mill, Harlow, Essex CM20 2JE Tel. Harlow 26721

Lutterworth Press, Luke House, Farnham Road, Guildford, Surrey GU1 4XD Tel. Guildford 77536

Macdonald & Evans Ltd., 8 John Street, London WC1N 2HY Tel. 01-242 2177

Macmillan Publishers Ltd., Houndmills, Basingstoke, Hants. Tel. Basingstoke 29242

Methuen & Co. Ltd., 11 New Fetter Lane, London EC4P 4EE Tel. 01-583 9855

Murray, John (Publishers) Ltd., 50 Albermarle Street, London W1X 4BD Tel. 01-493 4361

Nelson (Thomas) & Sons, UK Ltd., 36 and 40 Park Street, London W1Y 4DE Tel. 01-493 8351

NFER (National Foundation for Educational Research). Darville House, 2 Oxford Road East, Windsor, Berks SL4 1DE Tel. Windsor 69345

Nisbet (James) & Co. Ltd., Digswell Place, Welwyn, Herts AL8 7SX Tel. Welwyn Garden 25491

Oliver & Boyd (A Division of Longman Group Ltd.) Croythorn House, 23 Ravelston Terrace, Edinburgh EH4 3TJ Tel. 031-332 1211

Open University, The Marketing Division, P.O. Box 81, Walton Hall, Milton Keynes MK7 6AT Tel. 0908-74066

Oxford University Press, Walton Street, Oxford OX2 6DP Tel. 0865-56767

Pan Books Ltd., Cavaye Place, London SW10 9PG Tel. 01-373 6070

Panther Books Ltd., Frogmore, St. Albans, Herts AL2 2NP Tel. St. Albans 59101

Paternoster Press Ltd., Paternoster House, 3 Mount Radford Cres-cent, Exeter, Devon EX2 4JW Tel. 0392-50631

Penguin Books Ltd., Harmondsworth, Middlesex UB7 0DA Tel. 01-759 1984

Pergamon Press Ltd., Headington Hill Hall, Oxford OX3 0BW Tel. Oxford 64881

Pitman (Sir Isaac) & Sons Ltd., 39 Parker Street, Kingsway, London WC2B 5PB Tel. 01-242 1655

Routledge & Kegan Paul Ltd., Broadway House, 68-74 Carter Lane, London EC4V 5EL Tel. 01-248 4821

Schofield & Sims Ltd., 35 St. John's Road, Huddersfield HD1 5DT Tel. Huddersfield (0484) 30684

Temple Smith (Maurice) Ltd., 37 Great Russell Street, London WC1B 3PP Tel. 01-636 9810

Transworld Publishers Ltd., (Corgi, Bantam, Carousel etc.) Century House, 61/63 Uxbridge Road, London W5 5SA Tel 01-579 2652

University of London Press Ltd., St. Paul's House, Warwick Lane, London EC4P 4AH Tel. 01-248 5797

University Tutorial Press Ltd., 9-10 Great Sutton Street, London EC1V 0DA Tel. 01-253 6992

Van Nostrand Reinhold Co. Ltd., Molly Millar's Lane, Wokingham, Berkshire. Tel. Wokingham (0734) 789456

Ward Lock Educational Ltd., 116 Baker Street, London W1M 2BB Tel. 01-486 3271

Wheaton (A.) & Co., Hennock Road, Exeter EX2 8RP Tel. Exeter (0392) 74121

BBC Programmes

Many radio and television programmes for general listening and viewing are potentially useful in English teaching but, in addition to these, there is, of course, a range of educational broadcasting specifically designed for particular purposes and with defined age ranges in mind. The provision in English is especially varied and anyone interested should write for the Annual Programme Leaflet to:

School Broadcasting Council for UK, The Langham, Portland Place, London W1A 1AA Tel. 01-935-2801

In this booklet you will find detailed descriptions of each of the following English series:

Adventure (13-16 years)	Art and Humanities (13-16)
Animals Real and Unreal (10-12)	Books, Plays and Poems (14-17)
Drama Workshop (11-12)	Electric Company (10-16)
English (14-17)	Hello! Hello! (8-11)
Inquiry (13-16)	Inside Pages (10-12)
Listening and Reading III (11-13)	Listening and Writing (11-14)
Living Language (9-11)	Masterworks (14-18)
Movement and Drama II (9-11)	Scan (11-13)
Scene (14-16)	Speak (14-16)
Web of Language (10-12)	

Teachers' notes and pupils' pamphlets for these series may be obtained from: BBC Publications, 144-152 Bermondsey Street, London SE1 3TH.

Records and tapes

Argo (Division of Decca Record Co. Ltd.), 115 Fulham Road, London SW3 6RR 01-589 5293

CBS Records, 17/19 Soho Square, London w1v 6HE 01-734 8181
Catalogue only available for purchase.

Caedmon Spoken Word Recordings, Teakfield Ltd., 1 Westmead, Farnborough, Hampshire GU14 7RU Tel. Farnborough (0252) 41196
Free catalogue of wide range of English, American and other literature on record and cassette.

Decca Record Co. Ltd., 9 Albert Embankment, London SE1 7SW 01-735 8111

Saga Records Ltd., 326 Kensal Road, London w10 5BL 01-969 6651
Free catalogue. No spoken recordings.

Sussex Tapes, E.P. Ltd., Bradford Road, East Ardsley, Wakefield, Yorkshire WF3 2JN Tel. Wakefield (0924) 823971
Free catalogue of dialogues, tapes and tape-slide sequences for sale or hire. Mainly academic literary discussions and readings for older students.

Topic Records Ltd., 27 Nassington Road, London NW3 2TX 01-435 9983
Free catalogue of specialist folk music, including ballads and children's singing games.

Visual aids

See also Appendix One of Gordon Taylor's chapter for details of film distributors.

ABC Travel Guides Ltd., 40 Bowling Green Lane, London EC1P 1DB 01-837 3636
Excellent guide at small cost to *Museums and Galleries in Great Britain and Ireland*.

Athena International. P.O. Box 13, Raynham Road Estate, Bishops Stortford, Herts. Tel. Bishops Stortford (0279) 56627
Small charge for catalogue of prints, posters, cards and blocks of fine art reproductions.

Audio-Visual Productions, 15 Temple Sheen Road, London SW14 7PY 01-876 0064
Free catalogues. Materials on English Language, Social Studies, Literature.

CELPIS (Colleges of Education Learning Programmes Information Service).
Detailed catalogue for sale from: Councils and Education Press Ltd., 10 Queen Anne Street, London W1M 9LD
Range of a/v/a, relevant for all school subjects, produced by Colleges and Departments of Education, and available for use on terms negotiated between prospective user and the producing institution.

EAV Ltd. (Educational Audio Visual), Butterley Street, Leeds LS10

1AX Tel. Leeds (0532) 442944 Free catalogue of saleable materials including a/v sets on topics for General/Social Studies; English and American literature; Drama.

EFVA (Educational Foundation for Visual Aids. Also NCAVAE, National Council for Audio Visual Aids in Education), 33 Queen Anne Street, London W1M 0AL 01-636-5742
Services offered: hire of films and sale of multi-media kits; OHP transparencies; filmstrips, slides, tapes; monthly magazine, *Visual Education*; various other publications. Maintenance service available for a/v equipment. Teacher training courses arranged.

EP Ltd. (Educational Productions), Bradford Road, East Ardsley, Wakefield, Yorks. WF3 2JN Tel. Wakefield (0924) 823971. Free catalogue available illustrating variety of materials.

EPA Ltd. (Edward Patterson Associates), 68 Copers Cope Road, Beckenham, Kent. 01-658 1515 Free catalogue of tape-slide programmes in Humanities.

Pictorial Charts Educational Trust, 27 Kirchen Road, London W13 0UD 01-567 5343 Free catalogue of charts on English literature, Theatre, Library, Punctuation, as well as Social Studies.

Radio Times Hulton Picture Library, 35 Marylebone High Street, London W1M 4AA 01-580 5877 Ext. 4735 Over six million photographs, drawings, slides, manuscripts etc. available.

Slide Centre Ltd., 143 Chatham Road, London SW11 6SR 01-223 3457 Free catalogue of slide folios and filmstrips.

Slide Loan Service, National Art Slide Library, Victoria and Albert Museum, Cromwell Road, South Kensington, London SW7 01-589 6371 Reference only catalogue of over 90,000 colour slides for hire, free of charge, with nominal postage costs.

Theatre Association, British, 9 & 10 Fitzroy Square, London W1P 6AE 01-387 2666 Over 200,000 volumes, including 5,000 sets of plays, drama research information etc. for library subscribers. Quarterly theatre review. Holiday courses. Bookshop. Small number of dialect records for sale.

Theatre Museum, Leighton House, 12 Holland Park Road, Kensington, London W14 8LZ 01-602 3052 Due to open in the Flower Market, Covent Garden, in a few years' time, this collection is to be found at present in the Victoria and Albert Museum (Room 132) and Leighton House. There are over 9,000 library books on the theatre and allied subjects, and a changing display of objects showing the history and development of theatre, opera, ballet, circus.

Visual Publications, The Green, Northleach, Cheltenham, Gloucestershire GL54 1BR Tel. Northleach (045 16) 518 Free catalogue.

Woodmansterne Ltd., Greenhill Crescent, Holywell Industrial Estate, Watford, Hertfordshire WD1 8RD Tel Watford (0923) 28236 Free catalogue gives details of materials for sale, including slide-tape sequences, slide-books, and slides of classical paintings, means of transport, space exploration, the Holy Land and European countries, views of London and throughout the UK.

Multi-cultural material

I have the impression that, slowly but inexorably, more schools are beginning to think of providing courses and materials which reflect life and thought from a variety of cultures other than their own. This may be a response to the presence of many children, in certain schools, with overseas origins, or it may be part of a general move towards widening horizons and learning to appreciate the richness and variety of other cultures. Geographers have clearly had this objective all along but it's only recently that certain English stock cupboards have begun to acquire in any quantity literature from Asia, Africa, the Caribbean and the Americas, in addition to their European classics in translation.

What follows now is a list of sources for those interested in this area, excluding publishers given in Section 1, and also excluding addresses of Embassies, High Commissions and Tourist Offices, all of which could be useful. Some indication is generally given of what each agency has to offer.

Africa Centre, 38 King Street, London WC2E 8JT 01-836 1973
  Regular meetings and classes, plus information on school speakers.
Ann & Bury Peerless, 22 King's Avenue, Minnis Bay, Birchington, Kent CT7 9QL Tel. Thanet (0843) 41428 Slide sets for sale on world religions.
Bogle L'Ouverture Publications Ltd., 5a Chignell Place, Ealing, London W13 0TJ 01-579-4920 Books, posters, journals on Africa, the Americas, the Caribbean and Asia.
British Council, 10 Spring Gardens, London SW1A 2BN 01-930-8466 Information on many aspects of English education for overseas consumption and some material on education in Commonwealth countries.
Christian Aid, P.O. Box No. 1, London SW1W 9BW 01-730-0614 Conferences, speakers for schools, publications and AV aids.
CILT (Centre for Information on Language Teaching), State House, 63 High Holborn, London WC1R 4TN 01-242 9020
Commonwealth Institute, Library and Resource Centre, Kensington High Street, London W8 6NQ 01-602 3252 Information and ideas on direct application. No catalogue available other than a very useful select bibliography, *Race Relations in Britain*, 1976, Community Relations Commission.
CWDE (Centre for World Development Education), Parnell House, 25 Wilton Road, London SW1V 1JS 01-828 7611 Lists available of free and for sale publications, posters, filmstrips, slide sets.
Development Education Centre, Charles Gillett Centre, Selly Oak

College, Bristol Road, Birmingham B29 6LE 021-472 3255 Third World materials.

Hans Zell Publishers Ltd., POB 56, Oxford OX1 3EL Tel. Oxford (0865) 40512

ILEA Learning Materials Service Publishing Centre, Highbury Station Road, Islington, London N1 1SB 01-226 9143 Free catalogue indicating very wide age and ability range for multi-media materials for sale, not hire, including simulations, drama packs, and multi-racial booklets and broadsheets.

Institute of Race Relations, 247/249 Pentonville Road, London N1 9NG 01-837 0041 Reference library and a quarterly journal.

Islamic Cultural Centre, Regents Lodge, 146 Park Road, London NW8 01-723 7611

NAIY (National Association of Indian Youth), 46 High Street, Southall, Middlesex UB1 3DB 01-574 1325

NAME (National Association for Multi-racial Education). Details of membership, activities, local branches, publications etc., including the journal *Multiracial School*, published three times a year, from: Madeleine Blakeley, NAME Information Officer, Bishop Lonsdale College, Mickleover, Derby DE3 5GX

National Book League, 7 Albermarle Street, London W1X 4BB 01-493 9001 Multi-cultural book collection.

Oxfam, 274 Banbury Road, Oxford OX2 7DZ Tel. Oxford (0865) 54333 Publications, AV aids, artefacts for sale. Information concerning conferences, speakers for schools etc.

Race Relations Board, 5 Lower Belgrave Street, London SW1W 0NR 01-730 6291

RE Resources Centre, Westhill College, Selly Oak, Birmingham B29 6LL 021-472 7245 Major religions and third world materials.

Royal Anthropological Society, 36 Craven Street, London WC2N 5NG 01-930 6328 Teachers' resource guide for sale, with bibliographies, addresses for anthropological resources in the classroom, details of appropriate films, and some addresses of schools, colleges and universities with courses in anthropology/humanities.

Runnymede Trust, 62 Chandos Place, London WC2N 4HG 01-836 3266 Free list of publications on race relations, including a monthly bulletin.

School of Oriental and African Studies, Malet Street, London WC1E 7HP 01-637 2388 No loan system. Visits welcomed for information on all aspects of Africa, Asia, Latin America and the Caribbean.

Soma Books, 38 Kennington Lane, London SE11 4LS 01-735 2101. Bookshop specializing in Indian books for adults and children, the majority of which are published in India.

Third World Publications, 151 Stratford Road, Birmingham B11 1RD 021-773 6572 Free catalogue of useful materials for full age range.

Index